What a refreshing new look at culture and therapy! The model presented in this book is thoroughly relational and thus well-suited to the world of therapy. It's value-based and inspiring, it's field-tested with generations of students, and it's applicable to every clinical encounter within and across cultures.

William J. Doherty, Ph.D., Professor and Director, Minnesota Couples on the Brink Project, University of Minnesota; co-author of Helping Couples on the Brink of Divorce

Reaching out across gaps of culture, language, and power, and having that reaching out welcomed, can be the hardest challenge a therapist faces. *A Practice Beyond Cultural Humility* answers that challenge with ORCA practices for moving openness, respect, curiosity, and accountability, to create a safe space where mutual welcoming can occur.

James L. Griffith, M.D., Professor and Chair, George Washington School of Medicine and Health Sciences; co-author of Encountering the Sacred in Psychotherapy

This timely book offers a welcome alternative to traditional content-oriented "cultural competence" training. Practitioners, teachers and students in private practice, or in institutional and community settings, will change how they work with cultural diversity after reading this compassionate and practical book.

Celia Jaes Falicov, Ph.D., Clinical Professor, University of California, San Diego; author of Latino Families in Therapy, *2nd edition*

What a great book! *A Practice Beyond Cultural Humility* brings together a diverse group of authors to explore how to integrate openness, respect, curiosity, and accountability into their work with clients. This will be a valuable resource for both clinicians and trainees for years to come.

Joshua N. Hook, Associate Professor of Psychology, University of North Texas; author of Cultural Humility: Engaging Diverse Identities in Therapy

A PRACTICE BEYOND CULTURAL HUMILITY

A Practice Beyond Cultural Humility offers specific guidance to support students and practitioners in providing ongoing, culturally competent professional care.

The book introduces a cultural diversity-training model named the ORCA-Stance, an intentional practice which brings together four core components: openness, respect, curiosity, and accountability. Drawing on an array of influences, including theological and evidenced-based thinking, it showcases work with common clinical populations in a variety of contexts, from private practice to international organizations. Each clinical chapter offers a brief review of information relevant to the population discussed, followed by a case study using the ORCA-Stance, and a summary of recommended best practices. Topics such as poverty, immigration, and chronic illness are explored and, in each case, the practice of the ORCA-Stance is shown to allow relationships to become more culturally attuned and, therefore, more effective.

A Practice Beyond Cultural Humility provides practical examples, research, and wisdom that can be applied in day-to-day clinical work and will be valuable reading for graduates, marriage and family therapists, and mental health workers who seek to continue their professional development.

Claudia Grauf-Grounds, PhD, LMFT, is Professor Emeritus in the Department of Marriage & Family Therapy, Seattle Pacific University, and Lecturer/Faculty at the University of San Diego and Point Loma Nazarene University, USA.

Tina Schermer Sellers, PhD, LMFT, AASECT Certified Sex Therapist is Professor Emeritus at Seattle Pacific University, USA and founder of NW Institute on Intimacy.

Scott Edwards, PhD, LMFT, is Associate Professor in the Department of Marriage & Family Therapy, Seattle Pacific University, USA.

Hee-Sun Cheon, PhD, LMFT, is Associate Professor and Director of Clinical Training in the Department of Marriage & Family Therapy, Seattle Pacific University, USA.

Don MacDonald, PhD, LMHC, is Professor Emeritus in the Department of Marriage & Family Therapy, Seattle Pacific University, USA.

Shawn Whitney, MS, LMFT, is Assistant Director of the Center for Family & Couple Therapy, Human Development & Family Studies, Colorado State University, USA.

Peter M. Rivera, PhD, LMFT, is Assistant Professor and Director of Internships in the Department of Marriage & Family Therapy, Settle Pacific University, USA.

A PRACTICE BEYOND CULTURAL HUMILITY

How Clinicians Can Work More Effectively in a Diverse World

Edited by Claudia Grauf-Grounds,
Tina Schermer Sellers, Scott Edwards,
Hee-Sun Cheon, Don MacDonald,
Shawn Whitney and Peter M. Rivera

Routledge
Taylor & Francis Group

NEW YORK AND LONDON

First published 2020
by Routledge
52 Vanderbilt Avenue, New York, NY 10017

and by Routledge
2 Park Square, Milton Park, Abingdon, Oxon OX14 4RN

Routledge is an imprint of the Taylor & Francis Group, an informa business

© 2020 Taylor & Francis

Library of Congress Cataloging-in-Publication Data
A catalog record for this title has been requested

ISBN: 978-0-367-35643-9 (hbk)
ISBN: 978-0-367-35644-6 (pbk)
ISBN: 978-0-429-34090-1 (ebk)

Typeset in Bembo
by Taylor & Francis Books

To our families, colleagues, and those who have challenged us to develop good relationships.

We honor one lost too soon, Scott Green, who lived out the ORCA-Stance in our midst.

CONTENTS

CONTRIBUTORS

Alissa Bagan, MS, Licensed Marriage & Family Therapist and Licensed Mental Health Therapist; Western Psychological Counseling Services and Behavior Health Consultant, South Tabor Family Physicians; adjunct faculty, Portland Community College, Portland, OR; specializing in trauma, baganalissa @gmail.com.

Rachel Baska, MS, Licensed Marriage & Family Therapy Associate, Seattle, WA, specializing in eating disorder treatment, baskar@spu.edu.

Hee-Sun Cheon, PhD, Licensed Marriage & Family Therapist and AAMFT Approved Supervisor, Associate Professor in Marriage and Family Therapy at Seattle Pacific University, Seattle, WA, cheon@spu.edu.

William K. Collins, PhD, MS, Licensed Marriage & Family Therapist and AAMFT Approved Supervisor, Samaritan Center of Puget Sound, Pastoral Counseling Agency, Seattle, WA, https://samaritanps.org/therapist/bill-collins/.

Marcus Comer, MS, Seattle Pacific University MFT Alumni, focuses on Narrative Therapy methods; Commercial Construction Manager, Seattle, WA; managing teams and projects with awareness of the people and the stories that are part of everyday life and our engagement at work, comer.mp@gmail.com.

Charlie Delavan, MS, Licensed Marriage & Family Therapy Associate; group practice specializing in gifted children and families and LGBTQIA+ identity in the Seattle area, www.liveyourhopes.com.

Blake Griffin Edwards, MS LMFT, Behavioral Health Director, Columbia Valley Community Health, Wenatchee, WA, edwardsfamilytherapy@gmail.com.

Scott Edwards, PhD, LMFT, Licensed Marriage & Family Therapist and AAMFT Approved Supervisor, Program Director and Department Chair, Seattle Pacific University, Marriage and Family Therapy. Seattle, WA, sedwards@spu.edu.

Heather Fisher, MS, LMFT, Licensed Marriage & Family Therapist, Certified Medical Family Therapist, Interim Administrative Director of Medical Family Therapy Program at Seattle Pacific University; Mill Creek Family Services, specializing in trauma work. Seattle, WA, fisherh@spu.edu.

Claudia Grauf-Grounds, PhD, LMFT, Licensed Marriage & Family Therapist and AAMFT Approved Supervisor, Professor Emeritus of Marriage & Family Therapy, Seattle Pacific University, Seattle, WA. Lecturer II, University of San Diego, Department of Marriage & Family Therapy, San Diego, CA, claudiagg@spu.edu.

Scott Green, MS, MDiv, Pastor and Licensed Marriage & Family Therapist. Seattle, WA, c/o lynne.green@comcast.net.

Kyle Isaacson, PhD, Licensed Psychologist, Portland State University-Student Health and Counseling, Portland, OR, kisaacs2@pdx.edu.

Lahela Isaacson, MS, LMFT, Licensed Marriage & Family Therapist, Greenhouse Therapy Center, Children with Autism/DIR, Portland, OR, Lahela. Isaacson@gmail.com.

Kenneth Jaimes, MS, Licensed Marriage & Family Therapy Associate, Private Practice, Seattle, WA, www.ReStoryTherapy.com.

Kathleen Blair Jaimes, MS, Marriage & Family Therapy Associate, Community Mental Health, Seattle, WA, Kathleen.blair.jaimes@gmail.com.

Delene Jewett Galvin, MS, Licensed Marriage & Family Therapist; Mental Health Evaluator, Seattle Children's Hospital Emergency Department, Seattle, WA; Support Group Facilitator, Huntington's Disease Society of America, delene@spu.edu.

Kurt Johns, PhD, Licensed Marriage & Family Therapist, Private Practice, Bainbridge Island, WA, www.collaborativefamilytherapy.com/.

Jenny Johnson, MS, Licensed Marriage & Family Therapy Associate, Private Practice, Edmonds, WA, specializing in sex therapy and EMD, https://thesa getherapygroup.com/.

Rose Joiner, MS, Licensed Marriage & Family Therapist, MN Board Approved Supervisor, Private Practice, Saint Paul, MN, specializing in wellness, trauma and work with Native American populations, rose.joiner@gmail.com.

Mary Therese Kelleher, PhD, Licensed Marriage & Family Therapist, Private Practice, Seattle, WA, specializing in couple therapy with international and cross-cultural couples, mary@marykelleherlmft.com.

Lori Kimmerly, MS, Licensed Marriage & Family Therapist and AAMFT Approved Supervisor, Private Practice, Federal Way, WA, www.lorikimmerlytherapy.com.

Cassady Kintner, MS, Licensed Marriage & Family Therapist, Certified Medical Family Therapist, Private Practice, Seattle, WA, specializing in chronic medical conditions, www.cassadykintner.com.

Don MacDonald, PhD, Licensed Mental Health Counselor, Professor Emeritus, Seattle Pacific University; Seattle, WA, eieio@spu.edu.

Steve Maybell, PhD, Licensed Marriage & Family Therapist and AAMFT Approved Supervisor, adjunct faculty, Seattle Pacific University and Seattle University; diplomate in professional psychotherapy, clinical social work and Adlerian Psychology, stevenm@spu.edu.

Mary Moline, PhD, Licensed Marriage & Family Therapist and AAMFT Approved Supervisor, Professor, School of Behavioral Science, Loma Linda University, Loma Linda, CA, mmoline@llu.edu.

Robin Moore, MS, Licensed Marriage & Family Therapist and WA State Approved Supervisor, Bothell, WA, RMoore@Meierclinics.com.

Michelle Naden, PhD, Licensed Marriage & Family Therapist, Director of Counseling, Testing and Wellness, Walla Walla University, Walla Walla, WA, michelle.naden@wallawalla.edu.

Lauren Rimkus Pallay, MS, MHP, GC-G, Licensed Marriage Family Therapist, Private Practice, Tacoma, WA, ler.pallay@gmail.com.

Gerry Presar, MS, Licensed Marriage & Family Therapist, Private Practice, specializing in Blended Families, Divorce, and Men's Issues, Kirkland, WA, gerry@soundpsychotherapy.com.

Emily Rich, MS, Licensed Marriage & Family Therapist and Certified Medical Family Therapist, Private Practice, Faculty, Northwest Creative and Expressive

Arts Institute, specializing in eating disorders, body image, trauma, and couples, Seattle, WA. www.enrichmentcounselingandwellness.com,

Peter M. Rivera, PhD, Licensed Marriage & Family Therapist and AAMFT Approved Supervisor, Assistant Professor, Seattle Pacific University, Seattle, WA, riverap@spu.edu.

Leslie B. Savage, MS, Licensed Marriage & Family Therapist, Certified Focusing-Oriented Therapist and Medical Family Therapy, Medical Family Therapist, Private Practice, CoHear/BSC, Bellevue, WA, www.FocusingandSpirituality. com, LeslieS@CoHearGroup.com.

Tina Schermer Sellers, PhD, Licensed Marriage & Family Therapist, AASECT Certified Sex Therapist, Medical Family Therapist. Professor Emeritus, Seattle Pacific University; founder Northwest Institute on Intimacy, www.TinaSchermerSellers.com, DrTina@NWIOI.com. Family members: **Chloe Sellers** and **Christian Sellers**.

Becca Seuss, MS, Licensed Marriage & Family Therapist, Eating Recovery Center, Bellevue, WA, specializing in eating disorder and family support in recovery, beccasuess@gmail.com.

Christina L.P. Steere, MS, Licensed Marriage & Family Therapist and child mental health specialist. Founder of Eastside Family Services, a Private Practice specializing in attachment, trauma and elite athlete coaching in the Seattle, WA area, www.eastsidesfamilyservices.org.

Brittany Steffen, MS, Licensed Marriage and Family Therapist in group practice, Seattle, WA, and Adjunct faculty, Seattle Pacific University, specializing in the treatment of LGBTQ related issues, Brittanysteffenlmft@gmail.com.

Shannon West, MS, Licensed Marriage & Family Therapist, founding therapist at Speaking Pink, a Private Practice specializing in tween and teen girls, and women in their twenties, Seattle/Kirkland, WA, www.speakingpink.com.

Shawn Whitney, MS, Licensed Marriage & Family Therapist and AAMFT Approved Supervisor, Assistant Director of the Center for Couple and Family Therapy (CFCT) and a faculty supervisor, Colorado State University, Fort Collins, CO, www.restorationfamilytherapy.com.

Jackie Williams-Reade, PhD, Licensed Marriage & Family Therapist, Associate Professor, School of Behavioral Health, Loma Linda University, Loma Linda, CA, jwilliamsreade@llu.edu.

PREFACE: WE CALL IT THE ORCA-STANCE

Claudia Grauf-Grounds

An *ORCA-Stance* does sound a bit odd. But that's why we wrote this book, to explain ourselves. Learning from more than a decade of work within our training community, we wanted to voice our aspirations and address the questions: what kinds of interactions promote healthy, culturally sensitive relationships? In particular, how do we stay connected in relationships when there are significant differences between us?

We have discovered that an intentional practice demonstrates our aspirations and addresses our questions. In particular, the ORCA-Stance helps us to become less anxious when we are encountering discomfort. It helps us to become more settled within ourselves during an interaction and to proceed in a way that values the relational contributions of all those involved. The Stance invites us to learn from an encounter with others; it keeps us teachable. It reminds us to stay humble. As our world becomes more complex, we need to find ways to build bridges and to stay engaged with each other when we are uncomfortable. Although the focus of the book is for clinicians, we have found that this Stance helps us in many dimensions of our lives.

Carl Rogers coined terms like *congruence* or *unconditional positive regard* in the 1950s to inform mostly individual psychotherapeutic encounters, and this book similarly provides a framework to define a *relational* context of connection. We began by asking the simple question: "Upon graduation from our training program, how would our students interact with their clients?" If we observed our students doing therapy, what might we observe in the interactions? Later we developed our questions more broadly: "What interactional characteristics promote healing within therapy?" And, "What qualities promote trusting relationships across people groups and particular clinical populations, especially when there are significant differences between us?"

Originally, after brainstorming and synthesizing a list of core qualities, one faculty member jokingly said: *"An acronym for those four qualities could be ORCA"* – which was perfect because orca whales are part of our Pacific Northwest setting. And so it was. The definitions, practices, and implications for ORCA will be reviewed in the chapters that follow.

It became important to us to include a sense of humility and contextual understanding. By humility, we draw on a rich ecumenical and theological tradition of not valuing ourselves more highly than those we serve. Humility confronts pride. Humility takes a position that we can learn from the experiences of another. Humility is consistent with postmodern ideas, since each person is limited to their own context of understanding in particular ways. We are not all-knowing in all contexts. Although we may offer some expertise, there are limits to our knowledge. We must stay mindful of these limits and humble in our encounters. As we will discuss in Chapter 1, the conversations and definitions around cultural humility fit neatly with this intention.

We have experienced the value of practicing the ORCA-Stance in a variety of contexts, from our homes to international organizational consultations. As we introduced and used the Stance in a wide range of contexts, we have noticed a common reaction – particularly from those we train. Settings characterized by frustration relaxed into moments of more disclosure and ease in conversation. Where misunderstanding and reactivity abounded, traces of connection materialized. Particularly during difficult relational encounters, conflict of values, or even silence, the relationship persisted and did not implode. And these trainings appeared to be as helpful in settings from mainland China to suburban Seattle. We were onto something.

It is also important to punctuate that, philosophically, our educational program takes an "in-between" perspective of care. We interpret our experiences simultaneously close up and in context, aware that our interpersonal encounters affect us at multiple levels. From shedding tears during a poignant story to recognizing the power of gender during an interaction, we are impacted by, and in turn, we impact those around us. Thus, both intimate and broader social factors influence how we act and react.

We began with this assumption: *as we define and practice our core relational values, we will function better within our relationships, both therapeutic and personal.* As we work to describe the skills we need in order to be competent clinicians, we can identify and improve our professional services. By "naming" our practices, we begin to shape the contexts in which we live. As narrative thinkers might say, we are thickening our story as we name, deconstruct, and then develop our preferred ways of demonstrating who we are and how we choose to be in relationships. We feel compelled to share our ideas with you since they are pertinent to many of our lives in the twenty-first century.

There are three sections in this book. In the first, "Foundations," we define and explain the ORCA-Stance. We offer experiential exercises and descriptions for the Stance, explain how it came to be central in our training, and explore some of the philosophical underpinnings and research that support its usefulness. We also nest this discussion in the current thinking about cultural diversity training; we need additional ways to translate good ideas and information into actual practice. This leads us to the second section of the book, "Common Clinical Applications." Here we recommend specific ways to harness this practice with particular populations and topics. While we offer some conceptual information about these populations, we also focus on the applications and practical ways to work with them. In each group we note ways to stay responsive to a culturally humble posture. Finally, in the "Contextual Applications" section, we offer examples, from more intimate relationships (e.g., with our children) to larger social settings (e.g., organizations), that illustrate the opportunities to develop a stance of humility and cultural awareness in varied contexts. We also propose a process for you to take the ideas expressed in this book and develop them within your own context.

You will find a range of voices in this text. Authors either volunteered or were invited to write on a particular area of expertise and experience. Almost all are trained clinicians. Each person will emphasize particular lessons from the ORCA-Stance in their own unique way as they have internalized and used the relational processes distinctively. Please note that the clinical cases discussed have been described in a way to protect their confidentiality.

We share our ORCA-Stance to encourage you to become more intentional in the professional work you do and in the overall lives you live. We wish to empower you, as co-creators and narrators of your existence, to live purposefully, whether you are formally working or even playfully living.

ACKNOWLEDGEMENTS

What a collaboration!

With a thoughtful reflection and appreciation for the efforts of so many, we offer this brief acknowledgement, knowing we have missed some significant names along the way.

We appreciate the years of dedicated work and hundreds of faculty hours dedicated to excellence in the training of Marriage and Family Therapy students at Seattle Pacific University. In particular we note the significant legacies of Dennis Guernsey, Doug Anderson, and Bill Collins (previously with the Presbyterian Counseling Services).

We appreciate the students who have taught us to be a program that is sensitive to the varying populations that they serve with compassion. We note their integrity, vulnerability, and wisdom. Thank you for keeping us accountable.

We appreciate our committed graduate fellows who have walked alongside the faculty to help these ideas to become a publication. In particular we appreciate Abigail Lombardo, Rachel Baska, and Lillian Bailey.

Our thanks to Seattle Pacific University which offered the necessary resources to birth these ideas and to facilitate ways to communicate them within our diverse world. We are particularly grateful to Mícheál Roe and Katy Tannenberg, former and current Deans of the School of Psychology, Family & Community as well as our stellar Marriage & Family Therapy Program Coordinators, especially Kyleigh Gray and Amanda Hataway Smith.

We appreciate the vision of our key professional organization, the American Association for Marriage and Family Therapy (AAMFT), for publishing and recognizing some of our ideas in the October/November 2011 edition of *Family Therapy* magazine as "Innovations in MFT Training."

We appreciate the detailed and enthusiastic editing done by Gail Stillerman Weisman; her efforts helped us to blend into a unified mentoring voice.

Finally, we appreciate the active support and encouragement provided by Clare Ashworth, our wonderful mental health editor at Routledge, as well as her dedicated staff. Clare took our vision and championed our efforts throughout our journey.

SECTION I

Foundations

These four introductory chapters provide foundational information related to the rest of the book. Chapter 1 highlights key components of cultural diversity training, including cultural humility, and nests the **ORCA-*Stance*** into this framework. Chapter 2 is the heart of this text, taking the reader through experiential training to understand how the practices of openness, respect, curiosity and accountability operate in clinically-humble relationships. Chapter 3 ties philosophical concepts as well as common factors and empathy research to our perspective. Chapter 4 explains the initial development and context of this training.

1

DIVERSITY TRAINING

A Brief Overview

Peter M. Rivera and Claudia Grauf-Grounds

How Does One Prepare to Work with Clients in an Increasingly Diverse Society?

Within the United States, ethnic-racial groups continue to grow in size (US Census Bureau, 2019), sexual and gender minority groups are becoming more visible (McGill, 2016; Saad, 2012), couples are facing new challenges (Pew Research Center, 2014a), and diverse family forms continue to grow (Pew Research Center, 2014b). In light of such trends, it is now more important than ever for health care training programs to prepare students for an increasingly diverse society and an array of complex presenting problems.

Training programs usually offer students content- and process-oriented information as well as skills and perspectives in order to work more fluidly in cross-cultural relationships. Models that are content-driven target the therapist's knowledge and/or bias across various cultural groups (Sue, 2001). Such approaches often view therapeutic skills as a manifestation of increased awareness and knowledge of specific topics (Sue & Sue, 2003). Usually, this type of training is covered in a single course; however, training programs that have fully integrated topics related to diversity across courses are becoming more common.

Several issues have been raised in the critique of the content-oriented models, particularly since they are associated with "competency" language (e.g., Beagan, 2018). By implying that competence across cultural groups is obtainable, the student may limit their learning. Expectations of competence have the potential to increase power imbalances in therapy (Bogo, Tsang, & Lee, 2011; Furlong & Wight, 2011).

A content-oriented style of training can run counter to helping students to recognize and become accountable for the power and privilege that they bring into their therapeutic relationships. Additionally, an inflated sense of competence may cause therapists to overlook factors related to culture that may be clinically useful in treatment. Second, competence training is often limited by its focus on between-group differences. The assumption that heterogeneous groups can be described and understood by a set of observable traits may lead therapists to ignore or overlook important within-group differences. Diverse communities exist across the United States where within-group differences are common across variant and invariant characteristics (e.g., ethnicity-race, heritage, nationality, sexuality, gender, geography, age, sex). Such characteristics have the potential to shape how clients experience their families, communities, and presenting problems, and therefore may influence how a therapist conceptualizes a presenting problem or approaches treatment planning. The area of intersectionality has become a growing emphasis in diversity training as a result of this more complex understanding of persons (Chan, Cor, & Band, 2018; Gutierrez, 2018)

Finally, despite growing evidence that process-oriented components of working within cross-cultural relationships have a significant influence on the therapeutic alliance and the outcome of therapy (e.g., Hook et al., 2016), training programs often elect to focus on students' knowledge and awareness of cultural groups (i.e., content). Even though it is important to target students' knowledge and sensitivities through understanding, it would be a mistake to assume that these targets will automatically translate to intentionality and effectiveness in the process of entering into and maintaining cross-cultural relationships. It is therefore time for training programs to consider how process-oriented training can augment existing training models in order to better prepare students for the diversity that exists within our society.

Contrasting Content- and Process-Oriented Training

Content- and process-oriented training are distinctly different styles; therefore, they have different implications for the focus and objectives of training. Content-oriented training focuses on students' acquisition and retention of information, usually referred to as conceptual skills. This training focuses on what cultural knowledge is pertinent to students' development as therapists, and may include a range of topics related to diversity (e.g., ethnicity-race, socioeconomic status, sexual orientation) in the hope that students can translate this information into their practice.

In contrast, process-oriented training aims to develop students' capacity to appropriately and effectively function in cross-cultural relationships. Even though this training acknowledges the importance of content, it moves beyond students' acquisition and retention of knowledge by focusing on how students can translate content into relational processes. The outcomes focused on in process-oriented training would include perceptual (i.e., ability to perceive or discern what is happening in the client system), executive (i.e., what is done in therapy, such as behaviors and interventions), evaluative (i.e., ability to assess and appraise), and professional skills (i.e., how therapy is conducted, including attitudes and activities).

Cultural Humility: A Process-Oriented Model

Cultural humility is one process-oriented model that has been used by training programs to prepare students for working within cross-cultural relationships. Rather than helping students to obtain a certain level of expertise across diverse cultural groups, a cultural humility model trains a therapist in a relational stance that promotes culturally appropriate practices and interactions (Hook et al., 2016; Ortega & Coulburn, 2011). This relational stance involves highly related intra- and interpersonal components, which are conceptualized across dimensions of self-awareness, openness, and transcendence (Morris, Brotheridge, & Urbanski, 2005).

Self-Awareness

The first dimension of self-awareness involves a lifelong commitment to pursuing an understanding of one's experiences and worldviews in relation to individuals with different cultural backgrounds (Hook, Davis, Owen, Worthington, & Utsey, 2013; Ortega & Coulburn, 2011). This intrapersonal component involves developing and maintaining an accurate view of self (Hook et al., 2013). The tradition of self-of-the-therapist training in some clinical programs fits well within this domain.

Openness

The second dimension of cultural humility involves developing a capacity to adopt an "other-orientation" rather than focusing on one's self (Hook et al., 2013). This orientation requires therapists to be open to learning from the individuals and families they serve, which includes learning about the specific aspects of culture that are most important to their clients (Dyche & Zayas, 1995).

This position requires therapists to relinquish the role of expert on cultural differences and acknowledge and to accept the limitations of their knowledge about clients' cultural backgrounds (Hook et al., 2013). Moreover, this feature of cultural humility attends to many inter-group differences found within clinical populations. Listening closely to the client is central here.

Transcendence

The dimension of transcendence refers to embracing the complex and dynamic nature of life (Morris, Brotheridge, & Urbanski, 2005; Ortega & Coulburn,

2011). It is believed that an individual is able to understand and accept their limitations in knowing all that is to be known by acknowledging the existence of things that are greater than themselves (Hook et al., 2013). Through embracing the complex nature of life and the limited degree to which we can be assured that we *know* anything for sure, therapists may be able to accept that they will always fall short in fully understanding their client's lives, problems, and culture.

Moving Beyond a Cultural Humility Perspective

Existing scholarship on cultural humility has underscored its utility in assisting therapists with working in cross-cultural relationships. The emergence of cultural humility has also brought to our attention the need for training programs to move away from paradigms that view multicultural training from a linear either/or perspective, and adopting a dynamic perspective that considers how content- and process-oriented training models can be utilized together as part of an effective approach to training. The attention afforded to cultural humility also suggests a need for additional training models that build upon these efforts.

In this book, we offer the *ORCA-Stance* as a valuable model that has the potential to move us beyond cultural humility by attending to constructs that are captured by this model and that also align with some of the information about diversity that is relevant to content-oriented multicultural training. The next chapters invite you to consider this new movement.

References

Beagan, B.L. (2018). A critique of cultural competence: Assumptions, limitations, and alternatives. In C. Frisby, & W. O'Donohue (Eds.), *Cultural Competence in Applied Psychology*. Cham: Springer.

Bogo, M., Tsang, A., & Lee, E. (2011). Cross-cultural clinical social work practice. In J.R. Brandall (Ed.), *Theory and Practice in Clinical Social Work* (pp. 693–715). Thousand Oaks, CA: Sage.

Chan, C.D., Cor, D.N., & Band, M.P. (2018). Privilege and oppression in counselor education: An intersectionality framework. *Journal of Multicultural Counseling and Development*, 46, 58–73.

Dyche, L., & Zayas, L.H. (1995). The value of curiosity and naivete for the cross-cultural psychotherapist. *Family Process*, 34, 389–399.

Furlong, M., & Wight, J. (2011). Promoting "critical awareness" and critiquing "cultural competence": Towards disrupting received professional knowledge. *Australian Social Work*, 64, 38–54.

Grauf-Grounds, C., Edwards, S., Macdonald, D., Quek, K.M.T., & Sellers, T.S. (2008). Developing graduate curricula faithful to professional training and a Christian worldview. *Christian Higher Education*, 8, 1–17.

Gutierrez, D. (2018). The role of intersectionality in marriage and family therapy multicultural supervision. *American Journal of Family Therapy*, 46, 14–26.

Hewstone, M. (2002). Intergroup bias. *Annual Review of Psychology*, 53, 575–604. Retrieved from http://dx.doi.org.ezproxy.spu.edu/10.1146/annurev.psych.53.100901.135109.

Hook, J.N., Davis, D.E., Owen, J., Worthington, E.L., Jr., & Utsey, S.O. (2013). Cultural Humility: Measuring Openness to Culturally Diverse Clients. *Journal of Counseling Psychology*, 60(3), 353–366. Retrieved from https://doi.org/10.1037/a0032595.

Hook, J.N., Farrell, J.E., Davis, D.E., DeBlaere, C., Van Tongeren, D.R., & Utsey, S.O. (2016). Cultural humility and racial microaggressions in counseling. *Journal of Counseling Psychology*, 63, 269–277.

McGill, A. (2016). Americans are embracing transgender rights. *The Atlantic*. Retrieved from www.theatlantic.com/politics/archive/2016/08/americans are-embracing-transgen der-rights/497444/.

Morris, J.A., Brotheridge, C.M., & Urbanski, J.C. (2005). Bringing humility to leadership: Antecedents and consequences of leader humility. *Human Relations*, 58, 1323–1350.

Ortega, R.M., & Coulborn, K. (2011). Training child welfare workers from an intersectional cultural humility perspective: A paradigm shift. *Child Welfare*, 90, 27–49.

Pew Research Center (2014a). Couples, the internet, and social media. Retrieved from http://pewinternet.org/Reports/2014/Couples-and-the-internet.aspx.

Pew Research Center (2014b). Changing patterns in the U.S. Immigration and Population. Retrieved from https://www.pewtrusts.org/en/research-and-analysis/issue-briefs/2014/12/changing-patterns-in-us-immigration-and-population.

Pew Research Center (2017). Parenting in America: Outlook, worries, aspirations are strongly linked to financial situation. Retrieved from Retrieved from www.pewsocia ltrends.org/2015/12/17/parenting-in-america/.

Saad, L. (2012). U.S. acceptance of gay/lesbian relations is the new normal. *Gallup*. Retrieved from www.gallup.com/poll/154634/acceptance-gay-lesbian-relations-new-normal.aspx.

Sue, D.W. (2001). Multidimensional facets of cultural competence. *The Counseling Psychologist*, 29, 790–821.

Sue, D.W., & Sue, D. (2003). *Counseling the Culturally Diverse: Theory and Practice* (4th edn.). New York: John Wiley & Sons.

US Census Bureau (2019). *A More Diverse Nation*. Retrieved from www.census.gov/libra ry/visualizations/2019/comm/age-race-distribution.html.

2

THE ORCA-STANCE AS A PRACTICE BEYOND CULTURAL HUMILITY

Claudia Grauf-Grounds and Peter M. Rivera

> The ORCA-Stance provides a foundation, a basis, from which a clinician or layperson can engage in relationships – such that compassion for others and self is extended. I have found the ORCA-Stance, as introduced, to provide a quick and simple measure to check in with myself in sessions and in life so that I may be present with others as well as myself. This quick ability to check in via the ORCA-Stance comes after the introduction of the concept and reflection of the parts and ideas built into the acronym. Further, I have observed in my study of marriage and family therapy that the elements of ORCA permeate the theories and efforts of the therapeutic process; this creates a wonderful foundation by which to initially engage in clinical training and internship processes while the fundamentals are expanded on throughout the degree program. I suspect it could be derived that the ORCA-Stance provides us with a perspective that distills decades of theories into a more unified simple language from which to participate in therapy and relationships. I would venture further to state that ORCA is not a new idea but is a way of recalling in any moment something at the very fabric of human interaction and relationship.
>
> *(Marcus Comer, program graduate)*

The *ORCA-Stance* was originally developed to focus our training of marriage and family therapy students at Seattle Pacific University. The acronym ORCA stands for openness, respect, curiosity, and accountability. Starting first as a description of clinical values held by faculty (Naden, Callison, & Haynes, 2002), the ORCA-Stance has developed into a clinically applied and theologically influenced *relational stance* that we strive to have with others (Grauf-Grounds, Edwards, MacDonald, Quek, & Schermer Sellers, 2009). In a sense, it is our way of making overt our relational commitments.

The ORCA-Stance is not simply a group of values that we hold or teach. Rather, it involves practical interpersonal interactions that we strive to maintain in our daily encounters with clients, students, colleagues, family, and friends. The Stance can be thought of as skills that demonstrate our hopes for our relationships. In our program, the ORCA-Stance is initially taught experientially and subsequently it is then reflected upon and noticed throughout our clinical and professional interactions. At times, we reflect upon encounters so that we can demonstrate our commitment to this Stance and even change how we operate.

Similarly to the way in which we conduct our training process, this chapter will offer an overview of each component of the ORCA-Stance as well as a core exercise used to "experience" it. Afterwards, we will discuss how each core aspect relates to cultural humility and diversity training. Our hope is to develop a non-assuming and unpretentious posture in our relationships. (See the Preface and Chapter 1 for more about cultural humility, contextual awareness, and diversity training). Learning how to be present with others in their particular moments of life is a core of therapy; the ORCA-Stance offers us ways to practice this type of presence without relying only on our assumptions or knowledge.

To begin this chapter, each letter of ORCA must be defined: "O" stands for *Openness*, "R" for *Respect*, "C" for *Curiosity* and "A" for *Accountability*. For each experiential exercise, we hope that you, the reader, will stop and participate in some way rather than just reading the description.

A definition of openness: *Openness* is the interpersonal capacity to respond to and receive what others give.

An Experiential Exercise for Openness

Imagine yourself standing back-to-back with another person. You've never met this person before. As you notice their back to your own, you are aware of their height but that's about all. Now for a moment, with your eyes closed, consider how open you are to meeting this person. What do you experience as you encounter someone new? How available are you? How are you feeling in this moment? Do you already notice some level of energy or calmness from the other person as you stand there? What is it like for you to be in such close body proximity to another? Are your thoughts more about yourself or about your partner or do they switch back and forth?

Next notice your arms at your sides. When you feel ready, you are going to raise both arms in front of you. Reflect again about how open you are to this person. Now place your hands in front of you in a way that indicates your level of openness. Your arms may be close together or may be far apart. There is no right way to be. Just indicate your sense of openness to meeting the other by the placement of your arms. Now notice your hands. How might you want to hold them out in relationship to the other person as a way to symbolize your openness to this new relationship?

Finally, open your eyes and imagine turning around to face the other person while still holding your arms and hands outstretched. As you turn around, you see that the person who was standing behind you did the same thing as you; they are holding their arms out too. And as you turn, you notice that the other person has their arms less open than yours and their hands cupped. You feel for a moment that you want to match their level of openness, but you don't. Now stop and consider the differences without changing anything right away.

What are you feeling right now? What goes through your mind? What do you notice in your body? Do you want to change the location of your arms? Are you judging yourself or your partner? Does the way you are holding your hands indicate a different kind of openness than your partner's? Are you OK with the differences of where they are positioned? Do you imagine that the person you are facing has experienced some sort of trauma, leading to a more closed posture? If you had come into this experience at another time or day or another time in your life, how might your arms look differently than they do now?

Now take a few moments (maybe even writing down your thoughts) to reflect on what you were indicating by the way your arms and hands expressed your readiness to be open to your partner. You might use some of the questions below to help with this reflection.

Reflections on the Openness Experience

This experiential exercise begins our day-long ORCA-Stance training in our clinical program. The students have attended an overnight retreat and a week of classes together, but they don't know much about each other yet. Rather than lecturing about the concept of openness (or any other concept identified in the ORCA-Stance), we begin first with this simple experience of self and of other. The dyads in the room are randomly assigned and each pair has had only limited contact with each other, so the experience associated with this exercise usually solicits many reactions. In setting up the exercise for the students, we ask them to image the meeting of their first client as a "beginning professional therapist" in this experience. Often, the anxiety in the encounter is palpable.

After the experiential part of the exercise, we ask the participants the following questions:

- *Generally, how open are you to others?*
- *What opens you to another?*
- *What closes your reactions to another person?*
- *How well did this experience represent how you usually respond?*

A Discussion of Openness and Cultural Humility

Openness requires us to be interpersonally impacted by our relationships; it expands ourselves to begin to understand the perspective of the other. In order to be impacted, we must be humble enough to take in what the other offers to us. Empathic attunement might be a related term to the term Openness. Demonstrating empathy is a goal of many foundational therapeutic processes (Ivey, Daniels, Zalaquett, & Ivey, 2017; Gallese, Eagle, & Migone, 2007). As a movement towards healing, people choose to let others into their lives as a way to begin a process of change. In order to learn about the life experience of another, we must be teachable, attuned, and impacted.

The idea that openness is critical to effectively existing in cross-cultural relationships is not new and spans many disciplines (e.g., Wenger, 1999; Ridley, Mendoze, Kanitz, Angermeier, & Zenk, 1994). For instance, Fowers & Davidov (2006) argue that psychologists' capacity to be open is directly linked to their ability to achieve the aims of multicultural training. Others have argued that a lack of openness can be a barrier to working effectively in cross-cultural relationships (Hook, Davis, Owen, Worthington Jr., & Utsey, 2013).

From a systems perspective, relationships can be described along a continuum of connection, from very open to very closed (Bertalanffly, 1968). The degree of openness can define both the quantity of connection between persons and also the quality of that connection. When we connect often with another, we tend to become more socially and emotionally intimate with them. We feel closer to them and may depend on them for support. When we spend less time with them and disclose less personal information, we may become more distant in our experience of the relationship. Many of us can describe the strong impact of relating to an emotionally volatile or toxic individual and how the interaction can be felt within one's body, thoughts, and emotions. We can also make behavioral changes to shift the connection with this type of person. However, sometimes we react to another simply because of our unfamiliarity with them.

It is worth noting that the virtue of openness often runs counter to our experience of socialization, wherein group bias is often internalized at a young age (Hewstone, Rubin, & Willis, 1995). As such, the virtue of openness may often be absent in students, and developing students' awareness of implicit and explicit biases may be a necessary step in developing their capacity to be open in cross-cultural relationships. Additionally, appropriate levels of discomfort towards clients may benefit students by challenging them to increase awareness and skills in managing their levels of openness.

Burnout, compassion/empathy fatigue, or what is sometimes termed secondary trauma, can be common results of being very open to the suffering dimensions of another (Figley, 2002; Siegel, 2012; Grauf-Grounds & Edwards, 2007, van Dernoot Lipsky, 2009). Many of those in the helping professions take a stand to be open and impacted by the pain and trauma of others' lives. Beginning therapists commonly describe the "burden" or "weight" of the pain shared by their clients and even report how they feel it in their bodies or dream about this at night. In our training program, we have even developed a ritual to help beginning therapists to better manage the way that openness impacts them (Grauf-Grounds, Edwards, MacDonald, Quek, & Schermer Sellers, 2009). This suffering can be particularly weighty when it involves a combination of loss and trauma through issues such as racism, sexism, and classism.

A key clinical skill for clinicians to demonstrate is their ability to regulate the degree of openness they have with their clients. A balance between empathic connection and emotional limit setting is tricky. The amount of self-disclosure, the speed of responsiveness to phone calls or other digital communication, and the ability to manage appropriate professional boundaries relates to the degree of openness we have with our clients. However, openness is a core interactional component of all relationships as well and not just clinical encounters. When we mirror another and have connection emotionally, we are being human. We all make choices about the degree of connection and self-disclosure that we choose to share, and these choices impact how we define our relationships.

Research in interpersonal neurobiology documents the higher levels of empathy as well as trauma can impact both the client and their therapist. Findings suggest that engaging in a mindful, bodily based practice may contribute to the development and maintenance of empathy (Treleaven, 2018). Managing the impact of empathy (even as basic as the open-arm experience) can begin awareness of this powerful experience. As a therapist is able to become more aware of their internal state as well as to attune to their clients, there are many nonverbal processes at work at the subcortical level. The therapist has an experiential connection that allows for changes in understanding and the level of support needed in order to stay engaged.

Openness demands that we are willing to get close to another's experience. It requires us to be impacted from the outside, while still being attentive to our insides. Our experience is not the only one available to us and we need to surrender and embrace the others we connect with in order to begin a healing relationship. This is humble work. It is difficult work with a cost, and it is foundational to being a healer.

A definition of respect: *Respect* is the interpersonal capacity to see and respond to another as a unique and valuable creation.

An Experiential Exercise for Understanding Respect

Imagine yourself sitting on chairs placed in a fairly large circle, maybe 20 chairs. Within the interior of the larger circle is another circle of five chairs. You are sitting in the larger circle, and you begin to overhear the conversation of those within the smaller circle. The questions have been posed to the smaller group and are being answered aloud:

- *What were some of the messages that you received about respect when you were growing up?*
- *Which persons were to be respected more and which persons were to be less respected?*
- *Did you experience being respected or disrespected as you were growing up? How did you know?*

You hear the range of answers from each member of the smaller group – some younger and some older than you, some Caucasian and some not, some male and some female. You begin to consider how you were raised and what familial and cultural messages informed you.

Some of the stories you hear are familiar and some are different. You were chosen nearly last on a team sport once and were labeled as "not very coordinated." You've not experienced "micro-aggression" in an elevator due to your race. You were told to respect your elders, but didn't really talk to them very much. You are driving a junky car (and you don't own the ultimate driving machine) and you're not able to pay off your credit card right now. Education was important to your family because they had not been able to graduate from college.

You notice that within yourself you hold contradictions in the experience of respect. You notice that your current views have changed from your childhood, but you are aware that there are limited connections with those you respect less in your life. You notice how internal judgments, both negative and positive, operate in many encounters. You begin to wonder what messages have shaped your experiences of respect and disrespect.

Reflections on the Respect Exercise

This exercise is most powerful when done with others. By hearing stories from friends, family, or peers while asking yourself questions about the messages that you received about respect and disrespect, you expand the subtle and very common cultural messages about this domain. In fact, many nonverbal messages connect with the discussion of respect such as nodding the head, clapping hands, sneering or making particular verbal sounds (e.g., laughter, whistling).

It is often useful to write down or share some stories from childhood when remembering or (re)discovering messages about respect or disrespect. If you have less clear memories, call up family members or friends and ask some questions about this area. Also, it may be useful to go to a public place, such as a playground or grocery store, or to watch for "signs" of respect or disrespect in the actions or words you observe. Notice if any of the interactions that you observe seem to be familiar to your own experience.

In this exercise we ask our graduate students to identify people they might find (or have found) difficult to work with. We ask them to determine if messages about respect or disrespect might play into these difficulties. We ask the reader to do the same. (Again, you might pause again and document your reflections).

A Discussion of Respect and Cultural Humility

Respect begins by viewing the other as worthwhile, that is, with unconditional positive regard. This posture may be very difficult to hold when a person is displaying a behavior that one might "disrespect" or has been marginalized within society. It is easy at times to "label" a client as "dysfunctional" or as at least "very frustrating," which may be an indicator that we are struggling to develop and/or maintain respect for another. However, a posture of humility allows us to learn from our reactions and does not allow us to limit the worth of a person to behavior alone. It is through the practice of cultural humility that we can increase our self-awareness of experiences and individual characteristics that make it challenging to receive respect from or extend respect to others.

Our definition of respect moves beyond approval or acceptance of those who are different to one's self, and calls for training that allows students to develop a sense of esteem, honor, or awe for those who are different. Despite respect being part of the socialization of some children, we often struggle to live out this virtue in meaningful ways that are reflective of esteem, honor, or awe towards others. Therefore, multicultural training must be intentional with how it helps students to move beyond ordinary respect for members of various cultural groups. An example of such intentionality would be to move away from a deficit approach by adopting strength-based thinking when developing multicultural training. For instance, a strength-based approach does not allow the topic of oppression to just be about oppression, but calls for an acknowledgment of the strengths utilized and resiliencies demonstrated by various cultural groups who have been oppressed. Additionally, such training should challenge students to identify indicators of respect in the therapeutic process and to articulate how levels of deep respect for others influences their work in cross-cultural relationships.

Even when an individual's significant pathology brings about destruction (e.g., perpetrator of a mass shooting) or other behaviors that are hard to condone (e.g., verbal abuse of partner or children), cultural humility allows us to recognize the limitations of our understanding of others. It can also remind us that each person maintains inherent worth. Consequently, humility challenges us to look for facets of an individual's past and present life that may aid in extending and maintaining respect. For instance, we are mindful that all our clients begin as vulnerable children and many who challenge us may have been maltreated or traumatized in their vulnerability. Much of what psychotherapy hopes for clients is for healing and worth to be experienced afresh in lives that are often filled with disrespect and suffering.

Respect can operate at a subtle but pervasive way within relationships. Students-in-training often notice this and describe how they connect better to one family member rather than another. When explored, conversations about respect can show forth. When people are able to be humble and teachable within the encounter, exploring issues of respect and disrespect, more chances for connection can take place.

When therapists reference respect or disrespect, they often focus on cultural messages that privilege or marginalize others. Education might be privileged; poverty might be valued less. Having a lighter skin color might be more of an advantage in a particular community than being darker. It is useful to be culturally attuned to the messages from our background. Our fit or lack of fit with others may have to do with what is familiar within our own cultures. There is a tendency in human behavior to judge negatively and even disrespect those who are unfamiliar. What we try to keep in mind and to work to show is that we hold reverence for each individual. People not only carry a specific fingerprint, but a unique soul and identity.

Cultural diversity training assumes that various cultures, and therefore, people, are to be valued. Respect is central to the way we respond to another, as we understand them better. It also requires that we become humble and can learn from those who are different from us. The idea that therapists might appreciate and correctly interpret the culture of another in order to join with them is foundational in the establishment of a therapeutic environment. When judgment, misunderstanding, and disrespect are present, clients cannot trust the relational process. In particular, cross-cultural competency training requires those who grew up in dominant cultures to expand their experiences and to rely on humility in order to learn from those who are more marginalized.

In medical training, the finding that a physician must understand how a patient's culture impacts health care is a key ingredient in their ability to work with a patient and their family (see www.thinkculturalhealth.org.). A physician must be able to adapt and respect the cultural parameters in order to work effectively with a patient. Similarly, clinical research on why clients do not continue in psychotherapy services can sometimes be tied to respect. At times there are cultural messages at play that are unspoken. Asian families may seek a therapist who holds a particular status in order to respond to their interventions. Some African American families may listen for racial sensitivity and awareness of privilege in clinical encounters in order to experience respect for their own struggles. Some parents question whether or not young professionals can offer advice on parenting when they themselves do not have children of their own.

Respect is a foundational to a trusting relationship and clinical care. As we expand our own awareness of messages that shape those we respect or struggle to respect, we can improve our capacity to work with those who differ from us. This leads us into the foundational stance of curiosity.

A definition of curiosity: *Curiosity* is the capacity to wonder out loud as well as reflect within about the contexts of persons' lives without the need to fix anything right away.

An Experiential Exercise for Understanding Curiosity

In this exercise, we ask students to pair up with someone they do not know. For the purpose of this chapter, we ask that you imagine a person in your own life that you do not know very well. We ask that you use your imagination to hold a "meeting" with this person. For those of you who have a difficult time using your imagination for this exercise, we invite you to find someone, text someone, or call someone in order to create this experience and to attempt to practice this curious stance.

During the meeting you will focus on being curious about that person. You will need to develop questions that you might ask. You will imagine or hear their responses. Then, you will ask a follow-up question to *their answer* that enriches and expands your understanding of that person. In this aspect of the ORCA-Stance, you will choose not to make statements or share details about your own life. Instead you stand clearly in listening and asking modes of interacting and stay with their focus rather than your own once they begin to share.

In a sense you are being a detective about the person's life, wondering out loud at first, but also noticing the reactions and internal dialogue within yourself as you ask the questions and follow-up questions. You will notice choice points about the direction of your curiosity and your questions. You will take the lead from the person's responses rather than only your own perspective as they respond to you. You will need to drop the direction of your inquiries as they bring in another topic or story in response to your questions. Follow their lead and ask about words or the experiences they offer. Do not have a goal in mind except for understanding their experiences better.

Also, you need to notice your own internal reactions as they share. What questions do you have that have not been asked? Where has their experience been similar or different from your own? At any juncture, do you have the need to "fix" or "correct" what is shared or can you simply sit with what they have given you and be curious about it? Are you at ease with not sharing your own ideas and staying with their direction for the conversation, or do you find yourself struggling with this curious posture?

Reflections on the Curiosity Experience

This exercise highlights a difference in individuals who attempt curiosity. In polling our graduate students about this dimension of the ORCA-Stance, some find this exercise very easy and others find it more difficult. For many people, being with a person is easy; there is satisfaction in the time spent together and the information shared. No agenda is present and the experience together is enough. However, for others, there will be an internal pressure to move somewhere, to change things, and to bring an experience of something better to the encounter. There is an agenda present. Particularly for those who define their lives within the "helping professions," change is central. However, curiosity is a reminder that allows time to just be with another before moving towards something else. It is a reminder *to be and not just to do.*

Now take a moment to reflect on your experience. Where did you fail? Was it easier to just be with the other person and to follow their lead, or did you find yourself striving or pushing towards some sort of goal? In your life in general, is this true as well?

A Discussion of Curiosity and Cultural Humility

In the ORCA-Stance, our initial clinical position must include a posture of humility and of not knowing. We have not lived the full experience of those with whom we connect. We don't know everything. We all come from different contexts of life and we must recognize the limits of our own way of knowing, particularly when it comes to what others have experienced. Thus, humility allows us to recognize the limitations of our knowledge of others and is essential to being able to develop and maintain a curious posture in relationships.

Being curious in cross-cultural relationships means that we are able to rely on our wonderings to better understand the lived experiences of those who are different from ourselves; it fuels the process of discovery (Dyche & Zayas, 1995). Curiosity requires us to look beyond our assumptions, which helps with the problem of overgeneralization. It is important to move away from treating heterogeneous cultural groups as homogenous groups with no within-group differences. It is widely accepted that within-group variation exists as a function of nationality. For instance, there are over 20 different cultural groups among the Asian population in the United States (Lopez, Ruiz, & Patten, 2017).

Therapists need to be cautioned away from starting from an expert posture, particularly as they begin to hear clients' stories. We need to listen first to what our clients say, demonstrate empathy, and attend to their wisdom, notice their resources and expect that everyone can bring some sort of help to our work together. We need to hold back from our tendency to take a "convincing stance" (as Michael White calls it; see White, 2007) and be cautioned to slow down and to listen more than to speak. This is probably an important interpersonal quality needed in our world in general, yet can be very challenging when we are socialized to have excessive interests in our selves.

Most people enjoy responding to a good question. By starting with questions rather than statements, we demonstrate our willingness to engage in the life of another. However, particularly in the helping professions, there tends to be an urgency to "fix" the issue brought up rather than to understand it first. As mental health evaluators, we can be too ready to "diagnose" and to judge what our clients say too quickly. We may not take enough time to join and establish the relationship well before moving towards change. Particularly in our health care system that presses us to work quickly and efficiently, staying present and curious can be difficult.

A core skill related to curiosity is knowing how to ask questions, recognizing that not all questions are the same, and understanding that we do not always have to ask the right question. For example, there is skill in asking open-ended questions rather than close-ended ones (for example: *What did you think about that?* versus *Was that a good or bad choice?*). Also taking a solution-focused questioning position and listening for the potential exceptions and strengths that a client brings to our clinical work will be central to a curious practice. We don't have to and don't need to hold all the expertise. We believe that those we interact with can bring important resources to the situations they encounter.

Curiosity also invites us to challenge our implicit or explicit assumptions, which is especially important while working in cross-cultural relationships. Often cross-cultural competency training relies on knowledge about common patterns that a group holds (such as being collectivistic). A limitation of such an approach is that it overlooks within-group variations; by doing so, we may inadvertently assist with the development or maintenance of stereotypes. However, cultural humility allows us to recognize that we will never be able to obtain a complete understanding of between and within differences across cultural groups, and curiosity leads us to ask more questions about an individual's culture rather than offering unilateral prescriptions. It is a perpetual resource throughout just about any clinical or interpersonal situation. When stuck in a difficult encounter, it is vital for us to be able to move to curiosity as a way to stay connected.

A definition of accountability: *Accountability* is the ability to be responsible for the impact that one has in the relationship, particularly the unrecognized social power within the relationship.

An Experiential Exercise for Understanding Accountability

Imagine yourself sitting on chairs, side by side in a fairly large circle with about 15 other people. Some of the others are similar to you, close to your age, and dressed casually in jeans and a shirt. Others are a bit different due to their gender, dress, age, weight, or skin color.

A facilitator stands in the middle of the circle and begins to ask you to stand up from the circle and then move in response to the statements they make: If you have a college degree, take one step forward. If you own a car, take one step forward. If you live at home with your parents, take one step backwards. If you identify yourself as male, take two steps forward. If you identify as a racial minority in the United States, take one step back. If you have savings in a savings account, take one step forward. If you ever went to bed hungry as a child, take one step back. Think of some other statements you might add to this list and where people would move as a result of your statement.

You notice changes in the group configuration from where you began. Initially closely and evenly distributed around the circle, you now notice that some people are quite far away from you while others are much closer. You feel the shift in connections and discomfort in responding to some of the statements. Sometimes you feel privileged and sometimes you feel "less than." You also notice that some of these statements have to do with what you have chosen to do in your life (i.e., go to school) while others are out of your control (i.e., your race).

You are asked to express in brief statements how you feel about where you stand in relationship to the others. Some in the group say things like "left out," "uncomfortable" and "a victim." Others mention the unfairness of where they are in the group and that they desire to be somewhere else.

The facilitator then asks everyone to stay where they are but turn in relationship to the circle of chairs that has been left behind since the start of the exercise. Some are closer to the chairs and others quite distant from them. The group is then asked to imagine that there are people sitting on the chairs and to pick one chair to focus on. The person in that chair has come to seek their guidance. They are asked to reflect on the distance between themselves and their chair. They are asked to notice the distance between others and their chairs. Everyone standing is also asked to say how they feel about their ability to "close the gap" between where they stand and their chair. Finally, everyone in the central circle is asked to notice their position in relationship to each other and to move, if they wish, to another position that might feel more comfortable. If they stay or move, each is asked to explain how they made this decision.

At this juncture in the exercise, there is an opportunity to debrief in small groups about their experience of accountability to those around them. In particular, they are asked to reflect on the exercise as a way to understand the subtle and not so subtle ways that society gives power to certain people and not to others. They are asked to reflect on how they can be more accountable to this power within their relationships, particularly when they "hold" more power than the others around them.

Reflections on the Accountability Exercise

This exercise is familiar to many of those who have recently trained in business and the social sciences. Sensitivity to and awareness of power differentials within our world are necessary components to address racism, sexism, ageism, disability, and other domains in which injustices and bias can operate. Those who hold hierarchical power within organizations, in particular, must begin to notice where their decision-making impacts those around them. *Who gets a raise? What behaviors are pathological and who decides this? How do you rate a resume? Which students' experiences are to be valued more or less? What messages are carried through the words we use? How might my nonverbal behavior communicate my power?* These and countless other questions relate to how we operate each and every day and carry with them "answers" informed by those who hold power within a particular culture.

A Discussion of Accountability and Cultural Humility

It can be difficult to achieve accountability without cultural humility. Accountability recognizes the need to take ownership for our behavior at personal, interpersonal, professional, and societal levels. For instance, accountability calls us to recognize and be responsible for the various forms of privilege we bring into cross-cultural relationships, such as White, religious, or socio-economic privilege. Research has suggested that students often struggle to acknowledge their privilege (Ancis & Szymanski, 2001; Hays, Dean, & Chang, 2007; Hillock, 2012) and have a hard time understanding how their privilege impacts their therapeutic relationships (Hillock, 2012).

Accountability also takes seriously our ethical and legal responsibilities in our role as clinicians, teachers, supervisors, parents, and evaluators of those we live and work with as well as those we train. In particular, our understanding of accountability emphasizes the often-unrecognized *social power* that can be present in relationships due to domains such as gender, socioeconomic status, or race. Accountability helps us to understand that larger sociocultural constructs often show up within intimate interactions. When we fail to achieve accountability in our relationships, the practice of cultural humility makes us more able to receive and own constructive feedback from others in ways that translates into meaningful change. Ultimately, interpersonal communication can increase our accountability to unrecognized social power.

For professionals, there are standards of ethical and legal behaviors as well as recognized standards of clinical care. Clinicians must document and provide appropriate paperwork and hold defined confidentiality within their work domains. They must monitor and attend to the social dynamics. For example, one of our male training therapists was assigned a young girl who had been abused by several men within her life at a very young age. The family member responsible for the girl wanted the agency to refer the girl to a female therapist. The male therapist, in consultation with his supervisors, sensitively explored the family member's concerns and tentatively offered to start doing therapy as a way to provide a "positive" encounter with a male. The family member was given the authority to request a change in therapist if they had concerns at any time. The sensitivity to the power, both negative and positive, associated with gender in this case became a transformative for the girl, family members, and therapist. Prior to this encounter, the training therapist had been unaware of the power that he held in the relationship. All within this context began to recognize what was most often unrecognized or reacted to without becoming contextually observant and attentive of how power can be used appropriately.

Interpreting the ORCA-Stance Within a Faith-Based Community

The ORCA-Stance can readily fit within a humanistic framework. It punctuates the value of all humans and contexts them within the particulars of their community. Some of the students we train would embrace this worldview. Others, including our own training faculty and staff, hold a Christian faith worldview. We have attempted to examine the connection between this worldview and our professionally accredited training program in an article published in *Christian Higher Education* (Grauf-Grounds, Edwards, MacDonald, Quek, & Schermer Sellers, 2009).

Our training community appreciates the power of language in the understanding of how the world operates; our words are markers for larger, socially constructed meanings and values. Much of the work of social construction as well as narrative family therapy fit here (Berger & Luckman, 1967; White, White, Wijaya, & Epston, 1990). This leads us to the practice of building bridges between the humanistically oriented words (e.g., openness) and theologically informed ones (e.g., grace). This will be described in more detail below.

During our day of learning that introduces the ORCA-Stance we introduce each component of the Stance with a particular experiential exercise as described earlier in this chapter. At the end of the experiential exercise, we visually display the definition of each component and then make a Christian theological tie to that component. For example, we first guide the students through the Openness Exercise. After they turn with their arms and hands representing their level of openness, they debrief some with their partner about their initial reactions to the exercise. The exercise facilitator then defines the component of openness (i.e., the interpersonal capacity to respond to and receive what others give) on a visual display for all to read and briefly discusses it. The facilitator describes the dynamic of open and closed relational systems (Bertalanffly, 1968) and how those in the helping professions can suffer from compassion fatigue and burnout as a result of being too open to the suffering of others. Finally, the facilitator offers a theological tie. The facilitator briefly highlights how openness fits well with the theological concept of grace. Grace offers unconditional acceptance to those it touches and is central to the understanding of the saving sacrifice of Jesus, with arms wide-open on the Cross, from a Christian standpoint.

The first three components of the ORCA-Stance fit with a Trinitarian view of God. *Openness* is connected to grace and the work of Jesus. *Respect* stems from understanding God as the unique Creator of the universe and the Creator of each unique person. Everyone holds value and worth due to their being created in God's image (Genesis 1:26). The third component, *curiosity*, is tied to the function of the Holy Spirit in human life. It is the prompting for growth, health, and healing in each person. As we ask questions of our clients, they let us into their internal struggles and dreams for something to be changed and fixed. It the Spirit of God that spurs people to get help and to hope for a better life. Those within a faith-based orientation can see God at work even if our clients do not language or understand this to be the case. Therapists with this perspective trust that they are participating in God's work even when using more humanistic or professional words.

Finally, the *accountability* component of the ORCA-Stance fits with the second of the great Commandments cited by Jesus, namely to "love your neighbor as yourself" (Matthew 22:39). Professionals must monitor and explore the impact of the unrecognized social power that they hold in a relationship. They strive to care for (even love) that person and to not abuse the power in the relationship. Accountability in the relationship helps us to moderate our position in the relationship so that we can use our authority appropriately. Those holding power must conduct themselves with humility and adjust their position in the relationship at times. For example, we may need to use our professional role to "diagnose" a person with a mental illness; in this way we hold power over the client in order that they can receive insurance payments for the services they are receiving. However, at times we may come from a different culture than the person we are interviewing. We will need to take a "not-knowing" stance in order to learn from their wisdom and gain insight from them. In this way we take a lower position of power in relationship to become teachable ourselves. The reminder of cultural humility comes in handy at this juncture.

Although not a fully functioning Christian theological framework, the ORCA-Stance does assist those who hold a faith-based worldview to integrate their professional training and some of their core theological perspectives. In this way it helps some of our students to operate in both secular and faith communities less anxiously and more fluidly.

Moving from ORCA to an ORCA-Stance

When we first used ORCA within our clinical training context, we thought of each category as a value that we would hold in our relationships with our clients. Over time, however, we began to view the categories of ORCA as an overall way of relating to others, not only clients, but colleagues and other social relationships as well. Furthermore, we began to understand that each ORCA trait was akin to a type of dance step, and that it was the interaction among the traits where we experienced connection more like a dance style. A few years ago, we began to label our set of values as a holistic stance that intersected and co-informed our relationships. For instance, curiosity may be needed to identify things that we can respect about a person who is displaying a behavior that we have a hard time respecting. During this time we also began to identify interactional skills that might be associated with the ORCA characteristics.

The ORCA-Stance became a way of being within our relationships that manifested itself in particular types of behaviors that would support particular qualities in our interactions. For example, openness could be demonstrated in our nonverbal tone when we demonstrated an invitational tone, an accepting non-verbal posture, and clients would report that they felt understood. They might indicate that the therapist had empathy for their experiences. Respect might be quantified in the quality and quantity of the therapist's words. For example, if a therapist talked more to one particular client and less to the other, the client might interrupt the conversation. The client might even report that the therapist was taking sides and that their voice was not valued. In this context, a supervisor could explore how respect might be operating for the therapist as well as for the frustrated client. Next, curiosity might be noted in the style of questions asked; if a therapist jumped to a conclusion too quickly, without asking questions and getting feedback, a client might not experience much joining with the therapist in order to establish a foundation for their work together. Finally, accountability might sound like having an overt conversation during the session about the context of the clinical encounter. For example, a therapist might ask their Latino clients if a Caucasian therapist might be limited in their ability to understand and work with them. If so, they could explore how they might manage those limitations or offer a referral to a more culturally attuned resource.

Conclusion

Taken together, the dimensions of openness, respect, curiosity, and accountability not only inform the training practices in our program, but the journey towards equity and inclusion within our program. Openness challenges our faculty to recognize and increase their capacity to respond to and receive what others who are different give. Respect calls us to recognize and increase our capacity to see and respond to those who are at the margins as unique and valuable creations. Curiosity does not allow us to divorce behavior from the context in which people's lives are embedded. Finally, accountability calls us to recognize and be responsible for our privilege.

When operating well, taking an ORCA-Stance helps us to identify some of the conceptual information that may be useful in clinical care, but moves us beyond this limited understanding of diversity to engage interpersonally with those whom we serve. This engagement is affective, behavioral, cognitive, structural, strength-based, culturally attuned, socially just, and, hopefully, supports healing. The task is daunting at times and keeps us humble. It guides us in the demonstration of a way to stay productive and connected with each other, particularly when there are differences between us.

References

Ancis, J.R., & Szymanski, D.M. (2001). Awareness of White privilege among White counseling trainees. *The Counseling Psychologist*, 29, 548–569.

Bergan, P.L., & Luckman, T. (1967). *The Social Construction of Reality: A Treatise in the Sociology of Knowledge*. New York: Anchor Publishing. Available at https://books.google.com/books?id=Jcma84waN3AC&printsec=frontcover&dq=The+social+construction+of+reality:+A+treatise+in+the+sociology+of+knowledge&hl=en&sa=X&ved=0ahUKEwjqge TEr6XhAhVHllQKHVmCABoQ6AEIKDAA#v=onepage&q=The%20social%20constr

uction%20of%20reality%3A%20A%20treatise%20in%20the%20sociology%20of%20know
ledge&f=false.

Bertalanffy, L.V. (1968). *General System Theory: Foundations, Development Applications*. New York: George Braziller. Available athttps://books.google.com/books?hl=en&lr=&id=TBvjCwAAQBAJ&oi=fnd&pg=PA103&dq=General+system+theory:+Foundations,+Development+Applications.&ots=Igh9xSZKxk&sig=H0cwG_j2s4OcLSLKBOMhBGvoeeI#v=onepage&q=General%20system%20theory%3A%20Foundations%2C%20Development%20Applications.&f=false.

Dyche, L., & Zayas, L.H. (1995). The value of curiosity and naivete for the cross-cultural psychotherapist. *Family Process*, 34, 389–399.

Figley, C.R. (2002). Compassion fatigue: Psychotherapists' chronic lack of self-care. *Journal of Clinical Psychology: Psychotherapy in Practice*, 58, 1433–1441. Available at www.researchgate.net/profile/CR_Figley/publication/320290701_Journal_of_Clinical_Psychology/links/59e1359aaca2724cbfdb73cd/Journal-of-Clinical-Psychology.pdf.

Fowers, B.J., & Davidov, B.J. (2006). The virtue of multiculturalism: Personal transformation, character, and openness to the other. *American Psychologist*, 61, 581–594.

Gallese, V., Eagle, M.N., & Migone, P. (2007). Intentional attunement: Mirror neurons and the neural underpinnings of interpersonal relations. *Journal of the American Psychoanalytic Association*, 55(1), 131–176. Available at https://journals.sagepub.com/doi/pdf/10.1177/000306510705500010601?casa_token=ATd2J6YZuloAAAAA:Adl_wiEP5EjbKDrMg_QZm407qQrSlGhYseRLB9L9NgtMAX7XW40oQJOU1GKZYGQWgS-0IJwxQw.

Grauf-Grounds, C., & Edwards, S. (2007). A ritual to honor trauma: A training community's witness. *Journal of Systemic Therapies*, 26, 38–50. Available at https://guilfordjournals.com/doi/pdf/10.1521/jsyt.2007.26.1.38?casa_token=Aa0ghlgbvvIAAAAA%3AgNCUNNVUyyggm61Thzge7UgT0qcXEfvTRiBHX4vn1wL_8gnwEkGoTZvVwJf4aMAIAykR2mg&.

Grauf-Grounds, C., Edwards, S., MacDonald, D., Quek, K. & Schermer Sellers, T. (2009). Developing graduate curriculum faithful to professional training and a Christian worldview. *Christian Higher Education*, 8, 1–17. Available at www.tandfonline.com/doi/pdf/10.1080/15363750802134931?casa_token=PJMjVAcDUv4AAAAA:Cv6mCsfZDx76ZdAMHETPwKN7yPCGUY4H0dl49STrWHiVeYdfL8–XywB-yd9jxuDYHu-ZMloaw.

Hays, D.G., Dean, J.K., & Chang, C.Y. (2007). Addressing privilege and oppression in counselor training and practice: A qualitative analysis. *Journal of Counseling & Development*, 85, 317–324.

Hewstone, M., Rubin, M., & Willis, H. (2002). Intergroup bias. *Annual Review of Psychology*, 53, 575–604.

Ho, D.Y.F. (1995). Internalized culture, culturocentrism, and transcendence. *The Counseling Psychologist*, 23, 4–24. Retrieved from http://citeseerx.ist.psu.edu/viewdoc/download?doi=10.1.1.564.9053&rep=rep1&type=pdf.

Hillock, S. (2012). Conceptualizations and experiences of oppression: Gender differences. *Affilia*, 27, 38–50.

Hook, J.N., Davis, D.E., Owen, J., Worthington, E.L., Jr., & Utsey, S.O. (2013). Cultural humility: Measuring openness to culturally diverse clients. *Journal of Counseling Psychology*, 60, 353–366.

Ivey, A.E., Daniels, T., Zalaquett, C.P., & Ivey, M.B. (2017). Neuroscience of attention: Empathy and counseling skills. In T.A. Field, L.K. Jones, & L.A. Russell-Chapin (Eds.), *Neurocounseling: Brain-based Clinical Approaches* (pp. 83–99). Alexandria, VA: American Counseling Association. Retrieved from https://books.google.com/books?hl=en&lr=&id=4JkXDgAAQBAJ&oi=fnd&pg=PA83&dq=Neuroscience+of+attention:+Empathy+

%09and+Counseling+Skills.&ots=WOSRS-NtcA&sig=Sq4BitGzBnW2seW5OmoRo5
kguf4#v=onepage&q=Neuroscience%20of%20attention%3A%20Empathy%20%09and%
20Counseling%20Skills.&f=false.

Lopez, G., Ruiz, N.G., & Patten, E. (2017). *Key facts about Asian Americans, a diverse and growing population.* Washington, DC: Pew Researcher Center. Retrieved from www. pewresearch.org/fact-tank/2017/09/08/key-facts-about-asian-americans/.

Naden, M.G., Callison, K.M., & Haynes, C.M. (2002). Treasured awakenings: Reciprocity and the reflecting team process. *Journal of Systemic Therapies*, 21, 41–57. Retrieved from http s://guilfordjournals.com/doi/pdf/10.1521/jsyt.21.1.41.23097?casa_token=oevaJZsJ-fYA AAAA:ebpFXA5RWvw7u0nLFm8repE2CY9tRhnk6BkJHFeAnpGAppdPnP30Qy4lf0 VEu6W7yROe-x0.

Ridley, C.R., Mendoze, D.W., Kanitz, B.E., Angermeier, L., & Zenk, R. (1994). Cultural sensitivity in multicultural counseling: A perceptual schema model. *Journal of Counseling Psychology*, 41, 125–136.

Siegel, D.J. (2012). *The Developing Mind: How Relationships and the Brain Interact to Shape Who We Are* (2nd edn.). New York: Guilford. Retrieved from http://revistagpu.cl/2008/ GPU_dic_2008_PDF/THE%20DEVELOPING%20MIND%20HOW%20RELATIOI SHIPS%20AND%20THE%20BRAIN%20INTERACT%20TO%20SHAPE%20WHO %20WE%20ARE.pdf.

Treleaven, D.A. (2018). *Trauma-sensitive mindfulness: Practices for safe and transformative healing.* New York: Norton. Retrieved fromhttps://books.google.com/books?hl=en&lr=&id=m edHDwAAQBAJ&oi=fnd&pg=PT4&dq=Trauma-sensitive+mindfulness:+Practices+for +safe+and+transformative+%09healing.+&ots=YoycAVRxzR&sig=e3L1Xr6qE8CxGl3 61hzA0Hbm2is#v=onepage&q=Trauma-sensitive%20mindfulness%3A%20Practices%20f or%20safe%20and%20transformative%20%09healing.&f=false.

Van Dernoot Lipsky, L. (2009). *Trauma Stewardship: An Everyday Guide to Caring for Self While Caring for Others.* San Francisco, CA: Berrett-Koehler Publishers. Retrieved from https:// books.google.com/books?hl=en&lr=&id=92kzVqyiWHwC&oi=fnd&pg=PR2&dq=Tra uma+Stewardship:+An+everyday+guide+to+caring+for+self+while+%09caring+for+ot hers.&ots=a_fH9HAcV7&sig=uPzMpX-Jr3OSgy2IyqkNU5lmgW4#v=onepage&q=Tra uma%20Stewardship%3A%20An%20everyday%20guide%20to%20caring%20for%20self% 20while%20%09caring%20for%20others.&f=false.

Wenger, A.F.Z. (1999). Cultural openness: Intrinsic to human care. *Journal of Transcultural Nursing*, 10, 10.

White, M. (2007). *Maps of Narrative Practice.* New York: Norton. Retrieved from https:// books.google.com/books?id=qDdoLhCr7PgC&printsec=frontcover&dq=Maps+of+nar rative+practice&hl=en&sa=X&ved=0ahUKEwjaz-G1pKbhAhVpsFQKHS46BBoQ6AE IKjAA#v=onepage&q=Maps%20of%20narrative%20practice&f=false.

White, M., White, M.K., Wijaya, M., & Epston, D. (1990). *Narrative Means to Therapeutic Ends.* New York: W.W. Norton & Co. Retrieved from https://books.google.com/ books?hl=en&lr=&id=bhyFFL4uHZQC&oi=fnd&pg=PR7&dq=Narrative+Means+to +Therapeutic+Ends.+&ots=TuQBi_lDez&sig=vYxNmaIW5UHLi8OBuZzSfXVD8W I#v=onepage&q=Narrative%20Means%20to%20Therapeutic%20Ends.&f=false.

3

PHILOSOPHICAL UNDERPINNINGS AND EVIDENCE FOR THE ORCA-STANCE

Don MacDonald

Philosophical Underpinnings

The openness, respect, curiosity, and accountability (*ORCA-Stance*) model emerged from and functions in a multifaceted context of interactive facets: systems thinking, Narrative Therapy, postmodernism, cultural humility, philosophical personalism, common factors psychotherapy, and linkages between neural processes and human relationships. Insofar as ORCA originates from and is refined by Christian faculty who work in the context of a Christian university, a broad theological thread runs through the model as well. While the acronym is brief, the ORCA model's foundations are wide-ranging and complex. The four ORCA principles cut across these various approaches to common factors in family therapy, fitting neatly into a broad tradition that dates back to the 1930s. This chapter surveys these concepts.

Underlying the numerous and varied bases for ORCA is a prioritization of relationships, particularly as expressed in a systemic worldview. Systems thinkers hold that a system consists of dynamic, ever-changing relationships between members who mutually influence each other and, as such, are relationally linked. These reciprocal relationships function in such a manner that tends toward relational homeostasis of the entire collective or whole. A system, in turn, reciprocally interacts with other larger and smaller systems, often in predictable patterns, albeit occasionally in unpredictable forms. Systems and subsystems provide the essential context for human development and the understanding of individuals as affected by their current lives and significant influences (e.g., traditions) from the past. While the primary contexts for humans are their relations with other people, humans are linked with other life forms (e.g., owners and their pets) and other natural events (e.g., climate, geography).

A systems worldview underlies certain aspects of philosophy and is also a scientific framework used in physical sciences as well as social sciences (Bertalanffy, 1968; Magnavita, 2012). Thus, subjective-objective, empirical-metaphysical, and secular-spiritual experiences mutually affect each other continually, as predicted by a systemic view (MacDonald, 2014).

While a major starting point for the model is the work of James and Melissa Griffith (1994), as described in Chapter 4, the views of Narrative Therapy (White & Epston, 1990) also figure significantly. This theory of psychotherapy is rooted in a systems worldview as well as in postmodern philosophy.

Narrative Therapy (White & Epston, 1990) helped to organize the earliest framing of the ORCA model. The theory emphasizes three tenets: client empowerment, the therapist seeking to establish conditions that support clients telling their own stories in their own ways so that they can find their own solutions, and the therapist taking care to avoid adopting a superior and/or manipulative stance vis-à-vis clients. These tenets resonate clearly with all four aspects of ORCA as well as with principles of cultural humility (Tervalon & Murray-Garcia, 1998).

Narrative is a systemic approach. As such, all relationships experienced by client(s) and therapist affect the therapeutic relationship. It is, therefore, important to understand how client and therapist life stories interact so as to liberate clients to write or rewrite their own stories (White & Epston, 1990).

Narrative also derives from the French philosophical worldview of postmodernism. More specifically, Michel Foucault's version of postmodernity was an inspiration (White & Epston, 1990). Postmodernity holds that each individual's life is a collection of personal truths, acquired through direct life experiences and through language narratives about themselves, including relationships in life contexts. Each person's stories constitute their linguistically constructed internal realities that help to guide conduct, regardless of the views of others. People and institutions with power that do not care about or understand an individual's narratives will at times try to impose their own stories on the individual (Hayes & Oppenheim, 2003). An intent of Narrative Therapy as a postmodern approach is to help clients to liberate themselves from oppressive forces so that they can create or reclaim personal stories that are free from subjugation (White & Epston, 1990).

Relationships are at the core of an ORCA perspective. Relationships are also central to systems thinking and to the philosophical view of *personalism*. Personalism emerged in the later eighteenth century as a counter to the relationally detached mainstream of European philosophies. Personalism coincided and intertwined with the European Romantic Movement, which mounted similar protests to debasing influences of the Industrial Revolution and physical sciences (Tarnas, 1991; Williams & Bengtsson, 2009). Poet-artist William Blake and philosopher-musical composer Jean-Jacques Rousseau were prominent voices in this romantic dissent. The personalism movement continues today, suggesting that it remains meaningful to some philosophers and to those who respond to similar impulses (e.g., artists).

Personalism connects a diverse range of philosophers whose particular philosophies differ in details yet share basic similarities. Two characteristics of the movement date back to Jacobi and Schelling, spanning the eighteenth and nineteenth centuries. They held that humans optimally lived in relational communities and individuals exercised freedom of will. Personalism shares the latter view with existentialism and phenomenology (Williams & Bengtsson, 2009). Two additional commonly shared views are that each person has intrinsic worth or value simply by existing, so efforts to define humanity in materialistic terms is denounced; and that individuals are self-directing or self-guiding, as an expression of inherent free will. Rejection of dualism is another important consideration in the movement, as adherents believe that mind and body and temporal and transcendent mutually influence each other (Williams & Bengtsson, 2009). Many personalists hold religious views and/or focus on moral actions. Spiritual or moral views are not requisite, however, as seen in those who adhere more to a secular belief such as humanism (Sink & Dice, 2019).

Personalism persists into the present and is apparent in the work of twentieth-century scholars such as Buber ([1923] 1959), Levinas (1969), and Macmurray (1961); of public figures such as the civil rights leader Martin Luther King, Jr. and Pope John Paul II; and of psychologists such as William James, Gordon Allport, and Carl Rogers (Williams & Bengtsson, 2009). The movement's core emphasis on the primacy of relationships resonates well with the scientific worldview of systems thinking and ORCA, both of which also regard relationships as sine qua non.

Evidence

ORCA was developed through clinical observations and theoretical perspectives used at our university. The approach is a *treatment model* rather than a *theory*. A treatment model usually identifies therapy goals, processes, and methods thought to be helpful.

Unlike a theory, however, it lacks specific foundational theses and hypotheses grounded in research. Instead, the assessment of helpfulness for a treatment model usually follows from the clinical experiences of the person(s) who developed the model. While possibly useful and immediately applicable, a treatment model lacks the formal organization and verification of a theory. It is possible for a treatment model to develop into a theory (MacDonald & Webb, 2006).

The ORCA-Stance also squares nicely with a strong research tradition that dates back to the 1930s. The tradition is usually called a *common factors approach* to psychotherapy conceptual formation (Sprenkle, Davis, & Lebow, 2009; Wampold, 2011). The common factors approach assumes that what is helpful with different theories and practices of psychotherapy derive from similar or overlapping aspects of those theories. Several theorists might use varying words and definitions of the aspects, yet they are more similar than different.

Rosenzweig (cited in Wampold, 2011) initially framed the notion of common factors across the existing approaches to psychotherapy in 1936 and the movement grew. Rogers (1951) developed a theory of psychotherapy – client-centered or person-centered therapy – yet it was essentially a common factors approach, based on his clinical observations and research. Two of his doctoral students at the University of Wisconsin, Robert Carkhuff and Bernard Berenson (1977) extended this line of research, producing very significant, albeit relatively brief, studies that endorsed a common factors orientation. That orientation remained somewhat moribund until researchers like John Norcross (1986, 2011) revisited them. Norcross, under the rubric of *eclecticism*, produced and reviewed research which demonstrated that multiple theories or treatment models of psychotherapy were effective and that their effectiveness related to aspects of the therapeutic relationship, chiefly fostered by the therapist, that were similar across theories or models.

Until Norcross (2011), the idea of common factors resided almost entirely in the Cartesian or modernistic worldview realm of how the world works. That is, clients were diagnosed and treated as individuals, with little to no consideration of life contexts experienced by the client and therapist. Norcross, however, also provided a bridge to the next development: a systems worldview. Bruenlin, Schwartz, & Mac Kune-Karrer (1997) took a major step by interpolating common factors into a systemic worldview. This was a breakthrough in terms not only of family therapy, but also of psychotherapy in general. The authors recognized how common factors existed in systemic approaches to psychotherapy. This work has been continued by Duncan, Hubble, & Miller (1997), Sprenkle, Davis, & Lebow (2009), and Duncan, Miller, Wampold, & Hubble (2010). Hence, the movement remains strong and the ORCA-Stance, while not yet directly grounded in research, is entirely consistent with it. Again, the understanding of these four ORCA principles as cutting across the various systemic approaches to common factors in family therapy fits neatly into a broad tradition that dates back to the 1930s.

Another line of indirect support for ORCA appears in the research and reviews of research by such scholars as McGilchrist (2009) and Siegel (2012). Both neuroscientists hold that brain functions, emotions, actions, thoughts, and interpersonal relations are intimately and reciprocally influential (i.e., systemic). Both also contend that neural functions are flexible and capable of growth throughout life. Siegel considers these linkages at a more personal level, especially in relations between parents and children. McGilchrist has a more macro perspective, focusing more on civilizations and their by-products (e.g., humanities, arts, and sciences).

Siegel (2012) affirms the helpfulness of effective psychotherapy. Optimal therapy entails verbal and nonverbal connections between client and therapist, such that "there is a direct resonance between the primary emotional, psychobiological state of the patient and that of the therapist" (p. 334). Siegel also regards psychotherapy as optimally providing a safe support context for client exploration and growth. In such a context, both hemispheres of the participants may attune to and be of mutual benefit to one another. What Siegel describes in terms of interpersonal neural alignment and helping context are highly compatible with conditions fostered by therapist openness, respect, curiosity, and accountability – plus the common factors tradition in general.

McGilchrist (2009) attests to the importance of the neural hemispheres cooperating, rather than competing, with each other. When the hemispheres cooperate, an individual becomes more creative and more productive. When two or more individuals with cooperative hemispheres get together, they can foment changes for a group, a region, or an entire civilization. The European Renaissance, for instance, might have occurred when it did due to many people with cooperative hemispheres living and working together during that era.

While McGilchrist (2009) does not address psychotherapy per se, the bilateral intrapersonal functioning and the interpersonal mutual influencing effects resonate strongly with Siegel's (2012) work. Thus, conditions fostered by ORCA could (a) enable productive relationships between individuals and (b) have implications for societal functioning as well.

The ORCA-Stance is well grounded in a systems worldview, postmodern philosophy, Narrative Therapy, and cultural humility. It is also in agreement with research on common factors in psychotherapy and effects of neural functioning on relationships. The model has plenty of room to grow and diverse underpinnings for inspiration. It will be interesting to see how the model evolves.

References

Bertalanffy, L.V. (1968). *General System Theory: Foundations, Development Applications*. New York: George Braziller. Retrieved from https://books.google.com/books?id=N6-woQEACAAJ&dq=.+General+system+theory:+Foundations,+Development+Applications&hl=en&sa=X&ved=0ahUKEwjE47fvr6XhAhURLnwKHeVbAGsQ6AEIKjAA.

Brendtro, L.K., & Mitchell, M.L. (2012). Practice-based evidence: Delivering what works. *Reclaiming Children and Youth*, 21(2), 5. Retrieved from http://passageworks.org/wp-content/uploads/2015/05/Practice%E2%80%93Based-Evidence_Brendtro_Mitchell.pdf.

Bruenlin, D.C., Schwartz, R.C., & Mac Kune-Karrer, B. (1997). *Metaframeworks: Transcending the Models of Family Therapy*. San Francisco, CA: Jossey-Bass.

Buber, M. ([1923] 1959). *I and Thou*. Edinburgh: T & T Clark. Retrieved from www.burmalibrary.org/docs21/Buber-c1923-I_And_Thou-ocr-tu.pdf.

Carkhuff, R.R., & Berenson, B. (1977). *Beyond Counseling and Therapy*. Boston, MA: Holt, Rinehart&Winston. Retrieved from http://funpdfleon.com/beyond-counseling-and-therapy-register-now-to-get-free-access-to-our-books.pdf.

Duncan, B.L., Hubble, M.A., & Miller, S.D. (1997). *Escape from Babel: Toward a Unifying Language for Psychotherapy Practice*. New York: Norton.

Duncan, B.L., Miller, S.D., Wampold, B.E., & Hubble, M.A. (Eds.) (2011). *The Heart and Soul of Change* (2nd edn.). Washington, DC: American Psychological Association.

Griffith, J.L., & Griffith, M.E. (1994). *The Body Speaks: Therapeutic Dialogues for Mind-Body Problems*. New York: Basic Books. Available at https://psycnet.apa.org/record/1994-97405-000.

Hayes, R.L., & Oppenheim, R. (2003). Constructivism: Reality is what you make it. In T. L. Sexton, & B.L. Griffin (Eds.), *Constructivist Thinking in Counseling Practice, Research, and Training*. New York: Teachers College. Retrieved from https://psycnet.apa.org/record/1997-08618-002.

Levinas, E. (1969). *Totality and Infinity* (2nd edn.) Pittsburgh, PA: Duquesne University Press.

MacDonald, D. (2014). The importance to psychology of connections between relational theologies, personalism, and a systemic worldview. *Journal of Psychology and Christianity*, 34, 203–211. Retrieved from https://search.proquest.com/docview/1609199853?pq-or igsite=gscholar.

MacDonald, D., & Webb, M. (2006). Toward conceptual clarity with psychotherapeutic theories. *Journal of Psychology and Christianity*, 25, 3–16. Retrieved from https://web.b. ebscohost.com/abstract?direct=true&profile=ehost&scope=site&authtype=crawler&jrnl =07334273&AN=21387602&h=eb2di6EhTUAxgNgo3Fnc3M7SKhKYHrDteuLkkb1 LbC3mWvogxYa4%2bzfIoBAfeWhJVcBxW4HaHGMNeujwZQt%2fPQ%3d%3d&crl =c&resultNs=AdminWebAuth&resultLocal=ErrCrlNotAuth&crlhashurl=login.aspx%3f direct%3dtrue%26profile%3dehost%26scope%3dsite%26authtype%3dcrawler%26jrnl%3d 0334273%26AN%3d21387602.

McGilchrist, I. (2009). *The Master and His Emissary: The Divided Brain and the Making of the Western World*. New Haven, CT: Yale University. Retrieved from http://users.skynet. be/tony.aerts/images2/About_TheMasterAndHisEmissary_Iain McGilchrist.pdf.

Macmurray, J. (1961). *Persons in Relation: The Form of the Personal*. (Vol. 2). London: Faber. Available at http://betepub.info/persons-in-relation-in-search-of-free-pdf-john-macm urray.pdf.

Magnavita, J.J. (2012). Advancing clinical science using system theory as the framework for expanding family psychology with unified psychotherapy. *Couple and Family Psychology: Research and Practice*, 1, 3–13. Retrieved from https://psycnet.apa.org/record/2012-0711 5-002.

Norcross, J.C. (1986). Eclectic psychotherapy: An introduction and overview. In J.C. Norcross (Ed.), *Handbook of Eclectic Psychotherapy*. New York: Brunner/Mazel. Retrieved from https://books.google.com/books?id=cNJrAAAAMAAJ&q=Eclectic+psychotherapy: +An+introduction+and+overview.&dq=Eclectic+psychotherapy:+An+introduction+and +overviw.&hl=en&sa=X&ved=0ahUKEwjAzoT5tKXhAhVD4VQKHdmsC8MQ6AEI KjAA.

Norcross, J.C. (2011). *Psychotherapy Relationships that Work: Evidence-Based Responsiveness* (2nd edn.). New York: Oxford University Press. Retrieved from https://books.google. com/books?id=gtD8yUe1n5YC&printsec=frontcover&dq=Psychotherapy+relationship s+that+work:+Evidence-based++%09responsiveness&hl=en&sa=X&ved=0ahUKEwjx vceNtaXhAhUpj1QKHeXuCiUQ6AEIKjAA#v=onepage&q=Psychotherapy%20relati onships%20that%20work%3A%20Evidence-based%20%20%09responsiveness&f=false.

Rogers, C.R. (1951). *Client-Centered Therapy*. Boston, MA: Houghton-Mifflin.

Siegel, D.J. (2012). *The Developing Mind: How Relationships and the Brain Interact to Shape Who We Are* (2nd edn.). New York: Guilford. Retrieved from http://revistagpu.cl/2008/ GPU_dic_2008_PDF/THE%20DEVELOPING%20MIND%20HOW%20RELATIOI SHIPS%20AND%20THE%20BRAIN%20INTERACT%20TO%20SHAPE%20WHO %20WE%20ARE.pdf.

Sprenkle, D.H. (2012). Intervention research in couple and family therapy: A methodological and substantive review and an introduction to the special issue. *Journal of Marital and Family Therapy*, 38, 3–29. Retrieved from https://search.proquest.com/docview/1115574140?pq-origsite=gscholar.

Sprenkle, D.H., Davis, S.D., & Lebow, J.L. (2009). *Common Factors in Couple and Family Therapy*. New York: Guilford. Retrieved from https://pdfs.semanticscholar.org/ba76/bdd7eaa04d85f1dce7d694c30687f4a28c2 0.pdf.

Tarnas, R. (1991). *The Passion of the Western Mind*. New York: Ballantine. Available athttps://books.google.com/books?id=fPiZGAETdHMC&printsec=frontcover&dq=The+passion+of+the+western+mind.&hl=en&sa=X&ved=0ahUKEwiyx575taXhAhWE0J8KHSuiAxsQ6AEIKjAA#v=onepage&q=The%20passion%20of%20the%20western%20mind.&f=false.

Tervalon, M., & Murray-Garcia, J. (1998). Cultural humility versus cultural competence: A critical distinction in defining physician training outcomes in multicultural education. *Journal of Health Care for the Poor and Underserved*, 9, 117–125.

Sink, C.A., & Dice, R.T. (2019). A personalist orientation to school-based counseling policy research. *Journal of School-Based Counseling Policy and Evaluation*, 1(2), 1–7. Retrieved from https://doi.org/10.25774/ddxf-8y63.

Wampold, B.E. (2011). The research evidence for the common factors models: A historically situated perspective. In B.L. Duncan, S.D. Miller, B.E. Wampold, & M.A. Hubble (Eds.), *The Heart and Soul of Change* (2nd edn.). Washington, DC: American Psychological Association. Retrieved from https://psycnet.apa.org/record/2009-10638-002.

White, M., & Epston, D. (1990). *Narrative Means to Therapeutic Ends*. New York: W.W. Norton. Retrieved from https://books.google.com/books?hl=en&lr=&id=bhyFFL4uHZQC&oi=fnd&pg=PR7&dq=Narrative+means+to+therapeutic+ends&ots=TuQBi_mEkB&sig=rGAGygJFKzUTlKwLs6dT8pv3ZNg#v=onepage&q=Narrative%20means%20to%20therapeutic%20ends&f=false.

Williams, T.D., & Bengtsson, J.O. (2009). Personalism. In E.N. Zalta (Ed.), *The Stanford Encyclopedia of Philosophy*. Available at www.plato.stanford.edu/archieves/2009ed/entries/williams &bengtsson/.

4

OUR CONTEXT AND THE ORIGINAL DEVELOPMENT OF ORCA

Michelle Naden, Kurt Johns and Mary Moline

Like so many good ideas, the ORCA framework was created in the midst of great food and stimulating conversations between friends and colleagues. But it also emerged in response to great loss following the passing of our mentor and chair, Dennis Guernsey, who had worked tirelessly to fashion an on-campus program and trusted the Marriage and Family Therapy (MFT) faculty to reshape the program into a more coherent whole. The department was undergoing a period of considerable change and needed new definition as well as a structure that would help us to develop a fresh training model. There were countless conversations in those days about what constituted the best training for therapists, but on this particular day we gathered at a colleague's home to talk about what mattered most to us in shaping the program.

It was the mid-1990s and the MFT field was undergoing a tumultuous transformation with the poststructuralist wave that challenged many of the ideas undergirding family therapy theories. A critical lens increasingly highlighted gender, social class, race, and sexuality in an effort to challenge traditional hierarchies of influence in therapy practice. As faculty members, we represented many perspectives and had come from diverse backgrounds in training and teaching experiences. Perhaps it was partly due to the shake-up in the field and in the department that we all were open to explore something new for our MFT program. We felt free to start from where we were rather than having to tread carefully around already established training protocols.

Two members of our adjunct faculty facilitated our discussions to define our training philosophy and method. They had extensive experience of helping organizations to clarify their missions and visions. Kurt Johns reflects about his experience that day.

Kurt Johns Reflects

At the time I was working as an organizational consultant, guiding the leaders of academic, religious, and health care institutions through processes to define their mission. The beginning point for these discussions was identifying the core values of the institution. The values would be crucial for informing its mission or purpose. In facilitating the SPU [Seattle Pacific University] MFT discussion, a colleague (Ted Ewing) and I brought this same focus on values.

We began with questions like: "What does the SPU MFT program stand for?" "And what are the standards by which it can say it's doing a good job?" As noted below, our reflections on these questions came at a propitious time of change in the field, and on the heels of two influential books.

Our discussion began with a book, *The Body Speaks*, which had just been written by James Griffith and Melissa Elliott Griffith (1994). Several of us had read the book and were excited about it. James and Melissa brought their own personal backgrounds in dealing with chronic illness and their professional experiences in the medical field (James as a neurologist and psychiatrist and Melissa as a nurse) to the practice of family therapy. At the time of writing *The Body Speaks* they were co-directors of a family therapy training program. Being themselves the products of more traditional family therapy approaches, they were drawn to constructivist, language systems, solution-focused, and narrative approaches as the "more fruitful sources of inspiration" (Griffith & Griffith, 1994, p. 3) for their work.

A little more background is needed here in order to honor the influence that Griffith and Griffith's work had on our own. In their book, the authors addressed a very particular kind of problem that was highly resistant to treatment in medical settings: somatic complaints that seemed to have no clear physiological explanations and that were largely resistant to traditional medical treatments. They came to view "a somatized symptom as the public performance of an unspeakable dilemma" (Griffith & Griffith, 1994, p. 65). It was a personal "narrative," they said, that tightly held such dilemmas in place in people's lives. Through careful deconstruction of these narratives and reconstruction of new ones, the stories loosened their bind on people, and the symptoms resolved.

This transformative work required a certain "emotional posture" that would create a sense of safety for people suffering from distressing symptoms. The emotional posture grew out of a set of attitudes that structured the therapy – curiosity, respect, and openness. Together these attitudes pushed the clinician's "expert" knowledge and professional agendas to one side and made the knowledge and experiences of the clients the center of every conversation.

According to Griffith and Griffith (1994), conversations in therapy that are guided by these attitudes of curiosity, respect, and openness "constitute a political stance for therapy," and serve the following purposes: "Protecting the integrity of personhood of the participants; establishing egalitarian relationships; taking into account the impact of the clinical setting; and taking into account the relational impact of the clinician's expert knowledge" (p. 71).

Although it would be difficult to find a clinician who would disagree with the importance of these three attitudes, for the Griffiths they implied some very specific beliefs and practices. For example, these attitudes can lead to the belief that "patients and family members as human beings share more similarities than differences with the clinician"; that "persons and family members in their deepest desires do not wish to harm themselves or others"; that "a clinician cannot understand the meaning of the language a person uses until they have talked together about it"; that "change is always possible"; and that "a clinician cannot know for sure what actions family members need to take for the problem to resolve," in contrast to "a sense of certainty by the therapist about what does and does not need to happen" (Griffith & Griffith, 1994, pp. 91–92).

As our faculty explored these ideas we became aware that the authors were proposing more than just a set of attitudes for their therapeutic work. A fundamental set of beliefs about people and problems was put forth as well. We were invited into a worldview that would have us keep people's experiences at the center of the work while putting our beloved ideas about therapy and functioning to one side, at least long enough to really hear what people had to say about themselves and their preferences for their lives. Advocating these beliefs and practices configured the therapy in particular ways. In the authors' words,

> In this way one literally can choose a world whose atmosphere is one of openness, curiosity, and respect – perceptions, thoughts, and behaviors that best live in that atmosphere then follow. Selecting the reality, rather than enforcing the action, is the more therapeutic path to follow.
>
> *(Griffith & Griffith, 1994, p. 92)*

It is accurate to say that we "chose" such a world for our program that day in our faculty retreat. We enthusiastically embraced these attitudes as foundational stepping-stones for our training program.

A fourth attitude, "accountability to power," was added because of our faculty's commitment to notice and be responsible for our own use of power in the therapeutic relationship. Griffith & Griffith (1994) addressed power relations throughout the discussion of curiosity, openness, and respect, and challenged clinicians to "take responsibility for his or her epistemological stance in therapy" (p. 87).

Clinicians should strive to establish egalitarian relationships within the therapeutic conversation, while openly acknowledging the power differences between clinician, patient, and family members inherent in the structure of therapy. This therapeutic approach strives to restore a unity of language in which mind and body, public and private discourses can be rejoined. Hierarchies of power in human relationships tend to silence the non-dominant participants. It is therefore important for our therapeutic efforts to create therapeutic relationships that are as egalitarian as possible, with each participant in the process participating actively in decision making" (Griffith & Griffith, 1994, p. 73).

Adding accountably with power was in line with a growing number of voices in the field in the 1990s, a number of voices which had been growing steadily since at least the 1970s, with the influence of feminist thought (Hall, 2013); and the 1980s with the influence of narrative and more broadly, social constructionist, postmodern ideas (Doan, 1997). These conversations felt tremendously important to us as we were swept up in these larger movements that challenged the long-held assumptions about the therapist being a neutral, benign, and supportive presence. There was a sense of urgency about them, partly because we were so struck that we had been nearly oblivious to power for all the years of our training and teaching.

I was drawn to the prospect of fostering a greater awareness of, and account-ability for power on the part of the therapist in the therapeutic relationship. My own background in sociology had convinced me that we are never free of the influence of our sociohistorical contexts, and that, as Michael White compellingly argued in *The Politics of Therapy: Putting to Rest the Illusion of Neutrality* (1994),

> It is never a matter of whether or not we bring politics into the therapy room, but it is a matter of whether or not we are prepared to acknowledge the existence of these politics, and it is a matter of the degree to which we are prepared to be complicit in the reproduction of these politics.

Michelle Naden Reflects

For me, the conversation about power connected directly with my graduate studies in sociology and gender. I loved that we could begin to speak about our work more transparently than ever before. I felt relieved that there was an alternate epistemological stance to being in an all-knowing position as a therapist. Many in our teaching community shared the liberation I felt. We imagined a training sequence in which students were encouraged to hold their "knowing" tentatively and to create a wide-open space for client experiences and knowledge.

Several of our faculty had taught in other programs where the training sequence focused predominantly on students selecting and demonstrating mastery over one particular theoretical model in clinical work. Although we continued to emphasize learning and using theories in developing clinical competency, we were aware that a focus on therapist qualities in relation to clients was taking us in another important direction. We were not alone. Training in all American Association for MFT accredited programs was being heavily influenced by find-ings that the relationship between therapist and client was a highly significant variable in measuring positive therapy outcomes. The year *The Body Speaks* was published, Miller, Duncan, and Hubble (1996) published *Escape from Babel*. Based on a meta-analysis of research studies, they established that 30 percent of therapy effectiveness was accounted for by the therapeutic relationship, twice the percentage of explainable variance attributed to theories or techniques.

For us, the research documenting the significance of therapist qualities in treatment supported a focus on therapist Openness, Respect, Curiosity, and Accountability to Power relations and this framework became the foundation of our training program. When our colleague, Ted Ewing, directed us to reflect on the conversations that we had during the day of our faculty retreat, to name what stood out most as ideas that mattered to us, or moved us in some significant way, he wrote copious notes on big flip charts as we shared our thoughts. ORCA fairly jumped out to us as a shorthand acronym for what we were passionate about. I can still recall the excitement that we felt together as a community, as though we really were discovering something for the first time!

Footnote from Mary Moline

We held a faculty and student retreat that was influenced by ORCA after this faculty retreat. Students and faculty took the time to engage in collaborative conversation about the future of the MFT program, intentionally adopting an *ORCA-Stance*. The process was magical and as a member of the faculty, I wanted to engage in further retreats. It was illuminating and inspiring to hear the students' points of view about the program and how these would shape its future.

References

Doan, R.E. (1997). Narrative therapy, postmodernism, social constructionism, and constructivism: Discussion and distinctions. *Transactional Analysis Journal*, 27(2), 128–133. Retrieved from https://journals.sagepub.com/doi/abs/10.1177/036215379702700208.

Griffith, J.L., & Griffith, M.E. (1994). *The Body Speaks: Therapeutic Dialogues for Mind–Body Problems*. New York: Basic Books. Retrieved from https://psycnet.apa.org/record/1994-97405-000.

Hall, C. (2013). *White, Male and Middle Class: Explorations in Feminism and History*. New York: John Wiley & Sons. Retrieved from https://books.google.com/books?hl=en&lr=&id=5qUyXRTQZxgC&oi=fnd&pg=PA1977&dq=White,+male+and+middle+class:+Explorations+in+feminism+and+history&ots=jNQREjEGH5&sig=CDUbjnw_jFcZSZSwdS59u_BTBIs#v=onepage&q=White%2C%20male%20and%20middle%20class%3A%20Explorations%20in%20feminism%20and%20history&f=false.

Miller, S.D., Duncan, B.L., & Hubble, M.A. (1997). *Escape from Babel: Toward a Unifying Language for Psychotherapy Practice*. New York: Norton.

White, M. (1994). *The Politics of Therapy: Putting to Rest the Illusion of Neutrality*. Adelaide: Dulwich Centre Publications.

A reflective practice using the ORCA-Stance

Ask these questions:

- How is openness impacting us?
- How does respect/disrespect show up?
- How can we become more curious about what is happening?
- How am I demonstrating accountablity to the social power that is in this relationship?

SECTION II

Common Clinical Applications

The following section demonstrates the range of ways the *ORCA-Stance* can be applied to clinical work. We have selected populations that are commonly challenging for training therapists as well as topics or populations that are often treated in therapy. The focus of this section is to offer specific ways to ask questions, interact, and reflect on the work with clients who are frequently served.

Each chapter begins with a case example or quote. We then offer some information (content) that may be useful in understanding the clients concerned. We move to a case example that exemplifies ways that the ORCA-Stance can be taken. The emphasis of the chapter is on the process of relational engagement. We learn from the uniqueness of each situation and adapt ourselves accordingly. We hope to encourage the development of practical skills and a self-supervisory practice that is culturally attuned and holds a humble quality within our clinical encounters. All client stories have been modified in order to maintain confidentiality.

5

ETHNICALLY DIFFERENT CLIENTS

Inviting Creativity with Cultural Humility

Hee-Sun Cheon and Becca Seuss

There was a pause in our conversation and I knew this was my chance to ask my question, "What is it like for you to talk about racism with me, a white therapist?" I tried to keep my cool demeanor on the outside in order to project that I was culturally sensitive. Nevertheless, on the inside the roller coaster of anxiety was roaring through my stomach and all I could think was, "Wow, that came out so awkward." Waiting for a response, I was surprised when my client began telling me a story about a teacher who gave her a detention slip. She reported that she was the only student who got this slip and believes he gave it to her because she is Mexican. "Wait a minute." I said to myself in my head, "I just asked you a very direct question and I think you blatantly ignored it." My mind began spinning and trying to dissect where I went wrong in this interaction. I decided to try again. This time I rephrased the question using clearer language. I delivered my discourse and eagerly waited to hear my client's response. Once again, she replied with another story. This time a teacher had yelled, "Get moving. This is not a Quincenera" to my client and her Mexican friends in the hallway at school. "Oh no!" I said to myself in my head. "How could this happen again?" I tried my best to hide the confusion that I was experiencing and to sit with my client as she told these stories. Nevertheless, I found myself preoccupied with thoughts of my own inadequacies and expectations I had about how my client should answer these questions.

The unique and critical challenges that therapists encounter when entering the cross-cultural therapy space where clients are dissimilar racially and ethnically are paramount. Therapists are called upon to understand the clinical importance of inquiring into the effects of the contextual issues (e.g., race, ethnicity, gender, socioeconomic status, disability, and sexual orientation) on the lives of clients and on the therapeutic process. Whether named as "cultural competence," "cultural sensitivity," or "cultural humility," good cultural care is driven by several key realizations:

- General "good enough" counseling skills are, in fact, insufficient to provide responsible therapy to clients who are ethnically and racially marginalized (Sue & Sue, 2013).
- When clinicians work with those who are different from them on the basis of racial and ethnic differences, they are more vulnerable to "missed empathic opportunities" whereby a client reports emotional issues and the clinicians change the topic without addressing or reflecting the client's feelings (Comas-Diaz, 2006).
- Without the intentional self-examining process, therapists are at greater risk of behaving as a "culturally encapsulated counselor" lacking awareness of how sociopolitical differences impact the therapy process, and consequently disservice clients, thereby contributing to the mental health disparity issues (Wrenn, 1962).

A Competency Skill Model

Professionals in the field of multicultural counseling have put forward several models to guide therapists in developing their cultural competence. Possibly the most frequently used model of cultural competence is the Triparte model, which identifies self-awareness, knowledge, and skills as three essential tasks demanding attention (Sue & Sue, 2013).

Self-awareness requires a therapist's understanding of the significance of their own worldviews in shaping the way they counsel. Knowledge specifies the therapist's increased comprehension of the sociopolitical context in which they and their clients have existed. Skills refer to the concrete actions in a therapist's practice, although compared to self-awareness and knowledge, skill development has received the least amount of attention (Yeh, 2012). However, a body of competency literature has identified skills that are central and specific to working with culturally and ethnically diverse clients. Here are some examples:

1. Grounded in the awareness of cultural differences in communication styles, therapists need to determine effective ways to communicate with a client that may use a *different style of thinking, information processing, and communication* (Sue & Sue, 2013).
2. In order to be responsive to the needs of clients, therapists should be able to engage in a variety of helping styles and roles by modifying conventional forms of treatment (Hwang, 2006).
3. Therapists need to be open and able to use resources outside of the field of psychology, such as traditional cultural healing (Leong, Wagner, & Tata, 1995) and religious resources (Yeh, 2012),
4. Therapists need to discuss culture and cultural differences (e.g., race, ethnicity) early in and throughout the counseling process (Maxie, Arnold, & Stephenson, 2006).

What appears to be the common thread that cuts across the specified cultural competency skills is the therapist's ability to defer judgments and assumptions, step into an unfamiliar space to meet with clients, and above all to be flexible and willing to take risks with clients – requiring the therapist to look beyond and take the road less traveled. In these regards, Frey's assertion (1975) of counseling as a "creative enterprise" can be more applicable in cross-cultural therapy space.

ORCA Invites Creativity with Cultural Humility

Given that the impetus for cultural competence has been the inadequacy of service for members of ethnic minority groups, all the ethical concerns and clinical apprehension highlighted in the competency literature appear to be well deserved. However, the field of cross-cultural counseling has inadvertently constrained therapists with many "musts" and "shoulds." It has become a cautious enterprise seeking the right questions and right words while losing sight of cross-cultural counseling as a creative enterprise. Given that creativity is an inevitable part of the change process, reclaiming the creative aspect of cross-cultural work framed by the *ORCA-Stance* should offer culturally humble, and hopefully, liberating ways of connecting in difference.

Curiosity

The birthplace of a creative mind is curiosity. Curiosity is the capacity to wonder out loud as well as to reflect within about the contexts of people's lives without the need to fix anything right away. Curiosity is driven by a genuine desire to know and experience people we encounter. When curiosity is present in therapy, the dynamic process of interpersonal interactions opens up collaborative and exploratory engagements between clients and therapists, providing the source of power that keep therapists' assumptions at bay and sustaining creative conversations.

One caution that can be raised when practicing curiosity, however, comes from the idea of cultural mistrust – a construct conceptualized to describe minority groups' distrust of White Americans and mainstream American institutions such as the political system, the educational system, and the health care system due to the process of being exposed directly and/or indirectly to prejudicial and discriminatory practices (David, 2010). Hence, therapists' well-intentioned curiosity-driven questions can be misunderstood and taken in a suspicious way by culturally and ethnically different clients if transparency and openness about the intentions of the questions are not shared in the process.

Openness to Self and Others

Therapists are trained to attend to the resistance that clients exhibit in therapy, but they are frequently less prepared to deal with their own feelings of discomfort and anxiety in working with culturally dissimilar clients, let alone how to utilize them in the therapy process. As introduced in the case above, culturally and ethnically dissimilar clients may communicate in ways that are difficult for therapists to understand, such as directly or indirectly questioning the value of psychotherapy, or having radically different value systems. Consequently, therapists may feel confused, incompetent, frustrated, and even angry. Therapists often miss the immensely rich opportunities that the self-of-the-therapist brings to the therapy process when they are aware and willing to be open to exploration.

Therapists who are open and humble in their responses transform their discomfort into an opportunity to re-examine their work with clients, which fuels curiosity-driven questions throughout the therapy process. When therapists are open to include transparency about their experiences, safety and trust build within the therapeutic relationship. In response, clients feel accepted and heard, and are empowered to explore and share their experiences with therapists. Through this therapeutic process, therapists and clients open up new possibilities of creating different experiences, resulting in divergent thinking (creative thinking) that facilitates finding new ways to resolve the problems.

Respectful Curiosity

Respect is the interpersonal capacity to see and respond to each person with worth and dignity; the interpersonal space it creates invites a posture of cultural humility and acceptance. When respect is embodied, curiosity follows naturally because it is our intrinsic desire to know more about those who we view as unique and valuable. In fact, Dyche and Zayas (1995) described a posture of "respectful curiosity" as being equally important as learning about particular groups and specific techniques for working with culturally diverse clients. When they are uncertain of the cultural meaning of the symptoms, language patterns, and the approach to silence, therapists with respectful curiosity engage in collaborative work with clients to learn about and explore the lived experience of the clients – instead of forming premature conclusions. The questions therapists ask can be informed by their pre-existing knowledge, but therapists engage in dynamic sizing (Sue, 2006) when taking an informed not-knowing stance in order to avoid stereotyping members of a group while still appreciating the importance of culture. When cultural and ethnic differences are noted, counselors with respect approach the differences with cultural humility, viewing them as enriching instead of inferior or deficient.

Accountability to Unacknowledged Power

In order for the creative endeavor to be meaningful and responsible in cross-cultural counseling, it needs to be rooted in the comprehension of the socio-political contexts that the therapist and the client exists in. This stance indicates the sacred power that therapists hold in recognizing that their playing field is not level, and in initiating conversations to inquire into the effect that this has on the lives of clients and on the therapy process. Indeed, one of the skills unanimously recommended by the literature is the therapist's ability to engage in discussions regarding ethnic and racial differences. In fact, Day-Vines and her colleagues (2007) have coined the term *broaching* to describe counselors' ability to consider how sociopolitical factors influence the client's counseling concerns. An emerging body of research has indicated that the acknowledgement of cultural and racial differences during the counseling process enhances counselor credibility, client satisfaction, and the depth of client disclosure (Hernandez Morales, 2005).

Case Study

The following case study continues the interaction noted at the beginning this chapter. It illustrates challenges associated with different communication styles within the sociocultural context of cross-cultural therapy, and shows how the ORCA-Stance was embodied to connect with the client's system.

> I had been meeting with my client for about six months prior to having the described conversation. The client was a fourteen-year-old Latina-American girl who was referred to counseling by her school counselor due to symptoms of depression and self-harming behavior. Our sessions began to develop a theme where my client would tell stories each week that spoke to the racism she had experienced from teachers and students at her school. I shared this with my supervision groups and two supervisors suggested that I check in with my client concerning her experience of sharing these stories with a white therapist.
>
> After having the conversation with my client presented at the beginning of this chapter, I remember feeling like I had blown it. Initially I was so focused on myself and questioning my skills that I did not even consider how culture was interacting in the process of this conversation. Fortunately, I consulted about this interaction within my practicum group and my supervisor challenged me to lean into the ORCA-Stance during this time of confusion and feeling stuck.
>
> As I continued to work with this client, I found myself relying heavily on the principles of the ORCA-Stance. Cultivating a stance of respectful curiosity was essential. In sessions, I began to see a trend whereby I would ask my client a question and instead of answering my question with a direct answer she would typically tell a story. This made it difficult for me to decipher what was going on. However, the more I relied on respectful curiosity to guide what I thought were odd responses from my client, I began to see that my client was giving me answers to the questions that I asked. For example, I asked my client what it was like talking about racism

with a white therapist. Instead of responding, "Yeah, I feel comfortable doing that," she showed me her comfort by telling me another story about her experiences with racism. The answers to my questions were in her stories and it was vital that space was created for these stories to be heard.

Over the next few months, my client would continue to tell her stories during sessions in response to my questions. I realized that this was how she and her family communicated and processed things. Both her mom and dad would communicate indirectly during family sessions as well. Remaining curious about my client's stories encouraged and validated her to continue sharing. She reported that talking with someone and feeling heard contributed to a decrease in her depression symptoms and an elimination of self-harm urges.

Ideas for Best Practice

- Wield the ORCA-Stance yourself: remember that therapists can be well attuned at assessments and interventions when we are not afraid of facing our own reactions and responses to our clients and when we face the therapy process with humility. The practice is a commitment to go beyond examining ourselves as cultural beings and to be transparent when resisting culture and to create a new one when needed and appropriate. The process of embodying ORCA within us would be most similar to self-supervision. We stay engaged in our experiences in therapy, and we learn to share our authentic selves as a way of opening up space for collaborative conversations.
- Nobody can maintain their ORCA-Stance alone. Like the proverbial saying, "Nobody can practice alone," nobody can maintain their ORCA-Stance alone. Therapists' cultural engagement is likely to propel their growth through personal friendships with members of marginalized communities as well as through critical conversations with colleagues. After all, our cultural competence does not stop growing outside the four walls of a therapy room.

References

Comas-Diaz, L. (2006). Latino healing: The integration of ethnic psychology into psychotherapy. *Psychotherapy: Theory, Research, Practice, Training,* 43(4), 436–453. Retrieved from https://pdfs.semanticscholar.org/881c/ef8b3fdde8d13f0a7edad0ebd98aac89f815. pdf.

David, E.J.R. (2010). Cultural mistrust and mental health help-seeking attitudes among Filipino Americans. *Asian American Journal of Psychology,* 1, 57–66. Retrieved from www.resea rchgate.net/profile/E_J_R_David/publication/232498371_Cultural_Mistrust_and_Ment al_Health_Help-Seeking_Attitudes_Among_Filipino_Americans/links/00b4952fab83422 1fc000000/Cultural-Mistrust-and-Mental-Health-Help-Seeking-Attitudes-Among-Filipi no-Americans.pdf.

Day-Vines, N., Wood, S., & Grothaus, T. (2007). Broaching the subjects of race, ethnicity, and culture during the counseling process. *Journal of Counseling & Development,* 85,

401–409. Retrieved from www.researchgate.net/profile/Norma_Day-Vines/publication/263718280_Broaching_the_Subjects_of_Race_Ethnicity_and_Culture_During_the_Counseling_Process/links/5a52df73aca2725638c7b6b7/Broaching-the-Subjects-of-Race-Ethnicity-and-Culture-During-the-Counseling-Process.pdf.

Dyche, L., & Zayas, L. (1995). The value of curiosity and naiveté for the cross-cultural psychotherapists. *Family Process*, 34(4), 389–399. Retrieved from https://onlinelibrary.wiley.com/doi/pdf/10.1111/j.1545-5300.1995.00389.x.

Dyche, L., & Zayas, L. (2001). Cross-cultural empathy and training the contemporary psychotherapist. *Clinical Social Work Journal*, 29(3), 245–258. Retrieved from https://link.springer.com/content/pdf/10.1023/A:1010407728614.pdf.

Frey, D.H. (1975). The anatomy of an idea: Creativity in counseling. *Personal and Guidance Journal*, 54, 23–27. Retrieved from https://onlinelibrary.wiley.com/doi/abs/10.1002/j.2164-4918.1975.tb04166.x.

Hernandez Morales, A. (2005). Exploring and conceptualizing the negotiation of racial differences in counseling. *Dissertation Abstracts International Section A: Humanities & Social Sciences*, 65(8–A), 2907.

Hwang, W. (2006). The Psychotherapy Adaptation and Modification Framework: Application to Asian Americans. *American Psychologist*, 61(7): 702–715. doi:10.1037/0003-066X.61.7.702. Leong, F., & Lau, A. (2001). Barriers to providing effective mental health services to Asian Americans. *Mental Health Services Research*, 3(4), 201–214. Retrieved from https://link.springer.com/content/pdf/10.1023/A:1013177014788.pdf.

Leong, F.T.L., Wagner, N.S., & Tata, S.P. (1995). Racial and ethnic variations in help-seeking attitudes. In J.G. Ponterotto, J.M. Casas, L.A. Suzuki, & C.M. Alexander (Eds), *Handbook of Multicultural Counseling* (pp. 415–488). Thousand Oaks, CA: SAGE.

Sue, S. (2006). Cultural competency: From philosophy to research and practice. *Journal of Community Psychology*, 34(2), 237–245. Retrieved from https://onlinelibrary.wiley.com/doi/abs/10.1002/jcop.20095.

Maxie, A., Arnold, D., & Stephenson, M. (2006). Do therapists address ethnic and racial differences in cross-cultural psychotherapy? *Psychotherapy: Theory, Research, Practice, Training*, 43(1), 85–98. Retrieved from https://psycnet.apa.org/record/2006-05485-007.

Sue, D.W., & Sue, D. (2013). *Counseling the Culturally Different: Theory and Practice* (6th edn.). Hoboken, NJ: Wiley & Sons. Retrieved from https://books.google.com/books?id=OjDvvsJmm9gC&printsec=frontcover&dq=counseling+the+culturally+different:+theory+and+practice&hl=en&sa=X&ved=0ahUKEwjyrfK-u6XhAhWDAnwKHexqCpsQ6AEIMTAB#v=onepage&q=counseling%20the%20culturally%20different%3A%20theory%20and%20practice&f=false.

Wrenn, C.G. (1962). The culturally encapsulated counselor. *Harvard Educational Review*, 32(4), 444–449. Retrieved from https://psycnet.apa.org/record/1964-02905-001.

Yeh, J.C. (2012). Working with Asian American and Pacific Islander clients. In M.E. Gallardo, C.J. Yeh, J.E. Trimble, & T.A. Parham (Eds.), *Culturally Adaptive Counseling Skills: Demonstrations of Evidence-Based Practices* (pp. 139–154). Los Angeles, CA: SAGE. Retrieved from https://books.google.com/books?hl=en&lr=&id=2EcznQTwrVwC&oi=fnd&pg=PP1&dq=Culturally+Adaptive+Counseling+Skills&ots=W5DtCK68P-&sig=A6SnwxIJr1EWx5e7g0oJ3QW3nL0#v=onepage&q=Culturally%20Adaptive%20Counseling%20Skills&f=false.

6

IMMIGRANT CLIENTS

Mary Therese Kelleher

Lourdes arrived in the United States as an undocumented immigrant from Mexico at the age of three with her parents. A Deferred Action for Childhood Arrivals (DACA) recipient with a double major at a major Midwestern university, she has developed anxiety-related irritable bowel disorder. She has worried since adolescence that her parents will be deported someday without warning, and now is fearful that with the ending of the DACA program, she will be, too.

Mai came to the United States in 1985 as a refugee sponsored by the Lutheran Church, fleeing war and torture in her native Laos. She received lawful permanent resident status shortly thereafter. Thirty years later, she continues to suffer from post-traumatic stress disorder and depression with suicidal ideation caused by her war and migration experiences. She frequently has nightmares of watching her parents and eight siblings being tortured to death by Pathet Lao soldiers as she hid in the bushes; she believes she lost her soul at that moment (a traditional belief in her culture) and that the absence of her soul is the basis of her suffering. Lately, she has experienced strangers on the street angrily telling her to go back to her home country, and she is terrified of being forced to return to the scene of her torture. She daily considers suicide.

Fahten and Mahmoud both came to the United States on H-1B visas for an international tech company. After support from a therapist, Fahten ended her abusive relationship with Mahmoud and moved out. However, although he stalks and continues to threaten her, she finds she cannot report him to the police for fear that he will be in violation of the visa and deported to his home country, which is currently in a state of civil war. She is afraid he will die if he is deported; her therapist is afraid she will die if she does not report him.

More than ever, migrants and immigration policy are at the forefront of the civil discourse in the United States (American Psychological Association [APA], n.d.). Migrant populations within the United States are a widely diverse group with challenging and complex problems that extend beyond what most therapists will see in common practice situations (APA, 2013; Rodriguez, Paredes, & Hagan, 2017; Utrzan & Northwood, 2017). Yet therapists are rarely trained in the intricacies of this complex population and the special stresses and challenges they experience. Over the last 15 years, I have worked with migrant populations ranging from refugees to highly salaried economic immigrants within the technology field, and I have found that what has informed my work most strongly has been a combination of (1) training in trauma and loss, and (2) the practice of the core relational values enshrined in the *ORCA-Stance*.

Migrant populations are not homogeneous. They can be either authorized (i.e., those who have governmental permission to enter the United States, including those entering on a variety of visas) or unauthorized (i.e., without legal status in the United States) (APA, 2013). Within both these groups are individuals who are migrating for economic benefits, family reunification, or humanitarian issues (including war and/or violence, risk of persecution, or environmental disaster). Furthermore, demographic factors such as financial resources, education, employable skills, and age can range from very high to very low.

Most migrants – particularly economic migrants – are optimistic, have strong family cohesion, and highly motivated to learn English (if not their native language). They demonstrate resilience and, despite the inherent stress of the immigration process, score better than expected on a wide range of psychological and behavioral outcomes. However, all may experience a variety of concrete, emotional, and psychological stresses: loss of homeland, separation from family and friends, discrimination and racism (particularly for non-European migrants), loss of economic buying power, and decrease in level of employment.

The shift to American culture is often accompanied by global changes in cultural identity and pressure to rapidly assimilate to US culture, the loss of communication and heightened conflict with family, changes in gender and family roles (including role reversals between minor age children and parents), negotiation of cultural identity and loyalty, loneliness, isolation, and an indefinable sense of loss (known as ambiguous loss). Trauma may be experienced at all stages of the immigration process itself, from pre-immigration to post-settlement, independent of legal status. However, refugees, asylum seekers, and migrants without legal status (such as undocumented immigrants) often carry a higher burden of trauma; many are fleeing from violence or life-threatening situations, and most experience the high stress connected to the possibility of arbitrary documentation status checks, racial profiling, discrimination, immigrant raids (or threats thereof), the threat or reality of forcible removal and separation of families, detention camps, and forcible deportation (Cardoso & Thompson, 2010; Falicov, 2012; Mendenhall, Kelleher, Baird, & Doherty, 2008; Utrzan & Northwood, 2017).

Psychiatric pathology experienced by these groups includes anxiety, depression, and post-traumatic stress disorder, much of which is directly connected to increased situational stress and trauma (APA, n.d.; APA PI-GRO, n.d.; Chen &

Vargas-Bustamante, 2011; Utrzan & Northwood, 2017). Research has indicated that those with undocumented or questionable legal status experience much higher stress with increased symptoms (Momartin et al., 2006; Siemons, Raymond-Flesh, Auerswald, & Brindis, 2017). However, these same groups are often hesitant to seek out treatment owing to fears about disclosure of status, lack of knowledge of services, problems with accessibility, financial burden, and language barriers, or they may face other barriers to service based on a surfeit of trained or culturally sensitive providers (Chen & Vargas-Bustamante, 2011; Rodriguez, Paredes, & Hagan, 2017; Seimons et al., 2017).

As the therapist sitting across from a migrant client, we are often faced with someone culturally different from ourselves who has experienced stressors that we cannot fully comprehend. For example, when I met Mai, the Hmong refugee from Laos, I was unable to draw on my own 55 years of life experience to help me understand what it was like to have grown up in the middle of a bombing campaign, hidden and starved for years in jungles, watched your family die slowly and brutally by torture over a 24-hour period, lived in a displaced persons camp, shifted from a non-literate, agrarian Asian society to a highly literate, technologically driven urban Euro-American society within the space of one day, etc. I found that it was essential to work outside the box, questioning all of my assumptions and perceptions. You step into the role of student, with your client as your teacher. You know nothing. And you know that you know nothing.

ORCA became the net under my therapeutic tightrope. It was the structure I worked from as I sat with Mai and many, many other migrants over the years. In working with migrant clients – independently of their legal status or socioeconomic and educational background – I cannot stress more highly the importance of the ORCA concept of openness; I can say from experience that you will consistently have assumptions challenged in your work. You make it easier on yourself and your client when you adopt, from the first session, a state of humble unknowing, of cultural humility (APA, 2013).

Accompany this with accountability to power. If you are a US citizen, you hold a subtle type of power that your client may not have and may be sensitive to. This is your country. You know you fit in; you have a place. Remind yourself that you are working with someone for whom reality may be having no country, status, or power (Utrzan & Northwood, 2017). Depending on their immigration status, your client may also perceive you as a potential danger to themselves or their family members' status in your country. The problem of "medical repatriations" (i.e., health care professionals and administrators reporting Latinx undocumented patients, resulting in deportations) has recently been reported in the professional literature (Rodriguez et al., 2017) and is known within migrant communities. For many clients, therapy is a "both/and" situation: the therapist both represents a potential reduction of suffering *and* a potential source of suffering and trauma.

An awareness of the power differential can also help you to thoughtfully use curiosity. Disclosures may carry real risks – both concrete and psychological – for your client; this is especially true for undocumented migrants, DACA recipients, and refugees/asylum seekers (especially those who may have been victims of torture). While questions are essential to the therapeutic process, viewing your requests for information through the lens of the power differential can enhance your client's perception of safety and support. Stay curious, but clearly let your client know that they hold the power over the exchange of information within therapy (APA, 2013). I also provide space for naming episodes of discrimination or microaggressions early in the therapeutic relationship as a way of informing the client that I realize these episodes occur and may have an impact on them. And with those who are legal immigrants, I will often ask them how their experience with the immigration system has been.

While *respect* is essential with all clients, it is especially salient with marginalized migrant groups (Mendenhall et al., 2008). For many migrants, their experiences in the United States have caused the internalization of a belief that they are "less than" (APA, n.d.). I found over the years that overt respect (for example, using formal titles, like Mr./Miss/etc., rather than first names; using first names only with permission; and keeping sessions somewhat more formal until the therapeutic relationship is firmly established), combined with a stringent practice of cultural humility on the part of the therapist, can reinforce for many migrants that they have worth inside the therapy room.

Case Study: Maryam

Maryam, an international specialist in finance from South Africa who is culturally South Asian, had been married to her American husband, Michael, for nine years, during which time they lived overseas on multiple continents as Maryam went from position to position. For some of this period Maryam supported Michael as he finished an advanced degree in computer engineering. Their long-term plan was to depend on Maryam as the primary breadwinner until Michael landed a prestigious tech position in the United States, at which point Michael would sponsor Maryam for her green card, she would start her own business, and the couple would finally get pregnant. But after three months of being back in the United States, Michael made vague statements about how he was stifled by his wife and suddenly declared that the marriage was over, while refusing to delay filing for divorce long enough for Maryam to apply for permanent resident status.

When I first met Maryam, she was reeling from the rejection by her husband and the failure of her marriage, the loss of her professional dream (and path to US citizenship), and the knowledge she had to leave the United States (where all of her closest friends and her therapist were located) within a few months. In the Indo-African culture, parents are deeply involved in their children's marriages, and her parents responded to the crisis by flying to the United States to beg

Michael to reconsider his decision while attempting to recruit Michael's parents to join them in pressuring the couple to reunite. Both actions were seen by Michael and his family as bordering on harassment, and they pressured Maryam to make her parents stop (something which was antithetical to a good daughter's respectful stance). Her parents were also deeply confused and shamed by the failure of their daughter's marriage (something which rarely happens in their culture) and questioned her incessantly as to how she had failed Michael as a wife; she had her own doubts about herself as a wife, too, as she replayed arguments and lost opportunities over and over in her mind. At our first session, she was traumatized, guilt-ridden, depressed, grieving (the loss of the marriage, potential children, her dream career, and her long-planned home in the United States), deeply ashamed, and anxious about where she would work or live. She cried for hours daily, and some days she could not leave her bed.

Although I had worked for years with women from a variety of cultures, I knew that my previous experience would not carry over to Maryam, who was a sophisticated international professional from a culture very different from my Southeast Asian and Middle Eastern refugee clients and my own Christian-centric, Irish-American culture. With cases like this, it was necessary to consistently question my assumptions and examine my work for potential biases. For example, my cultural programming and professional training informed me that there was a problem with boundaries between Maryam and her parents; however, if I acted on that belief, I would (a) be culturally biased, (b) increase my client's suffering, and (c) cause potential harm to an essential family connection when Maryam needed as much emotional support and love as possible. Therefore, I took an informed one-down approach: I educated myself as much as possible on Indo-African family culture and on US immigration law while asking Maryam to help me to understand the cultural and political issues as they appeared in our sessions. I listened carefully, humbly, and with curiosity to the expert – my client – while examining and challenging my own perceptions. If I mis-stepped (and I did at times) I would acknowledge it, apologize, and ask to be educated about the finer points of her situation. For example, I was too quick to apply Western pathology to Maryam; what I diagnosed as depression as her daily hours of tears went on for months was actually an appropriate way of mourning her multiple losses based on her cultural background. When she pushed back on my suggestion of medication, I re-evaluated my stance, acknowledged her expertise on her own grieving process, and shifted my treatment plan to an increased use of meditation, yoga, and social connection, which worked with her cultural world view and which helped her to find relief.

Maryam and I worked together for a year, during which time she relocated temporarily to Thailand after her visa expired. Mostly we used an internet-based E-therapy platform, with occasional face-to-face work when she was in the country on temporary visas. I concentrated on using mindfulness- and attachment-based interventions along with statements of normalization and compassionate concern. Six months into therapy, we appeared to have stalled; I sought supervision from an internationally based licensed marriage and family therapist with wide cultural competency whom I respected. He suggested a short course of Eye Movement Desensitization and Reprocessing with a Bangkok-based therapist, which was successful. Although I suggested that Maryam might want to continue working with her local therapist, she preferred to return to working with me; I believe that was because of the strength of the therapeutic bond as well as my open attempt to practice cultural humility and work within her cultural context.

Shortly afterwards, Maryam's grief began to lift. She overcame the damage to her self-esteem and began job searches for executive positions in US-based companies close to where her friends lived; she started the complex H-1B visa application process after she was offered a position. During the nail-biting visa waiting period we explored her choices between an arranged marriage (which would give her stability and would immediately allow her to attempt pregnancy) and Western romantic dating (with its unknown outcome and the possibility of failing to find a partner before she lost her fertility). She ultimately decided to date again, while gently sidestepping her mother's attempt to arrange a marriage for her; after several tries, she connected with a man who she grew to love. When her visa was finally approved, she relocated to the New England area. Surrounded by loving friends, challenged by a fascinating new career, and exploring a new relationship, she blossomed, and we agreed to end therapy.

Ideas for Best Practices

- Openness: Assume that your client's experiences and worldview may be significantly different than yours. Guard against any judgment on your part, including in your nonverbal presentation.
- Respect: Do not rush into casual friendliness. Use formality with great warmth and empathy to instill a sense of respect between yourself and the client.
- Curiosity: While you stay constantly curious, use care when asking for information; disclosure should be seen as a privilege to be earned.
- Accountability to power: Always be aware of hidden power differentials.

References

American Psychological Association (APA) (n.d.). *Understanding attitudes toward recent arrivals to the United States*. Washington, DC: APA. Retrieved from www.apa.org/advocacy/immigration/prejudice-facts.pdf.

American Psychological Association (APA) Presidential Task Force on Immigration (2013). *Working with Immigrant-Origin Clients: An Update for Mental Health Professionals*. Washington, DC: APA. Retrieved from www.apa.org/topics/immigration/immigration-report-professionals.pdf.

American Psychological Association, Public Interest Government Relations Office (PI-GRO) (n.d.). *Immigration policy: A psychological perspective*. Washington, DC: APA. Retrieved from www.apa.org/advocacy/immigration/fact-sheet.pdf.

Cardoso, J.B., & Thompson, S.J. (2010). Common themes of resilience among Latino immigrant families: A systematic review of the literature. *Families in Society: The Journal of Contemporary Social Services*, 91(3), 1–9. doi:10.1606/1044-3894.4003.

Chen, J., & Vargas-Bustamante, A. (2011). Estimating the effects of immigration status on mental health: Care utilizations in the United States. *Journal of Immigrant Minority Health*, 13, 671–680. doi:10.1007/s10903-011-9445-x.

Falicov, C.J. (2012). Immigrant family processes: A multidimensional framework. In F. Walsh (Ed.), *Normal Family Processes: Growing Diversity and Complexity* (pp. 297–323). New York: Guildford Press.

Mendenhall, T.J., Kelleher, M.T., Baird, M.A., & Doherty, W.J. (2008). Overcoming depression in a strange land: A Hmong woman's journey in the world of western medicine. In R. Kessler, & D. Stafford (Eds.), *Collaborative Medicine Case Studies: Evidence in Practice* (pp. 327–340). New York: Springer.

Momartin, S., Steel, Z., Coello, M., Aroche, J., Silove, D.M., & Brooks, R. (2006). A comparison of the mental health of refugees with temporary versus permanent protection visas. *Medical Journal of Australia*, 185, 357–361.

Rodriguez, N., Paredes, C.L., & Hagan, J. (2017). Fear of immigration enforcement among older Latino immigrants in the United States. *Journal of Aging and Health*, 29(6), 986–1014. doi:10.1177/0898264317710839.

Siemons, R., Raymond-Flesh, M., Auerswald, C.L., & Brindis, C.D. (2017). Coming of age on the margins: Mental health and wellbeing among Latino immigrant young adults eligible for Deferred Action for Childhood Arrivals (DACA). *Journal of Immigrant Minority Health*, 19, 543–551. doi:10.1007/s10903-016-0354-x.

Utrzan, D.S., & Northwood, A.K. (2017). Broken promises and lost dreams: Navigating asylum in the United States. *Journal of Marital and Family Therapy*, 43, 3–15. doi:10.1111/jmft.12188.

7

POVERTY AND HOMELESSNESS

Heather Fisher

I have found few things more culturally humbling in my life than accepting that, as a therapist and human being, I am not always able to provide help to my clients in a way that feels satisfactory to myself and/or my client; I am limited by what the available social resources allow me to provide. I distinctly remember the first time I experienced this feeling. During one of our sessions my client, a teenage girl, reported to me that she and her mother were being evicted and would be living in their car. This was not the first time they had experienced eviction but it was the first time they had no prospective housing options. Her mother was undergoing breast cancer treatment for the third time and they had simply run out of money. In my new intern-therapist fervor, I immediately jumped into action and contacted every community resource I could think of only to find out that there were two-year waiting lists for housing, even for the highest needs population, and few resources they could access right away. I was devastated and felt helpless as I informed my client that there was little I could offer her other than my advocacy and support. She cried and pondered what they were going to do. Working in community mental health serving low-income, high-trauma, under-resourced clients for the last four years, I have become far more familiar with this feeling than I would like.

The homeless and extremely poor populations are growing in size, creating a working poor distinction. Of the homeless population, 40 percent are children under the age of seven. Family homelessness is emerging as the most prominent population utilizing social and public services (Haskett, Armstrong, & Tidsdale, 2016; Bradley, McGowan, & Michelson, 2017). Interim housing and shelter options are ill equipped to handle families and children. Public misconceptions and assumptions – such as homelessness being the result of laziness, mental health issues, drug use, or the image of the single person sleeping on the street – fuel public debates to find solutions to the homeless populations encroaching into both urban and suburban neighborhoods (Bradley et al., 2017; Hyde, 1985). Unfortunately, public anxiety and outcry often demands immediate, and short-sighted solutions rather than longer-term, sustainable solutions. There is not one easy, quick solution to a national problem of distressing and growing proportions. What is needed are quality and accessible community resources coupled with further data regarding family homelessness and the impact of homelessness on child development.

Children and parents experiencing homelessness tend to struggle not only with anxiety, depression, and post-traumatic stress disorder (PTSD), but also with increased health risks. Social determinants of health such as lack of or low income, high stress levels, lack of social support, ineffective transgenerational models of parenting and resiliency, as well as lack of understanding or access to health care, create a high risk for the development of both acute and chronic illness or mental/social instability for those experiencing homelessness or poverty (Larkin and Park, 2012). Pathology for homeless families often includes anxiety, depression, PTSD, and behavioral issues (Haskett et al., 2015; Rafferty and Shinn, 1991). Families experience issues of hunger and poor nutrition, developmental delays, educational underachievement, and sleep disorders (Rafferty and Shinn, 1991; Haskett et al., 2015). Furthermore, homeless children are more likely than their adequately housed peers to be exposed to violence, parental mental health difficulties, and drug use.

In my work with homeless families I have found the primary complaint to be the overall feeling of invisibility, a sort of nothingness. Families feel that social workers, school counselors, doctors, and teachers do not want to look them in the eye because there is little they can do. I have found the ORCA principle of *respect* to be crucial in building rapport with homeless families. Parents, in particular, need to feel that I respect their role as parent, because shelters often make them feel undermined and scrutinized, and create challenges to autonomy and self-efficacy (Bradley et al., 2017). I make no assumptions about how they became homeless and my *accountability to power* in the room provides opportunities for cultural humility, noticing how easily I could be in this same situation myself. Parents who are able to move past their societally imposed feelings of shame and failure, and who adapt their parenting practices, tend to be more resilient and experience less traumatizing mental health impacts than those who do not. Peer support and spiritual/faith-based support have proven useful to parents in this population for removing the stigma and discussing adaptive parenting skills with others who have similar lived experiences. The emotional toll on homeless parents and children is often mutually reinforcing, creating situations in which children require more from their already emotionally taxed parents (Bradley et al., 2017; Rafferty and Shin, 1991).

In my research for this chapter I became frustrated by the fact that the research from 1985 shared similar concerns and solutions for this population as current research. However, little seems to have changed in our social systems to meet the social emotional needs of this population. The most impactful solution I have found was the McKinney-Vento Act (MVA) implemented in 1987, which meets the transportation, educational, and nutritional needs of homeless students by ensuring that all children have access to education and resources within our public school system (Canfield, Teasley, Abell, & Randolph, 2012). The MVA provides liaisons within school systems to help families to access social resources as well. I could debate the efficacy of the available programs and resources for many hours and quote all manner of research to show how the system is failing this growing population. However, what is needed most is humanity, moving beyond cultural humility, and making space to find connections in our differences. We need to spend time helping this population to feel seen, heard, and valued; as therapists, advocacy and social/emotional support are the most impactful resources we can offer.

Case Study: Elizabeth

Elizabeth ("Lizzie"), a teenage refugee from Haiti, came to the United States through a sponsor family after the big earthquake in 2010. Prior to the earthquake, Lizzie had been living in an orphanage with her "brother" for about three years. Her mother had died suddenly leaving them homeless in their small town, fending for themselves for 18 months until local police arrested them for stealing food. Following their arrest, they were placed in an orphanage, as no known family existed. A couple of years later the earthquake happened and they were again left to fend for themselves until rescue teams made it to the orphanage. They walked and slept amid the rubble and the remains of their caretakers and fellow orphans for a week before rescue teams came and found them.

When I first met Lizzie, she was accompanied by her social worker and was a ward of the state. Her sponsor family had "returned" her after a few years due to the emotional and behavioral issues she and her brother exhibited. Her brother went to live in a facility for kids with behavioral issues and Lizzie was in search of a new home. She was separated from the only family she had ever known. Her experiences had taught her to stay quiet and not share her pain in order to be considered suitable for living with other families. While she was guarded and untrusting, her eyes revealed that she was craving connection and affection, although she had no idea how to receive it. During the intake assessment she reported that she had been verbally/emotionally abused the entire time she lived with her sponsor family, and that she had witnessed all kinds of atrocities (including execution and child labor) while living in the orphanage. After our two-hour intake I diagnosed her with PTSD and depression. The weight she was carrying seemed unbearable to me, but she bore it with great strength. She had already incorporated these stories into her overall sense of being as a means of survival.

While writing up her diagnosis paperwork I realized that I knew very little about her lived experience. Our intake questions did not leave much room for anything other than what we needed for a diagnosis. I relied heavily on all of the ORCA principles to guide my practice with her. During our next session I entered the room with curiosity and openness, eager to hear what she had to say; my only assumption was that she was the expert on her life, not me. I had researched Haitian culture and spoken with a special populations consultant who specialized in Haitian refugees. I had a plan for treatment, but wanted to hear Lizzie's plan and goals before presenting my own plan. I was very aware of the need to be *accountable to my power in the room* so that she did not see me as another adult telling her what to do and who to be. Much to my surprise, with tears in her eyes, she wanted to talk about her hair. You read that right – her hair. She reported that most Haitians wore natural hair and she did not know how to do her hair any other way. She had only lived with white families since being in Haiti and was embarrassed to ask for help with something they could not understand. This radiantly beautiful teenage girl who sat before me was being bullied by the other Black girls in her school because she did not wear her hair like they did. She was Black but not African American, further reinforcing that she still did not belong. That was her biggest stressor. Without curiosity and openness to what she was bringing into the room, without the capacity for cultural humility, I would have completely missed the thing that was hurting her the most in that moment.

I spoke with a local Black hair stylist who agreed to teach her about her hair, however she chose to wear it. I worked with Lizzie for the rest of the school year. She found another sponsor family and really started to come into her own and open up a bit. Once I was able to mediate Lizzie's immediate concern of acceptance at school, we were able to explore the impact of her experiences, including homelessness and her refugee journey.

By the end of the school year she had opened up to me and shared information she had never told anyone else. I could see the pain and struggle on her face every time she shared sacred pieces of her story. I was overwhelmed with a feeling of great respect every time she trusted me to share. My greatest goal was to create a space where she felt safe, respected, and cared for, a kind of holding space for her to envision a different future for herself. It was an honor to walk alongside her during this time in her life.

Ideas for Best Practice

Incorporating the ORCA lens into my worldview has helped me to learn so much about myself, and my clients. I use the principles so often that I have used ORCA as verb to explain how I "ORCA'd my way through a session" with an issue/population I knew little about. The *ORCA-Stance* is not just a set of rules or principles; it is a way of looking at the world through a lens of cultural humility, searching for connections where on the surface you see only stark contrast with what your lived experience allows you to perceive. No other tool available to me has been more beneficial or grown me as a person and clinician more than the ORCA-Stance.

- Openness: The client is always the expert on their life, not the therapist. Strive to be open to whatever the client is bringing into session that day.
- Respect: Treat the information that clients disclose with respect and dignity. Respect their journey by creating an environment in which they do not feel invisible but rather seen, held and respected. Anticipate and welcome the opportunity to connect in our differences.
- Curiosity: Their normal is very likely to be different than our normal. Look for opportunities to learn about each client's lived experience. Approaching clients with curiosity allows them to share without feeling threatened by cultural assumptions.
- Accountability to power: Constantly seek to explore your biases and blind spots in regard to each individual client. Address differences in session when it feels appropriate. Seek connection.

Allow the ORCA-Stance to be your first consideration when entering into a relationship with new clients. The homeless and extremely poor populations require, and deserve, the best care that we have to offer. You may provide the only available outlet they have to express themselves free of judgment; treat that responsibility with the honor it deserves.

References

Bradley, C., McGowan, J., & Michelson, D. (2017). How does homelessness affect parenting behaviour? A systematic critical review and thematic synthesis of qualitative research. *Clinical Child and Family Psychology Review*. doi:10.1007/s10567-017-0244-3.

Canfield, J.P., Teasley, M.L., Abell, N., & Randolph, K.A. (2012). Validation of a McKinney Vento Act Implementation Scale. *Research on Social Work Practice*, 22(4), 410–419. doi:10.1177/1049731512439758.

Haskett, M.E., Armstrong, J.M., & Tisdale, J. (2016). Developmental status and social emotional functioning of young children experiencing homelessness. *Early Childhood Education Journal*, 44(2), 119–125. doi:10.1007/s10643-015-0691-8.

Hyde, P.S. (1985). Homelessness in America: Public policy, public blame. *Psychosocial Rehabilitation Journal*, 8(4), 21–25. doi:10.1037/h0099665.

Kidd, S.A., & Scrimenti, K. (2004). Evaluating child and youth homelessness: The example of New Haven, Connecticut. *Evaluation Review*, 28(4), 325–341. doi:10.1177/0193841X04264820.

Larkin, H., & Park, J. (2012). Adverse childhood experiences (ACEs), service use, and service helpfulness among people experiencing homelessness. *Families in Society: Journal of Contemporary Social Services*, 93(2), 85–93. doi:10.1606/1044-894.4192.

Mowbray, C.T. (1985). Homelessness in America: Myths and realities. *American Journal of Orthopsychiatry*, 55(1), 4–8. doi:10.1111/j.1939-0025.1985.tb03417.x.

Rafferty, Y., & Shinn, M. (1991). The impact of homelessness on children. *American Psychologist*, 46(11), 1170–1179. doi:10.1037/0003-066X. 46. 11. 1170.

8

QUEERING THE ORCA-STANCE

Charlie Delavan and Brittany Steffen

In an intake session, I see the ring on my client's finger and ask him, "How long have you and your spouse been together?" He shares that he and his husband have been in a committed relationship for 17 years, but were only recently married when Washington state legalized same-sex marriage in 2012. It is in moments like this, when swapping in a gender-neutral term for a gendered one, that the therapist demonstrates their commitment to the practice of openness, respect, curiosity, and accountability to power, in which our queer clients can begin the long process of feeling secure in the therapeutic relationship.

Even as therapists, one who identifies as queer and who works with this population (Charlie Delavan) and the other from a gay-parented household (Brittany Steffen) and who specializes in working with the lesbian, gay, bisexual, transgender, and queer (LGBTQ) community, it takes a moment's consideration to mentally edit the assumption of heteronormativity from our interactions with clients. As our LGBTQ clients assess for safety in therapy, language can be especially informative. Being thoughtful about these subtle details in language demonstrates the conscious effort by the therapist to take a culturally humble, not-knowing stance with clients.

The word "queer" has three distinct but related meanings. First, it can refer broadly to anyone who identifies as part of the LGBTQIA+ community (this does not include allies, despite the common misunderstanding that the "A" refers to this group of people). Second, it can refer to a conscious repurposing of a derogatory term that was used against the LGBTQIA+ community in order to reclaim its power for our own. Third, it can refer to beliefs, practices, attitudes, and so on that specifically go against and attempt to dismantle the dominant cultural standards and narratives that exist around us (Rudy, 2000). Like many labels, but especially because of its charged political history, queer is a word that should be used to describe your client only if they have used this word to describe themselves. When we use the term "queer," we use it with each of these meanings hovering just under the surface.

Queer people have a different set of challenges to face when attempting to receive mental health care. For years, our very existence was deemed a pathological condition, something that made us not quite human, perhaps broken, in the eyes of others. Our identities were used as a means to alienate, oppress, dehumanize, and sometimes even to kill us. You have likely already worked with a client who grew up in the not so distant past, when homosexuality was a diagnosable mental health issue, and was treated by therapists using conversion therapy. Although all major psychological associations now ban conversion therapy, it is worth being familiar with this treatment as it is likely that one day you will work with a client who has experienced some version of this damaging practice. Defined briefly,

> conversion therapists view gay and lesbian persons as needing to be fixed or repaired. Instead of respecting these clients, practitioners using conversion therapy violate the value of dignity and worth of the person when they lose sight of gay men and lesbians as individual persons. The homophobia and heterosexism of the practitioner takes center stage when gay clients are viewed as pathological and flawed.
>
> (Jenkins & Johnston, 2004, p. 559)

While the methods used to impose this practice varied wildly, the outcomes experienced by clients share similarly damaging themes.

Following a vote in 1973 by members of the American Psychiatric Association, the diagnosis of homosexuality was replaced by "Sexual Orientation Disturbance" as a compromise to those who believed that some form of the diagnosis should remain in the Diagnostic and Statistical Manual of Mental Disorders (DSM). It wasn't until 1987 that homosexuality was completely removed from the DSM, and it wasn't until 1992 that the World Health Organization removed homosexuality from its International Classification of Diseases and Related Health Problems. Even more recent was the removal of "Gender Identity Disorder" from DSM-5, published in 2013; it was replaced by "Gender Dysphoria" in an attempt to reflect the cultural shift to viewing the dysphoria as the object of treatment, rather than the client's identity itself.

As members of a profession that has historically discriminated against queer clients, therapists are in a position of needing to be accountable to this past. Because of this history, there is still a sense of mistrust on the part of queer people when they consider reaching out for the help they need. This baseline lack of a sense of safety is essential to understanding the experience of a queer person sitting in your office, and it is from this place that we wish to think about what the *ORCA-Stance* has to contribute. We have become obsessed with the idea of "safe space." We are at a cultural moment where we can put up a rainbow sticker or include the words "open and affirming" on our websites and think we have created a safe space for queer people. However, there is so much more nuance that goes into actually helping queer people to feel safe. ORCA offers tools, both in the form of a therapeutic stance and in actionable directives, that can help us to consider ways to actually *be* open and safe for our queer identified clients.

Openness

Odds are if you are a cisgender (i.e., a person whose gender identity matches the one assigned to them at birth) heterosexual therapist seeing a queer identified client, you are going to hear some things that are outside of your experience and culture. This can apply to any client, but with a queer identified client, these differences in experiences may be highlighted. Openness is what you do when those moments of difference happen. It is easy to react in ways that reveal our biases, our lack of knowledge, sometimes even our disgust. This includes the words we say, our facial expressions, and our body language. Our queer clients often have years of practice in assessing for safety, and are practiced in picking up on unspoken, subtle prejudices. Because of this, it becomes increasingly important that openness is communicated – not just verbally, but nonverbally in our actions (Kort, 2008).

How are you communicating that you are open to listening to your client? To knowing your client? To holding space for your client? And what kind of space are you creating for them in the room? Even before you sit with a client, they are gathering information about your openness, or lack thereof. Prejudice and heteronormativity can creep in through intake paperwork, bathroom signage, and waiting room literature – creating negative experiences before therapy has even begun. Take a moment to read through your intake paperwork and critically examine your office spaces. Up until recently, a question about "marital status" could have led to a moment's hesitation for a gay client in a committed, long-term relationship, who was legally denied marriage. Asking clients to circle one option for gender, male or female, leaves out those who identify as queer. Making small changes to communicate your openness tells your clients that you are aware of the possibility of difference.

Openness is a posture that acknowledges the personhood of the other, including the intricacies and details of their story. Openness remains steady in anticipation of the possibility of the mutual impact of my story interacting with theirs. A person who can be freely open to others is a pleasure to encounter, leaving you feeling seen, heard and known. Openness is about honoring the validity of each person and each story that walks in the room, regardless of how different it is from your own. It is an essential posture when working with queer clients. If you do not remain open to hearing a story that is different from yours, your closed-mindedness will be palpable to your queer client, because they are in the position of being well attuned to those subtle signs of discrimination.

Respect

In some ways, you must be able to accomplish openness in order to fully demonstrate respect to a queer client. You cannot respect a person for who they are if you cannot open yourself to the nuance of existence. The reality is that queer people tend to have experienced multiple ways in which their lives are difficult. Childhood trauma is prevalent; poverty, homelessness and job/health care/food insecurity are more likely to be present; and comorbid conditions can also impact a client's health. The ORCA-Stance of respect places these difficulties squarely within the context of a culture that is steeped in prejudice and discrimination. Respect in the ORCA-Stance externalizes these difficulties in a way that communicates to the client that these problems are the problem – the client is not the problem.

Transgender clients face especially pervasive discrimination, even in the therapy room. In my experience as a provider specializing in transgender care, we frequently encounter clients who have been shuffled from one therapist to the next, because their providers claim not to have the training or experience to be able to work with transitioning clients. One client stands out. After 15 months of weekly therapy to address trauma, this particular client asked her provider if she would help with a letter for hormone replacement therapy. The therapist referred her out, saying that she didn't have any experience of writing these letters. In doing so, this therapist missed a significant opportunity to show respect for her client's long-term investment in their therapeutic relationship. Respect in this case could have been achieved by collaborating with a specialist, attending training, or collaborating with the client's physician to inquire about requirements for treatment. Even the busiest clinician can find time to honor a long-standing therapeutic relationship in a way that respects both their time, and the client's.

Respect is also about understanding what health looks like for the person sitting in front of you, and helping your queer client succeed toward that definition. Do not make the mistake of assuming that what you believe is or should be an issue for them is actually an issue. Do not assume that their queer identity is the reason they have come in for services, or that their coming out or transitioning should happen on anyone's timeline but theirs. Respect allows space for the client's specific needs and desires, and avoids privileging the clinician's assessment of how the client should be living.

Curiosity

Demonstrating curiosity with queer clients is perhaps the finest line to walk in the ORCA-Stance. If curiosity is a spectrum, we can say that making assumptions about our clients' lives lies at one end, and being uninformed, or ignorant, to the point whereby we rely on our clients to provide education in the therapy room, is at the other end of this spectrum. Becoming too curious runs the risk of either fetishizing your client's life, or asking your client to educate you about the realities of life for queer people. Both of these things set the client's experience so far outside of what you consider "normal" that they are now being asked to divulge information that isn't relevant to therapy, or to do the work of teaching you with the time they are paying you for.

To clarify this stance further,

> there is an important difference between taking a not-knowing stance of curiosity to refine and fine-tune a client's meanings and understandings, to the therapist just not having any knowledge about SGM [sexual and gender minority] issues. Bernstein (2000) reports that clients can resent having to educate their therapists about their lives, and so it is the responsibility of the therapist to gain some background general knowledge.
>
> *(Butler, 2009, p. 344)*

Taking a not-knowing, or curious stance, means that you do not assume the sexual orientation or gender identity of your client, and once your client has shared their identities, that you do not assume that these are problems that your client wants or to discuss in therapy. However, it is noteworthy that the stance of curiosity should not extend to inquiries about your client's identities themselves.

To highlight this point, let's use the example of learning that your client is a straight cisgender female, in a heterosexual relationship. It's very unlikely that a therapist would ask this client questions along the lines of, "How did you know you were straight? Why are you so sure?" In short, avoid putting your clients in the position of having to justify themselves (Ryan, 2009). When you want to be curious, ask yourself what purpose it is serving. Is it genuinely helping you to understand what your client is talking about, does it fetishize, or is it something you can look up later? Curiosity with queer clients should benefit the client's therapeutic journey, while the therapist's journey in their LGBTQ education should occur outside of the therapy room.

Accountability to Power

It could be argued that most, if not all, clients enter the therapy room from a one-down position in relationship to their therapist. This is highlighted by the client's experience of being labeled by a provider who then assigns a formal diagnosis for insurance coverage, and the initial vulnerability of sharing personal stories with a stranger. Many modern therapy theories suggest that clients benefit when therapists actively hold themselves accountable to, and compensate for, this power differential – and the ORCA-Stance is no different.

There are many ways to actively demonstrate accountability to power, and therapists would benefit from critically examining what power structures they bring into the room. The heterosexual cisgender therapist brings the power of a dominant status as a sexual and gender identity majority, in addition to racial identity, membership to a professional, expensively educated class, and a position as an "expert" meeting with clients in a familiar and comfortable office space. In addition, the queer client may have had a long history of therapists who were uneducated and uninformed at best, or openly discriminatory and prejudiced at worst.

In addition to the above elements, another piece of power that is wielded in the room, both consciously and unconsciously, is heteronormativity. Heteronormativity refers to the dominant cultural paradigm that suggests that marriage/partnership is between one cisgender man and one cisgender woman, and that the most important goal of this partnership is to rear children. Heteronormativity is restrictive and can be oppressive to everyone, including cisgender heterosexual people, but is particularly so for queer people. Consider the fact that queer clients live in a world designed in so many ways, both big and small, to meet the needs of heterosexual cisgender individuals and couples. It is so much a part of the culture that active steps must be taken to demonstrate accountability to the power of this construct in therapy. As it stands, this places them in the position of "other" and has historically translated into discriminatory practices in housing, employment, and health care – including the treatment they've received in counseling, referenced above. The very definitions of queer love exist outside of heteronormative expectations. Whether you are aware of it or not, the assumptions that come with the heteronormative paradigm show up in the room with queer clients, and it is something that should be both acknowledged and actively dismantled.

How does one even begin to hold themselves accountable to their power as a therapist working with a queer client? One way is to inquire about your client's past experiences in therapy – were they positive or negative? If they were negative, it is essential that the therapist should understand both the impact of this experience and the fact that these experiences leave the new therapist at a deficit. Whenever possible, educate yourself and work to become LGBTQIA+ culturally competent so that you do not have to refer out queer clients – such clients face discrimination on a regular basis and a referral out because of a skills deficit will feel like, and arguably is, a repeated experience of this discrimination. Consider our belief that your good intent does not negate the impact of this referral out on your client. Any referral based on a lack of cultural competency perpetuates the marginalization of minority clients. Lean on the stance of cultural humility and demonstrate accountability to power by learning about your client's culture with them.

For those transitioning clients navigating the complex world of health care, we recommend providing a copy of the World Professional Association for Transgender Health guidelines. This guide is for health care providers to learn about best practices/standards of care for transgender client, but it can also be a great way for transitioning clients to learn about the kind of care they're entitled to. Knowledge, for those transitioning clients, really is power.

Case Study

The principles comprising the ORCA-Stance described here have greatly benefited our therapeutic work with queer clients. Consider the case of Kelsey, a 15-year-old girl diagnosed with an adjustment disorder following the breakup of a long-term relationship. When treatment began, Kelsey reported mood issues stemming from both the breakup, and from conflict with her mother. Treatment consisted of individual sessions with Kelsey, and family sessions with both her and her mother, Catherine. Working from a stance of openness, when Kelsey started to describe the breakup, the therapist did not assume that Kelsey's former partner was male. Appearing to visibly brighten at this opening, she shared that she had recently come out to her mother as bisexual, even though she had been "passing" as straight as a girl with a boyfriend. Showing both curiosity and respect to this experience, the clinician inquired about both the experience of "passing", and the coming-out experience, having previously learned about the struggles that bisexual individuals face from within the LGBTQ community at a local National Alliance on Mental Illness (the organization known as NAMI) training session.

Kelsey shared that although the conversation with her mother had initially gone well, Catherine's mood quickly changed, and she ended up threatening to send Kelsey to boarding school. The conversation ended with them both in tears, and her mother left the house for several hours; neither had brought up the topic of sexuality in the five months that had since passed. The clinician expressed curiosity about the experience Kelsey had during and after this conversation, as well as about Kelsey's perception of her mother's experience. She shared that her mother had a history of leaving during conflict, and they wondered together what kind of conflict style her mother had developed as a result of her own childhood.

After prepping for a family session, which consisted of discussing what Kelsey hoped to accomplish in the session, and what the possible outcomes – good and bad – might be, her mother was invited to therapy. The clinician prepared some material from the Family Acceptance Project in advance of the session, in order to provide Catherine with the latest research conclusively demonstrating what clinicians have known for years – that family support of their LGBTQ child is directly linked to that child's wellbeing. Working from the stance of openness to

Catherine's experience and needs, the clinician saved this material for an as-needed option to provide at the end of the session. As it turned out, these materials weren't necessary.

After Kelsey shared that she wished to discuss their coming-out conversation, her mother was able to share that she often found herself overwhelmed by direct conflict, and that her conflict style was one of avoidance, learned as a child. She shared that she was in fact completely open to Kelsey's identity as bisexual, and she cried as she sincerely apologized for how she had handled that conversation. Showing respect to Kelsey's experience, the clinician encouraged Kelsey to move forward with her desire to share the negative impact of her coming-out experience with her mother, while supporting Catherine in listening from a place of non-defensive curiosity.

Ideas for Best Practice

Taking all this information into account, there are a few things that we believe are imperative to working with queer clients.

- Demonstrate openness to difference before your work with a new client begins. Therapists working with any clients, queer identified or not, would do well to screen their marketing materials, waiting room environment, intake paperwork, and in-office décor for inclusivity. Language, our bread and butter as therapists, changes quickly. Begin the standard practice of using gender-neutral terms during your intake sessions, and stay up to date on best practices for inclusive language.
- Respect your queer client's experience of growing up in a culture that privileges the heterosexual, cisgender experience by inquiring about the possible impact of this context and presenting mental health issues. Respect their right to choose their own therapy experience by letting go of assumptions regarding what their goals "should be."
- Check your curiosity – is it for your benefit, or for your client's benefit?
- Make yourself accountable to the powerful position you hold by exploring the impact that internalized homophobia and transphobia may have had on your work as a therapist in the past, and prevent this from recurring with current or future clients.

References

Butler, C. (2009). Sexual and gender minority therapy and systemic practice. *Journal of Family Therapy*, 31(4), 338–358. doi:10.1111/j.1467-6427.2009.00472.x.

Grant, J.M., Mottet, L.A., Tanis, J., Harrison, J., Herman, J.L., & Keisling, M. (2011). *Injustice at Every Turn: A Report of the National Transgender Discrimination Survey*. Washington, DC: National Center for Transgender Equality and National Gay and

Lesbian Task Force. Retrieved from https://books.google.com/books?id=wQvWngEA CAAJ&dq=Injustice+at+Every+Turn:+A+Report+of+the+National+Transgender+Di scrimination+Survey&hl=en&sa=X&ved=0ahUKEwjrrqTOvKXhAhVI654KHcnvDT8 Q6AEIKjAA.

Israel, T., Gorcheva, R., Walther, W.A., Sulzner, J.M., & Cohen, J. (2008). Therapists' helpful and unhelpful situations with LGBT clients: An exploratory study. *Professional Psychology: Research and Practice*, 39(3), 361–368. doi:10.1037/0735-7028.39.3.361.

Jenkins, D., & Johnston, L. (2004). Unethical treatment of gay and lesbian people with conversion therapy. *Families in Society: The Journal of Contemporary Social Services*, 85(4), 557–561. doi:10.1606/1044-3894.1846.

Kort, J. (2008). *Gay Affirmative Therapy for the Straight Clinician: The Essential Guide*. New York: W.W. Norton & Company. Retrieved from https://books.google.com/books? hl=en&lr=&id=BrWj-fTk1DkC&oi=fnd&pg=PA1&dq=Gay+affirmative+therapy+for +the+straight+clinician:+The+essential+guide&ots=yHFYCp3slj&sig=W4WqR0M_E W0sWFxx-20Zsoilg9s#v=onepage&q=Gay%20affirmative%20therapy%20for%20the%2 0straight%20clinician%3A%20The%20essential%20guide&f=false.

Rudy, K. (2000). Queer theory and feminism. *Women's Studies*, 29(2), 195–216. doi:10.1080/00497878.2000.9979308.

Ryan, C. (2009). *Supportive Families, Healthy Children: Helping Families with Lesbian, Gay, Bisexual & Transgender Children*. San Francisco, CA: Family Acceptance Project, Marian Wright Edelman Institute, San Francisco State University. Retrieved from https://books. google.com/books?id=D2yTAQAACAAJ&dq=Supportive+families,+healthy+children :+Helping+families+with+lesbian,+gay,+%09bisexual+%26+transgender+children.&hl =en&sa=X&ved=0ahUKEwiOs8jnvKXhAhVEnZ4KHSo6BRcQ6AEIKjAA.

9

SURVIVORS OF TRAUMA

Alissa Bagan

> The human response to psychological trauma is one of the most important public
> health problems in the world.
>
> *(Bessle A. van der Kolk)*

Traumatic events can often alter our ability to cope. As a clinician, I am repeatedly reminded of the vastness revealed in our capacities for both sensitivity and
resilience. This is especially apparent when working with those who have survived trauma. Trauma events can include family and social violence, rapes and
assaults, disasters, and war.

Sometimes trauma is specified as "complex," which indicates that it is interpersonal in nature, involves the feeling of being trapped, and is ongoing or
repetitive. Trauma not only affects psychological functioning but often impacts
physical and social health. For instance, a study of almost 10,000 patients in a
medical setting, now known as the *Adverse Childhood Effects Study*, reported that
people who had survived being severely maltreated as children showed a 1.4 to
1.6 times greater risk for obesity, but a 1.6 to 2.9 times greater risk for heart disease, cancer, chronic lung disease, skeletal fractures, hepatitis, stroke, diabetes, and
liver disease (Felitti et al., 1998).

Fortunately, more recent neuroscience research offers us a look at how trauma
impacts the brain and nervous system. This is an invaluable resource as it allows us to
imagine what is happening inside the body of someone suffering from trauma in
order to make sense of otherwise confusing behaviors. For example, the criterion
for post-traumatic stress disorder (PTSD) includes hypervigilance, which in terms of
neurobiology reflects the chronic activation of the sympathetic branch of the nervous system – or the "fight/flight" response – whereas dissociation is associated with
an activation of the parasympathetic nervous system called dorsal vagal activation.

Understanding what is happening in the body offers us support by grounding the therapist's feet in the relevant scientific literature, which can be very valuable when waves of overwhelming emotion fill the room and the therapist's own body. Without this understanding, it can be all too easy to distance ourselves from this vulnerable population, adding insult to injury as those who have survived trauma are often stigmatized and ostracized as they try to cope. Understanding what is happening inside the brains of those who have survived trauma allows us to respond with cultural humility; we are more able to stay with their suffering as our compassion is increased by a clearer understanding (Badenoch, 2008).

Treatment of Psychological Trauma: Considerations from Neurobiology

We have known for several decades that the therapeutic alliance accounts for more change, in terms of outcomes, than do our theories or interventions (Miller, Duncan, & Hubble, 1997). More recently, the neuroscience research is providing a bridge between the disciplines of psychology and biology that Freud foreshadowed, by demonstrating the centrality of the therapeutic relationship. James Coan, director of the Virginia Affective Neuroscience Laboratory at the University of Virginia, states that it is possible to think of the entire human brain as a neural attachment system, since so many neural structures stem from attachment behavior (Coan, 2010). We are social beings to our core and our Open and Respectful stance with our clients is at the heart of treatment regardless of the interventions or theories we use.

There is a growing body of research on trauma that strengthens the stance regarding the primacy of relationship. It suggests that, even with survivors of combat and torture, the environment after the trauma – specifically, those who respond to the survivor – may be just as crucial as the traumatic event itself to the development of post-traumatic symptoms (Dobbs, 2012). In one study that followed the fates of 141 Nepalese children who had served in the 1996–2006 civil war, all of the children experienced violence and other events considered to be traumatic, yet their post-war mental health depended not on their exposure to war, but on how their families and villages received them after the war. Those who were stigmatized or ostracized suffered persistent PTSD, while those who were readily and happily re-integrated via rituals or conventions designed for that purpose suffered no more mental distress than did their peers who had never gone to war (Dobbs, 2012). The power of warm, unconditionally accepting relationships cannot be underscored enough in the treatment of trauma.

Arguably one of the greatest discoveries in neuroscience research over the last 400 years is that of neuroplasticity. Neuroplasticity refers to the fact that the brain can change in both structure and function through our experiences including our actions, our perceptions and sensing of the world, and even our thinking and imaginings (Doidge, 2007). This is very hopeful news and has implications about how we relate to our clients. The embodied offerings of the *ORCA-Stance* are not just nice sentiments, but rather have the power to rewire the brain.

The Relational Brain and Our Early Years

Our brains are constantly monitoring the environment for safety. At a minimum of once every quarter of a second, it surveys and completes an assessment. Because some of these nerves are innervated with the face, throat, and chest, we have built-in ways to quickly send signals to each other about our relative safety. Our nonverbal ways of communicating – including our facial expressions, eye gaze, tone of voice, breath rate, and posture – are ways that we express both how we are on the inside as well as the quality of our connection with each other. A gentle voice and a calmly beating heart signal to our clients our readiness to engage.

During infancy the still-developing brain and nervous system contain a very limited ability to regulate shifting emotional and bodily states (Badenoch, 2008). These capacities for emotion regulation are built and are dependent upon consistent attunement with a caregiver. Attunement, or the ability to be aware of and responsive to another, literally wires into the developing brain the ability to self-regulate (Schore, 2012). During these first few years of life the brain forms a sort of template, or mental model, which is held below our level of conscious awareness and serves to aid us in anticipating how events will unfold. This formation is adaptive: each experience is not a brand-new experience to navigate, which would use up our resources that we need in order to be prepared for potential threats. Based upon the experiences we have, this template answers the most fundamental questions about the nature of the world and relationships. It answers questions like, "Is the world a safe place in which to take risks? Are relationships trustworthy? When things go wrong, do they get better or do they continue to get worse?" Because these encodings occur early on in life, and are thus held below our conscious awareness, they feel like "the truth" about the way things are, thus influencing all areas of our lives.

Trauma and the Social Brain

To a social brain, having our caregivers attune to us is paramount. Social baseline theory asserts that the experience of being alone has health implications like having an increased need for food, sleep, decreased immune functioning, and decreased physical activity, to name but a few (Coan, 2011). Fitting into one's family is about survival. To be clear, while we may be close to one another in terms of proximity, if attunement isn't available, the experience inside is one of being alone. So, while we may have others physically in our presence, if we are not attuned to them, we adapt in the service of fitting in, but to the detriment of our developing mind, brain, and body. This has implications for the development of the nervous system and thus the ability to develop self-regulation and sometimes our self-concept. This may be, in part, why we have a genetic drive toward attachment (Badenoch, 2011).

In the face of trauma, children will adapt in myriad ways. For instance, they will make themselves "the bad one," "the disgusting one," or, paradoxically, "the invisible one" in order to fit into the family. Again, fitting in is about survival to the social brain. These adaptations are perfectly designed for negotiating the intricacies of early relationships with caregivers. A child whose parents are emotionally dismissive learns to not notice his or her emotions because to do so would be to risk noticing the pain associated with the void of connection as well as to risk not fitting in. A child whose parent is unpredictably violent learns to be anxiously watchful even when things are quiet, in order to anticipate the next explosion. When children are faced with these dilemmas, they adapt in the service of staying connected, but at the expense of their developing brain and nervous system. As children grow into adults, if not addressed, these lived dilemmas remain inside as inner conflicts that, while not visible or necessarily conscious, can be observed on the outside as behavioral patterns.

Children's natural tendencies are to move toward connection and they continue to move outward toward others until they are met with anything other than acceptance (Badenoch, 2008). Children who experience childhood abuse or neglect, especially at the hands of their caregiver, are faced with an impossible dilemma: when stressed, their biological drive for attachment moves them toward their caregiver for support via co-regulation, but the very person who is supposed to offer this brain-integrating regulation is also the source of the fear or pain, thus creating a double-bind. In the disorganized attachment style, this can be observed outwardly; for example, when a child averts its gaze while running toward a parent, or cries while smiling.

Hebb (1949) notes that "what fires together wires together" in the brain. Again, since one of the primary jobs of the brain is to anticipate our ongoing experience, repetition of these early experiences leads to neural firings accumulating into mental models that become our embodied expectations about others and the world. How this plays out and how it can change, which has implications for therapeutic intervention, has to do with implicit memory.

Implicit Memory

Typically, when we think about what memory is, we think about a kind of memory where there is a beginning, a middle, and an end. This is explicit memory. When explicit memory is operating, we have a sense of "past" associated with it. The signature of implicit memory, on the other hand, is that it does not have the subjective internal experience of recalling which is associated with it. Additionally, implicit memory does not have a sense of "I," or self, associated with it. Rather, implicit memory is held in our emotions, our perceptions, and our bodily sensations. For example, when you ride a bike, you don't have the experience of recalling how to ride a bike, you have the experience of just knowing how to ride the bike, even though it is through the help of implicit memory that your body is able to recall this action.

Implicit memory contains procedural aspects of behavior just as riding a bike does (Solomon & Siegel, 2003) and it also contains emotional and perceptual aspects. For example, during your earliest years, your parents may have reacted to your crying by becoming anxious. In their anxiety, they may have tried to cheer you up rather than first attuning to your upset, and thus signaled that painful emotions are to be avoided. Consequently, therefore, you may have internalized an emotion of fear that accompanies the sensations of painful emotions, and as an adult you have a vague but familiar anxiety when others are uncomfortable, as well as having a hard time accessing your own painful emotions.

Additionally, implicit memory takes specific experiences and generalizes them into broad categories. For example, a single relationship with our parent is generalized to all relationships or the sound of an explosion is generalized to all sounds. Since we don't have to pay conscious attention in order to form implicit memories, we experience implicit memory as the truth of things or "just the way things are." One of my clients stated when we were talking about the trouble in her romantic relationship that "You can't rely on people. They act like they care but really they don't." The foundational nature of implicit memory cannot be underestimated. Becoming aware of our implicit memory via our felt sense in our bodies takes some practice. It might be compared to a fish trying to become aware of the water it's swimming in. It's not that it's hidden; on the contrary, it's so interwoven into how we experience the world that it's difficult to notice.

A more detailed example may be illuminating.

One of my clients, who I will call Stella, came to see me after having broken up with her fiancé. She was confused and didn't know what to do because she wanted to marry him, yet also felt anxious about getting married. I mention this example because it highlights the foundational nature of implicit memory. It plays out not so much within the content of the therapeutic conversations, but through the therapeutic relationship itself, and so has implications for use of the ORCA-Stance. Understanding the relevant neurobiology can aid us not only in making sense of the destructive patterns we sometimes see with those who have suffered relational trauma, but also in remaining in an ORCA-Stance, even in the midst of intense emotion in the consulting room.

Case Study: Stella

Stella explained that she had been anxious all her life and sometimes couldn't sleep. She would have nightmares and couldn't go to work some days. After a few months of sitting together, Stella's eyes would fill with tears at the outset of our meetings despite her efforts to stop them. Coupled with her emotional expression, I had become aware over the weeks of a mounting palpable and yet general feeling of pressure in myself, as if I needed to do something more and that somehow I was not being helpful, despite my sincere wish to help. With my feet grounded in the neuroscience, I was able to access my curiosity about these swells of emotion. My curiosity coupled with Stella's bravery allowed us to explore together.

Stella was able to notice that she felt anxious because she also felt angry with me. As I offered my curiosity and respect for the anger, encouraging her to say more about it, Stella envisioned the feeling as a stubborn little girl with her hands over her ears, refusing to listen to me. This sense of not wanting to listen to me was initially confusing to Stella, because she also felt desperate for me to say something to help her in making a decision about her engagement. Over the weeks, as I continued to offer my respect for her budding assertiveness expressed in the anger, she was able to also be respectful and curious about why she felt she needed the anger at me. With our joined curiosity and respect for her angry feelings, Stella became aware that the way that she felt was a familiar bind. She explained that the feelings of anger and desperation represented in that image in her mind was exactly how she felt growing up —desperately in need of help. The help that was offered, however, was not relevant to her concerns; it felt intrusive, hence, the need for the hands over the ears in the image. To aid Stella in getting to this clarity, I used my curiosity and respect to come to ask Stella what it felt like would happen if the little girl in the image took her hands off her ears, and she said it would feel like she'd be steamrolled with irrelevant and intrusive information. Stella immediately connected this to the dynamic she had with her mother – one where she felt in need of help, but the help offered tended to not be connected to her experience. My hope in sharing this example is that it illuminates how implicit memory is woven into the way we experience life, including the therapeutic relationship.

Challenges in Working with Trauma

Because implicit memory doesn't have a sense of past associated with it, we tend to view whatever is in front of us in the present moment as the cause of our upset. Not only that, but because we can only imagine what we have experienced, we tend to act in ways that elicit the precise response we fear. With Stella I could feel the pressure to do something to help her, which, had we not had curiosity on our side, might have looked like I was offering suggestions about how to make decisions or cope with anxiety symptoms, all of which would've been experienced by Stella as irrelevant intrusions – a repetition of the unhelpful pattern.

The ORCA-Stance was invaluable with Stella because without curiosity and respect for her autonomy and inner knowing, the intensity of the emotional pull to "do something" may have taken its toll and pulled us into repeating an unhelpful pattern.

Respect Imagines the Image Bearer

When we can appreciate the way in which the brain encodes our experiences and is wired for connection, symptoms begin to make sense and take on new meaning. Rather than having an anxiety disorder, for example, we might be able to view anxiety as the nervous system's wise, ancient, and protective way to signal that we are in need of another's calm presence beside us. Similarly, what on the surface might look like manipulation can be appreciated with cultural humility as a clever way to glean as much nurturance as possible from the relationships available and protect against being alone. Being dramatic takes focus as a way to protect oneself from being forgotten. Cultural humility views trauma symptoms in context and believes that behind challenging behaviors are adaptions to past impossible situations.

Scripture tells us that we are image bearers of God. Respect sees the other this way, as one who bears the image of the creator, regardless of whatever less-than-pleasing behavior might be on the surface. Respect has faith that what is seen is not the whole. Because respect embodies the faith that we are image bearers – image bearers of a God who heals – we can rest in this knowing that inside of the other is a wise system. Rather than pathologizing, respect views symptoms and destructive patterns as a wise system's adaptations to past circumstances in the service of protecting an image bearer.

The Bible also paints a beautiful picture of a God who is deeply relational. So intimate is this relationship that our very genes bear witness in our genetic drive toward one another. Thankfully, as is seen in complex trauma, our spirit knows when this image is not treated with respect as we set out to protect ourselves from being hurt again. It's as if our wise spirit knows that what has been hurt is worth being protected. But again, this protection comes at a cost. We all suffer in a myriad of ways, and with trauma, symptoms like anxiety, hypervigilance, substance abuse, or depression, to name but a few, remain to tell the story of an image bearer who has been denied his or her true nature – a nature of being wired for interconnectedness.

While trauma constricts the deepening of relatedness, respect sets the stage for restoration. Respect understands the therapeutic relationship to be what Badenoch (2011) calls "a partnership of mutuality" as it grasps the humility of our own minds and knows that none of us are the healer, but that we bear the image of the One who heals. This is reassuring news because it means that neither client nor therapist needs to be the healer, but instead we can trust that we have been given wise systems that will point us in the direction of healing if we will listen with cultural humility and an ORCA-Stance.

Ideas for Best Practice

Since therapy is a relational endeavor, our patients will inevitably touch our attachment templates that, in turn, impact our clients. Our ongoing insight and healing of parts of ourselves is relevant. Here are some best practice suggestions:

- Become familiar with your own attachment history so that you are aware of the places where you might still need supervision and support. Without doing so, it is easy to wind up inadvertently going down the implicit route to repeat unhelpful patterns with our patients. For those who like concrete exercises, you can identify your attachment style using the Adult Attachment Inventory (AAI) available cost-free online. Become familiar with the relational patterns you are likely to fall into in light of your attachment style.
- Become familiar with some of the basic neurobiological research on attachment and relationships. Allan Schore, Dan Siegel, Bonnie Badenoch, Jaak Panksepp, and Stephen Porges all provide a wealth of information on this subject. When emotion intensifies, having your feet grounded in the relevant neurobiological research on relationships and trauma provides a solid, invaluable resource. When this knowledge becomes second nature and we can imagine what is happening inside our patients, our compassion grows and we are all the more able to offer curiosity and respect to them, and thereby the possibility of literally rewiring the brain.
- Here's a more in-depth, inner-work exercise for after you've reviewed your attachment style and the relevant neurobiological literature: When you find yourself stuck with an emotion (anxiety, for example) that doesn't change despite trying to reason your way out of it, practice offering yourself curiosity about how this feeling might have served as an adaptation. Once you're able to offer curiosity toward it, practice listening to the part of yourself that has the emotion as you ask, "what would I have to feel if I didn't have this feeling" (i.e., anxiety)? For Stella, for example, it was the feeling of anger. This endeavor is an exercise in differentiation of the implicit binds, or inner conflicts that remain inside for us, and can aid us not only in our own healing, but equips us further in offering the *ORCA-Stance* to the brave clients we sit with.

References

Badenoch, B. (2008). *Being a Brain-Wise Therapist: A Practical Guide to Interpersonal Neurobiology.* New York: Norton. Retrieved from https://books.google.com/books?id=9_ra fueEC6QC&printsec=frontcover&dq=Being+a+brain-wise+therapist:+A+practical+guid e+to+interpersonal+%09neurobiology&hl=en&sa=X&ved=0ahUKEwjOxJfelKbhAhXL 854KHXC5DCAQ6AEIKjAA#v=onepage&q=Being%20a%20brain-wise%20therapist% 3A%20A%20practical%20guide%20to%20interpersonal%20%09neurobiology&f=false.

Badenoch, B. (2011). *The Brain Savvy Therapist's Workbook: A Companion to Being a Brain-Wise Therapist*. New York: Norton. Retrieved from https://books.google.com/books?id=9_ra fueEC6QC&printsec=frontcover&dq=The+brain+savvy+therapist%E2%80%99s+workb ook:+A+companion+to+being+a+brain-wise+therapist.&hl=en&sa=X&ved=0ahUKEw iJ1sX8lKbhAhWFlp4KHf1sBkQQ6AEIKjAA#v=onepage&q&f=false.

Coan, J. (2010). Adult attachment and the brain. *Journal of Social and Personal Relationships*, 27(2): 210–217.

Cozolino, L. (2006). *The Neuroscience of Human Relationships: Attachment and the Developing Social Brain*. New York: Norton. Retrieved from https://books.google.com/books?id= rnb0AgAAQBAJ&printsec=frontcover&dq=The+neuroscience+of+human+relationship s:+Attachment+and+the+developing+social+brain&hl=en&sa=X&ved=0ahUKEwjS7Y 2JlabhAhXWsJ4KHQHvBvkQ6AEIKjAA#v=onepage&q=The%20neuroscience%20of %20human%20relationships%3A%20Attachment%20and%20the%20developing%20social %20brain&f=false.

Dobbs, C. (2012). Toni Morrison (Review). *College Literature*, 39(4), 148–149. Retrieved from http://muse.jhu.edu.

Doidge, N. (2007). *The brain that Changes Itself: Stories of Personal Triumph from the frontiers of Brain Science*. New York, NY: Penguin Group. Retrieved from https://books.google.com/ books?id=Qw7qj5nXSPUC&printsec=frontcover&dq=The+brain+that+changes+itself:+S tories+of+personal+triumph+from+the+frontiers+of+brain+science.&hl=en&sa=X&ved =0ahUKEwjv8LeUlabhAhUUpJ4KHQ3lCrEQ6AEIKjAA#v=onepage&q=The%20brai n%20that%20changes%20itself%3A%20Stories%20of%20personal%20triumph%20from%2 0the%20frontiers%20of%20brain%20science.&f=false.

Felitti, V.J., Anda, R.F., et al. (1998). Relationship of childhood abuse and household dysfunction to many of the leading causes of death in adults: the adverse childhood experiences (ACE) study. *American Journal of Preventative Medicine*, 14(4), 245–258.

Hebb, D.O. (1949). *The Organization of Behavior: A Neuropsychological Theory*. New York: Wiley.

Miller, S.D., Duncan, B.L., & Hubble, M.A. (1997). *Escape from Babel: Toward a Unifying Language for Psychotherapy Practice*. New York: Norton.

Schore, A.N. (2012). *The Science of the Art of Psychotherapy*. New York: Norton. Retrieved from https://books.google.com/books?id=tCmBTeHVpjkC&printsec=frontcover&dq= The+science+of+the+art+of+psychotherapy&hl=en&sa=X&ved=0ahUKEwiS-ajSlabh AhWIwVQKHWwxDlEQ6AEIKjAA#v=onepage&q=The%20science%20of%20the% 20art%20of%20psychotherapy&f=false.

Siegel, D.J. (1999). *The Developing Mind: How Relationship and the Brain Interact to Shape Who We Are*. New York: Guildford Press. Retrieved from https://books.google.com/books? id=1F-BA_cdEO0C&printsec=frontcover&dq=The+developing+mind:+How+relation ship+and+the+brain+interact+to++%09shape+who+we+are.&hl=en&sa=X&ved=0ah UKEwjFwLrllabhAhUjMXwKHWCEDAwQ6AEIKjAA#v=onepage&q=The%20dev eloping%20mind%3A%20How%20relationship%20and%20the%20brain%20interact%20 to%20%20%09shape%20who%20we%20are.&f=false.

Solomon, M.F., & Siegel, D.J. (2003). *Healing Trauma: Attachment, Mind, Body and Brain*. New York: Norton. Retrieved from https://books.google.com/books?id=eqRjX-Kl0 vEC&printsec=frontcover&dq=Healing+Trauma:+Attachment,+mind,+body+and+br ain&hl=en&sa=X&ved=0ahUKEwi9hczNlqbhAhXB6Z4KHSMZDiIQ6AEIKjAA#v= onepage&q=Healing%20Trauma%3A%20Attachment%2C%20mind%2C%20body%20a nd%20brain&f=false.

10

SUBSTANCE USE DISORDERS

Jenny Johnson

"I don't think I have another relapse in me," said Heather, sitting in a group during her inpatient treatment for an opioid addiction. "One more relapse will probably kill me. I have to make it work this time," she said flatly, as if stating a dry and obvious fact. This was her ninth inpatient treatment for substance abuse. Her matter of fact tone belied her typical vivaciousness. She was by nature boisterous, energetic, playful, teasing, and full of life. She evoked strong emotions in others; almost everyone in the treatment group loved Heather, but a few hated her. It was hard, sitting in group therapy with her, to imagine the havoc that addiction had wreaked on her life.

The language of addiction is broadly and sometimes inappropriately used in our culture; for example, "these cookies are addictive." For the purpose of our discussion here, addiction refers specifically to a disease that necessarily involves a chemical hook, such as opioids, meth, alcohol, or prescription painkillers, which biologically impacts brain functioning (Volkow, Koob, & McLellan, 2016). Addiction is a diagnosable mental illness. In the fifth edition of *Diagnostic and Statistical Manual of Mental Disorders* it is called substance use disorder, with various classifications for the type of substance and the current stage of addiction as well as qualifiers for the severity of the disorder (American Psychiatric Association, 2013). Addiction is also a chronic disease that can be fatal. It is important when working with addiction to bear in mind that it is both a mental and medical illness. Hence, best practice treatment for substance use disorders combines medical, pharmacological, and psychotherapy interventions. Despite our best and multi-faceted treatments for substance abuse, there remains no cure and relapse is often a part of the disease and disorder.

Substance use disorders do not discriminate. They affect people across cultures, races, genders, ages, and of all socio-economic statuses. A therapist often cannot accurately assess whether a person has a substance use disorder from that person's outward appearance or self-reported behaviors, which can make it difficult to identify. We know that a person's genetics can make them more vulnerable to the disease, but environmental factors, such as family history, also influence the development of the disorder (Volkow et al., 2016). Many addicts have both the genetic predisposition to developing the disorder as well as a family tree rife with those who suffer from substance use disorders, which makes them even more susceptible to it. A final factor that is significant in the etiology of this disease is the presence of a history of abuse, trauma, post-traumatic stress disorder (PTSD), depression, anxiety, and other mental illnesses. There is a high rate of comorbidity of mental health and substance use disorder (Brooner, King, Kidorf, Schmidt, & Bigelow, 1997).

Heather grew up with a mother who used opioids regularly and illegally. Members of her extended family also struggled with drug and alcohol use. Her mother's use of drugs not only exposed her to them, but also created perpetual instability in her life. It also created traumatic experiences for Heather in the form of neglect and sexual abuse from the other drug users with whom her mother associated who floated in and out of her life. By the time she was in high school, she was drinking regularly and using drugs as a way of coping with the trauma she had experienced and the intense emotional distress that accompanied it. She not only had a diagnosis of substance use disorder, but also met criteria for depression, anxiety, and PTSD.

It is profoundly humbling to work with those suffering from substance use disorders. The effects of addiction are broad and deep in a person's life, ravaging their personal lives, relationships, mental health, careers, and physical health. The fewer resources an addict has economically and socially, the more likely they are to face the loss of housing and employment, time in jail and even the loss of custody of their children. Often compounding these issues is a personal history of abuse, neglect and/or trauma. A desire on the part of a clinician to help to alleviate the suffering of those seeking treatment for substance use disorders is natural and visceral, but also fragile. This disease will bring every therapist up against the limitations of their best training, interventions, and skill in providing treatment and motivation for change. As is commonly said to family members of addicts, "you did not cause it, you cannot cure it, and you cannot control it."

Twofold Application of Respect

The ability to remain useful to clients seeking therapy for substance abuse is predicated on respect. Respect for the client, despite a history of self-destructive behaviors, is an obvious necessity, but just as critical to your relationship with the client is a robust respect for the disease of addiction itself. Balancing respect for both the client and the power of this disease helps you to maintain realistic expectations for yourself and your client. When working with an addict, you run two essential risks. The first is becoming discouraged and despondent owing to a client's lack of change or recurrent relapses into the disease. Just as risky to quality care, but subtler, is the risk of colluding in the disease with the client out of a desire to align and alleviate suffering. Respect for both the client and the disease is the key to enabling you to walk the fine line of unconditional positive regard for the client, while not colluding in a disease that by its nature is manipulative and seducing.

Respect for a client in the grips of addiction and respect for the tenacity of the disorder itself can be made operational with the useful conceptualization of "the addict self" and "the true self." Every addict has these two selves within them. The power of addiction lies in its ability to overpower a person's true self. Author and father of a son with a substance use disorder, David Sheff, describes this process in his memoir *Beautiful Boy* (2008). His son, Nic, is a loving, caring, and devoted older brother. Sheff knew his son as a person who would never hurt or intentionally harm anyone, certainly not his family and friends. However, as his addiction took hold, he engaged in behaviors that were painful and devastating for his family. Sheff describes the pain of realization dawning on his younger son's face as he realizes that his older brother Nic had broken into his room and stolen all the money he had been saving.

Nic has a true self. By his father's account, his true self is a kind, generous, and caring person, self-sacrificing and nurturing where his younger brother was concerned. Nic's addict self is none of these things. His addict self does not care who he hurts or what pain he causes. He cares for only one relationship – his relationship with meth. His addict self will go to almost any length to procure and preserve his relationship with meth. The addict self requires the relationship with meth to be maintained even at the expense of loss of family, job, housing, or indeed the physical need to stay alive.

It is a universal experience when working with addiction to be lied to, manipulated or distracted with ploys, minimalizations, and pleas for sympathy. Experiences like this can feel like a betrayal to a clinician who has been working so hard to help a client. This feeling of being betrayed and manipulated by a client can compromise your respect for your client if you cannot cognitively separate your client's addict self from their true self. Identifying and honoring a client's true self can help to preserve your regard and respect for your client. Simultaneously respecting the addict self's ability to subvert their true self will help you not to fall prey to the manipulations and subversive tactics that help an addict to avoid responsibility. It is important to remember that the "addict self" has a hidden agenda – to maintain the addiction at any cost. Maintaining positive regard while not colluding with the disease is the aim of respect when treating substance use disorders. As with good parenting of a small child who is prone to tantrums, we do not concede and let a toddler have ice cream for dinner, but neither do we begin to loathe them because they make us miserable in their attempts to procure ice cream for dinner.

Cultivating Cultural Sensitivity through Curiosity and Openness

Substance use and substance abuse must also be treated with cultural sensitivity. It may not be obvious at first that substance abuse, while a diagnosable disorder, is also a culture unto itself. Substance use/abuse has its own social norms, rituals, practices, roles, and rules that govern belonging in this subculture. When working with any culture that is not one's own, it is important to attend to the ways in which acceptance in the culture is mediated. Curiosity and openness are key to approaching the issue of addiction as a culture you may know little about. It takes humility to be curious and open to learning about that culture. Being curious about the culture of drug use will help you to understand and anticipate the impact that a client's move toward sobriety will have to their status and belonging within the group. Psychotherapy assists a client in changing their drug seeking and using behaviors. Unfortunately, it does not attend to the social impacts that this will have, and it can promote a relapse as the client faces the loss of status, ritual, routine, and acceptance within their group.

Cultural humility is expressed in a curiosity and willingness to learn about the cultural norms of those using and abusing substances. This curiosity will often reveal the thrill and excitement of this way of life. One of the very common complaints of addicts working to get themselves clean is a pervasive and consuming sense of boredom. An active addict often throws off caution and societal restrictions. They live in frenetic chaos. Of course, they get high and when they come down the effects and collateral damage of that chaos is devastating and ruinous. However, there was the thrill and the thrill will be there again as they run from that devastation back to their drug. They can feel disconnected from their peers and simultaneously experience the tedium of "normal" life as they move into sobriety.

Heather struggled in sobriety to rebuild a life with meaningful connections and purpose. Her romantic relationship and the father of her children were both physically violent toward her and still in active drug use. Her family members used drugs and alcohol, which made contact with them difficult. Despite the connections she made in treatment, with her sponsor and in Narcotics Anonymous meetings, she often felt lonely and tremendously bored. She expressed not knowing what to do with herself and said sometimes that the hardest thing was "just dealing with how boring normal life is!"

If you are working with someone entering recovery, be curious about how the rituals and socialization of their lives operated while they were in active addiction. Also, be open to learning about the highs, the perceived "good times," and the relationships formed during their addiction. Addicts entering recovery may be losing not only a substance but also status, a way of life, and a tribe that they belonged to. Curiosity about this with your client will help you to plan interventions to remedy and mitigate those losses, which are real and painful. The research is overwhelmingly clear that involvement in 12-step groups is essential to successfully staying in recovery, particularly in early recovery. This may be largely due to the fact that it provides an entirely new community and place to gain belonging and human connections that replace those lost when leaving a life of active addiction. A competent therapist will support and actively encourage a transition into 12-step groups and other forms of community that will support sobriety and replace the loss of a cultural identity.

Quality Care Is Collaborate Care

Most ORCA principles find their meaning and relevance in the client-therapist relationship. However, when treating substance abuse, openness has another and broader application. As previously mentioned, substance abuse is both a mental and medical illness. Treatment of addiction will very often be done in conjunction with other professionals, including medical doctors, chemical dependency counselors, government agencies that provide drug replacement therapies (such as methadone or suboxone), and sometimes Children's Protective Service workers and the legal system.

Each of these professions approach the treatment of addiction with their own set of tasks and treatment protocols. Chemical dependency professionals and the legal system are often responsible for holding clients accountable for being in compliance with their treatment plans and abstinent from alcohol and other drugs. Medical personal may treat withdrawal symptoms, manage replacement therapy drugs, provide urine analysis, and treat the physical results of the client's previous drug use. Your role as a therapist also provides a unique part of the treatment. Therapists are rarely the ones to hold clients accountable for their addict behavior. We do provide an emotionally and physically safe space where the client has the opportunity to be more honest with themselves and where they can receive treatment for other mental illnesses that may be compounding their addiction.

Substance abusers receive the best care and treatment when all these professionals work in concert with one another and are open and receptive to input and feedback from one another. This reduces the possibility that you will collude in the disease as a result of a client's deceptions. Your perspective as a therapist may be quite different from that of a medical provider or a chemical dependency counselor. You will be a better therapist if you open yourself up to collaboration with these professionals and are open to hearing their perspective, experience with your client, and how they are approaching the treatment. Likewise, sharing your perspective respectfully can be valuable to these other professionals in treating your client.

Sometimes in your role as a therapist, you will be one of a very few individuals who will ever bother to peer through the chaos and pain of addiction to see the true self of your client lying beneath the ruin. It can be grueling work with little reward seeking out an addict's true self. But glimpsing it can take your breath away and may give your client a foothold to begin climbing out of a pit of self-loathing and shame. If you enter the work of treating substance use disorders with lofty ideas of what a difference you will make, you are likely to become demoralized in your work. ORCA offers another path.

Utilizing the principles of respect, openness, and curiosity will enable you to be accountable to the power you hold by honoring the best in your client, while maintaining boundaries that keep you useful in the treatment of this disease. Seeing a client's true self and helping them to reclaim even a small piece of that have given me some of the most gratifying moments of my life, professional or otherwise. ORCA was the modality that unlocked those moments.

Ideas for Best Practice

- Addiction creates two "selves" of each client – a true self and an addict self. Respect your client's true self, but never underestimate the impact and influence of their addict self.
- Be open to collaboration with other professionals. Substance use disorders are a medical and mental illness and require coordinated care from medical and mental health professionals.
- Be curious about the cultural significance of drug culture. Seek to understand how drug culture mediates belonging and status for your client and attend to the social impact it will have for them to leave a life of active addiction.

References

American Psychiatric Association (2013). *Diagnostic and Statistical Manual of Mental Disorders* (5th edn.). Arlington, VA: American Psychiatric Publishing. Retrieved from https://books. google.com/books?id=-JivBAAAQBAJ&printsec=frontcover&dq=Diagnostic+and+statis tical+manual+of+mental+disorders&hl=en&sa=X&ved=0ahUKEwjku9filqbhAhXEjp4K HQh_CzkQ6AEIKjAA#v=onepage&q=Diagnostic%20and%20statistical%20manual%20 of%20mental%20disorders&f=false.

Brooner, R.K., King, V.L., Kidorf, M., Schmidt, C.W., & Bigelow, G.E. (1997). Psychiatric and substance use comorbidity among treatment-seeking opioid abusers. *Arch Gen. Psychiatry*, 54(1), 71–80. doi:10.1001/archpsyc.1997.01830130077015.

Sheff, D. (2008). *Beautiful Boy: A Father's Journey through his Son's Addiction*. New York: Houghton Mifflin. Retrieved from https://books.google.com/books?id=bi5SRm2EA0g C&printsec=frontcover&dq=Beautiful+Boy:+A+father%E2%80%99s+journey+through +his+son%E2%80%99s+addiction&hl=en&sa=X&ved=0ahUKEwi14Kv8lqbhAhUI7J4 KHQ2ZC-AQ6AEIKjAA#v=onepage&q=Beautiful%20Boy%3A%20A%20father%E2% 80%99s%20journey%20through%20his%20son%E2%80%99s%20addiction&f=false.

Volkow, N.D., Koob, G.F., & McLellan, A.T. (2016). Neurobiological advances from the brain disease model of addiction. *New England Journal of Medicine, 374*: 363–371. doi:10.1056/NEJMra1511480.

11

CHRONIC PAIN IN ADULTS

Leslie B. Savage

> A retired Seattle anesthesiologist once told me that if you choose to treat patients
> with chronic pain, be prepared to fail. I have carried this notion with me and have
> found it to be true as a health care provider with a goal to cure pain.

In Western culture, particularly in the United States, the medical model predominantly centers on acute care. Most of us have learned to expect a diagnosis
and treatment plan to cure or resolve our medical issues. In these cases, pain is
believed to have an identified cause and treatment to resolve the pain. Yet mil-
lions of people live with chronic pain, whereby pain lasts beyond the expected
time for healing of an injury or illness. When pain is perceived as curable, it is
something intolerable and the only pursuit is to eliminate pain. There seems to be
no space in our culture to tolerate or accept pain.

Chronic pain is an experience, not a thing. According to the International
Association for the Study of Pain (2019), pain is an unpleasant sensory and emotional experience associated with actual or potential tissue damage, or described in
terms of such damage. Our experience of pain is influenced by everything that is
going on in our life in the present moment, what has happened in our past, and
in our perception of the future. Our painful experiences from the past have been
stored; they are experientially and emotionally grafted into and inform the current pain experience and our outlook for the future. Chronic pain is complex and
the experience of pain is unique to each person. No one can fully know another's
experience of pain; each person is alone in his or her pain.

I have been fortunate thus far – my injuries and illnesses have resolved and I do
not live with residual pain. I have no personal experience of what it is like to
endure pain beyond the expected time for healing. Everything I know about pain
has come from an open, curious, respectful place where I am among others who

have chronic pain. I have learned how my judgments, agendas, assumptions, and expectations can become dead ends or roadblocks to helping patients. When I let go of my preconceived notions to be present with openness and curiosity, I learn more about the complexity that chronic pain creates in patients' lives. My early teachers were a group of patients at the Seattle Arthritis Clinic who had rheumatic conditions that caused inflammation of the tissue lining around joints and who lived with residual pain. All were excited to participate in a group and they became my teachers of cultural humility as I entered into their shared experiences of living with chronic pain. Shortly after beginning, I had prepared a session for the group and no one showed up. I was embarrassed, hurt, and angry all at once, and wondered if I had done something to offend them during the previous session or if they were non-compliant. At the following session, I had to put aside my assumptions and inquire about their absences. My first lesson in cultural humility was making space to tolerate pain. I learned that patients have flare-ups that are extremely painful, but other than seeing a doctor for relief, the best position in which to reduce pain is a horizontal one. It turned out that their greatest fear was that they would all be absent on the same day. I discovered that in general Monday was their recovery day after overexerting themselves on the weekend, and rather than fighting the reality of their circumstances we found another day that would have better odds for their attendance.

As I look back now on that time, I realize that my group was teaching me to be prepared to fail. It was a spiritual journey for me in perseverance and humiliation, finding my strength through my inadequacy. It was during my last quarter at Seattle Pacific University, when I was completing a course in Beliefs, Health & Spirituality, that I became intrigued by mindfulness and chronic pain. How can one find joy and harmony when one experiences pain on a daily basis? This question sparked a curiosity that has shaped my professional and spiritual growth and my endeavor to help people to live well with chronic pain. The path to healing did not come from reading books, articles, and trying different therapeutic approaches, although these did help me to formulate my inquiry. It came from fully immersing my attention on understanding patients' experiences with pain. I had to admit that I did not know. With genuine openness and curiosity, it is vital to hold a culturally humble position that is nonjudgmental and ready to listen to and believe the experiences of others. The group became my petri dish to learn cultural humility and I am forever grateful for their patience and perseverance to stumble along with me.

My first challenge was to believe that my patients' experiences with pain were real and not feigned. This was a step in faith, to trust something I could not know. I learned to be fully present, like a satellite dish: open and receptive to the whole person. Now I attune to the external material, the story, and the energy of how it is being told. And simultaneously I am curious about the internal material that is less visible and underlying. I listen for the essence of what is missing, what is shy, and what has been denied, avoided, or shamed. I have become more sensitive to the patient's experience: reflecting back and using what I have learned from others about living with chronic pain to get a closer understanding of the patient's experience. I discovered that many patients do not fully understand their experience and for many this is the first time that they have begun to put words to it. I help them to describe their experience by tentatively offering what I am sensing and have them use my suggestions as stepping-stones to guide them to a closer narrative that resonates within them. I remember one patient who described his experience with pain like that of a *bully*; something in him remembered when he was teased in high school and how that filled him with shame, worthlessness, and internalized messages of *I will never be good enough* and *I must not matter*. His current experience with pain brought on those same feelings, along with depression and hopelessness. In attempting to kill the pain with medication, he almost died.

How does one hold a vital culturally humble position with openness and curiosity that can be genuinely felt and trusted by patients? This is what the *ORCA-Stance* implores me to do. I would be remiss if I did not share that presence is a state of being versus a theoretical framework. Presence integrates body, mind, and spirit and is grounded in my spiritual relationship with God, Christ, and the Holy Spirit – the Divine. There is a spiritual *felt sense* of being connected to the universe, to creation, to something greater than my patients and me. I allow my body to spontaneously sense the relational whole of a situation or experience, embracing the entire interacting web of complex linking and connecting that goes along with each and every part. It is like my body knows, in a great gulp, something more than what my mind can analyze, comprehend, or reason.

According to Eugene Gendlin, philosopher and psychologist of experiential psychotherapy and founder of the International Focusing Institute, he describes the felt sense this way:

> Your physically felt body is in fact part of a gigantic system of here and other places, now and other times, you and other people – in fact the whole universe. This sense of being bodily alive in a vast system is the body as it is felt from the inside.
>
> *(1981, p. 77)*

In presence, I am tapping into a unique way of *felt-knowing* that is quite different; it links me to spiritual truth and wisdom. When I am connected to the Divine, my heart is filled with love, compassion, empathy, patience, and acceptance. According to Gendlin, "every organism is carried forward by being loved or cared for. The body will take a carrying-forward step if it can happen in the interaction [with the therapist]" (1996, p. 281). There is a *good enough* sense of safety and security that allows patients to go deep and share the most sensitive and vulnerable places within them. Light comes into the darkness of what they have been keeping to themselves, most often to something that is subconscious. There is an exhale, an ease in tension, and a shift as the body releases what it has been holding, sometimes described as *having been locked in a vault* or *stuck behind a concrete wall*. In presence, I am attuned and attending to what is vulnerable in the patient; I am not the fixer. I am more like a conduit connected to the universe, to the Divine, to God's creation, and there is a linking to the *true seeds of self* that God has planted in everyone, waiting to be found and nurtured. In this place, my fears take a side seat to trust, which fosters a genuine openness with interested curiosity. I am okay with not knowing what will come next, and I allow things to unfold.

> This means [therapists] do not need to have an answer to the [patient's] stuck places. Sometimes there are real answers. However, usually we have answers because we have not yet understood the problem. When we reach the stage where we have no answer either, then we have really understood the problem.
>
> *(Gendlin, 1996, p. 290)*

I have found that through this process patients feel safe, heard, validated, and respected enough to uncover what it is like for them to live with chronic pain. It raises awareness to how their current experience with pain may carry with it underlying past memories of painful experiences. In staying present and attuned with the process that is unfolding – the body's experiential knowing or felt sense of their circumstance – there may be a sense of injustice in how one was mistreated, a knowing of what would have been more right, or repressed memories of pain and/or resilience which offer a way forward in the present. According to Gendlin, if patients "are responded to so as to continue the present interaction in a way that goes beyond their old pattern [then] this enables [them] to discover themselves living in new ways" (1996, p. 291). In the case example mentioned earlier of the patient who identified pain as a bully, the insight that unfolded was how he escaped his tormenters and drove his motorcycle up into the mountains to be with nature. He remembered that being in nature is where he found peace, harmony, acceptance, and his worth. This was a revelation to him that shifted everything; his experience with pain became just that – pain, an element in his life that was there and that was no longer associated to his past experience of being bullied. In his journey towards acceptance of pain, he realized that he needed to take trips into the wilderness to counterbalance the persistence of pain. These trips became his spiritual filling station when he would become discouraged, depleted, and exhausted from daily demands and pain management – they assisted him in living well with pain.

Another spiritual truth uncovered in my chronic pain group is the existential isolation and disconnection that patients experience from others, loved ones included. Reflecting on his life-long practice of working with chronic pain patients, David Sinclair, the retired Seattle anesthesiologist I mentioned earlier, acknowledged an inescapable truth for people living with pain: no one can know what another's experience of pain is like. It is their own experience, and it is in relation to other experiences of pain that they can communicate how they subjectively experience it. All that another person can know or quantify is the effect of pain on the person's behavior (mechanical and emotional aspects). According to Sinclair, "the tentacles of chronic pain invade aspects of life and person inaccessible to the observer, trapping the patient in a realm of existential loneliness that is difficult to accept even for the philosophically sophisticated individual" (2010, p. 19). Because pain is invisible to others and there is no visual clue like a cane, wheelchair, cast, or crutches, people are often unaware of a person's debilitating pain. The paradox of living with pain comes from the social assumptions, judgments, and expectations we hold for a *normal* person. Whether it is conscious or unconscious, we unfortunately misjudge people living with chronic pain as lazy, slow, forgetful, unreliable, weak, and negative. The essence of who they are is not truly known in the present moment by another because their life is limited by pain; it hinders a spontaneous unobstructed expression of self because pain is a constant element that demands attention. What we see and judge is a modified or adjusted expression of who they are.

Kaethe Weingarten, a psychotherapist, wrote a reflection of her own experience with chronic pain that included those of her chronic pain patients and described the existential isolation and disconnection as living with a painful gap. This gap is related to a loss of identity as patients lose the things that define them. It is living between who you have been and who you are now, of how you want to be and how you can be now, and of who you dreamt to be and who you still long to be. Weingarten named it *chronic sorrow*. She defined it as "a normal, nonpathological state of pervasive, continuing, periodic, and resurgent sadness related to loss of self" (2012, p. 3). When I shared this article with my group of chronic pain patients, we expanded the definition of chronic sorrow as *living between life and death*. They described a gravitational pull that has them turning inward, away from others; it is like wanting to curl up in a fetal position with their pain and be alone, not move or do anything, just be in a position that does not hurt. Yet there is another force that propels them to engage with life; it senses danger in succumbing to the pain because it could lead to further isolation, even death. Every day involves waking up and choosing life, establishing and hooking onto *lifelines* that engage them to live. Lifelines include a redefined sense of purpose, the pursuit of interests that are important to them, and picking an inner circle of people – a life partner, family members, and friends – who validate their pain on a daily basis by acknowledging and offering to accommodate it.

This is easier said than done. Part of the hardship comes from the lack of tolerance for pain in our culture. Early on, most of us are taught that pain is a negative experience and it is quickly dismissed, brushed aside, minimized, or ignored. The *double whammy* for people living with pain is that it is an element in their life and they are not allowed to talk about it; it is heard as a complaint or an excuse. The external social messages we have all heard growing up become internalized as "should" which evoke embarrassment, shame, and self-doubt when they do not apply to patients living with pain. Instead, statements like *"there is a medical cure"* or *"you will get better if you stay busy,"* or *"you will be alright, so pull yourself up by your bootstraps and strive for the best results,"* or *"fake it until you make it,"* have the potential to increase depression and anxiety. These comments can hinder acceptance and a chance to find joy when living with pain.

When one's focus is on getting rid of the pain, pain may become the enemy and invite a sense of defeat and victimization. When pain is validated, acknowledged, and accommodated, it fosters a befriending of the pain – to admit it is there, own it, and take responsibility for it. Thus, the patient is liberated from only having to get rid of it to learning how to live with it, manage it. In the present moment, the patient has more freedom to make choices about what is important to them, including surrendering to the pain and resting as long as necessary without shame or guilt. As pain is befriended, it becomes an element in the patient's life that no longer has the foothold to define them, making room for joy and well-being.

Case Example

In order to help to clarify the complexity of living with chronic pain and the various parts that accompany it, I will share an excerpt from a recent group session. I invited a patient to turn inward and describe where she finds herself in the context of her circumstances. She told me that she fluctuates between feeling discouraged and hopeful. When she is in the present moment and is doing something she knows she can do (without much pain), she has a sense of accomplishment and it brings her a sense of well-being and hopefulness.

Discouragement comes when the critical part makes a judgment about her: *You should be able to do this; if the kids can, why can't you? It is so simple.* Tasks like juicing a lemon, mashing potatoes, carrying the laundry basket, and unloading the dishwasher cause pain in her arm, shoulders, and neck. This critical part is worried: *Why is it so hard when you could easily do these tasks before?* This critical concern comes from remembering what the doctor said about her injury: *He does not know if you will fully recover, you may plateau and not be able to do certain things.* Every time she could not accomplish something simple, this critical part let her know: *What the doctor predicted is not acceptable; it is an excuse you are using to just give up!* Identified with this critical part, the patient would push through the pain to complete tasks to excruciating levels that brought a sense of defeat.

Then the patient noticed something else there, a wise part that acknowledged her physical pain when doing these tasks, and it told her: *When the pain is escalating you need to slow down or stop that motion and not complete the task right now.* As this patient listened to both parts, she acknowledged the inner conflict and empathized with both parts, realizing that each part's perspective is valid. With more self-awareness, the patient was able to articulate her desire with clarity: *I want to persist with my recovery, not have it defined by the doctors, continue to make progress, and not give up.* She described her recovery as something like training for a marathon, although there is no race or finish line. It is more like an everyday push to strive and keep it in balance with what her body can tolerate.

When I am present, I am able to help patients to notice, identify, and name the different parts they carry in association with their experience with pain. This creates space for the parts to be heard, honored, and accepted without judgment or punishment. Feelings of helplessness, fear, anger, and discouragement dissipate as we listen and empathize with the parts that carry their own thoughts, memories, and emotions from past painful experiences. There is a noticeable shift in the body, a release of tension in being heard and seen, like a heavy sigh, lightness in posture, or a smile. As patients gain clarity around their internal struggles, battles, or conflicts, a next step is revealed: a way forward that is more right for them. They become more confident in who they are and they take more responsibility for their pain and how to accommodate it. It is not a resignation, it is an acceptance that allows them to make their own choices and accept the consequences in pushing forward to engage with life, having a sense of purpose, accomplishing things that are important to them, making adjustments for pain, respecting and testing the boundaries of pain, and having gratitude for the people and small things that bring them joy amid their pain.

Ideas for Best Practice

- To be able to admit when I do not know and engage the ORCA-Stance to invite my clients to share more as I seek to understand more fully their circumstances. Some of my emotional *warning signs* include confusion, frustration, or a judgmental attitude; they alert me to pause and consider that I may be impatient and trying to fix my client.
- The notion that each client has an inner client, *the client's client*; the one in there that may have unmet needs, longings, and primal protests. To use my felt sense of their circumstance to understand the mystery of this one, relating in an empathic and compassionate way to spiritually call forth and speak to the client's client (Preston, 2014).
- To remember first and foremost that I am a person, part of the human predicament, with my own gambit of longings, needs, dashed hopes, prejudices, wounds, vulnerabilities, dreams, and inspirations. My ability to be present and receptive to my clients with empathy and compassion

happens when I have shamelessly accepted my own foibles (Preston, 2014). Then, in a more undefended way, I can give myself more fully in the ORCA-Stance.

- To intentionally invite trouble and work with what clients bring into therapeutic interaction. When I sense that the client may be angry, bored, disengaged, or disappointed with me, I will tentatively let them know what I am sensing and trying to learn from their experiences.

References

Casarjian, R. (1992). *Forgiveness: A Bold Choice for a Peaceful Heart*. New York: Bantam Books. Retrieved from https://books.google.com/books?id=KoAsUoobZ6AC&printsec=frontcover&dq=Forgiveness:+A+bold+choice+for+a+peaceful+heart&hl=en&sa=X&ved=0ahUKEwjA-K_jnabhAhWzwcQHHdYSDXQQ6AEIKjAA#v=onepage&q=Forgiveness%3A%20A%20bold%20choice%20for%20a%20peaceful%20heart&f=false.

Edwards, S., Savage, L.B., & Schermer Sellers, T. (2014). Client relationships with chronic pain, mindfulness, wellbeing. American Association for Marriage and Family Therapy, Milwaukee, WI, October 18.

Gendlin, E.T. (1981). *Focusing* (2nd edn). New York: Bantam Books. Retrieved from https://books.google.com/books?id=eN55GY2O2twC&printsec=frontcover&dq=Focusing&hl=en&sa=X&ved=0ahUKEwjfi5CLnqbhAhVLsVQKHbT3AfIQ6AEIKjAA#v=onepage&q=Focusing&f=false.

Gendlin, E.T. (1996). *Focusing-Oriented Psychotherapy: A Manual of the Experiential Method*. New York: Guilford Press. Retrieved from https://books.google.com/books?hl=en&lr=&id=0gMIl2vAVgoC&oi=fnd&pg=PA1&dq=Focusing-oriented+psychotherapy:+A+manual+of+the+experiential+meth&ots=Qr0S4tvDIw&sig=sSlC0er1ZkSbEyP-vPphYGEY9ac#v=onepage&q&f=false.

McMahon, E.M., & Campbell, P.A. (2010). *Rediscovering the Lost Body-Connection within Christian Spirituality: The Missing Link for Experiencing Yourself in the Body of the Whole Christ Is a Changing Relationship to Your Own Body*. Minneapolis, MN: Tasora Books.

Pelez-Ballestas, I., Prez-Taylor, R., Aceves-Avila, J.F., & Burgos-Vargas, R. (2013). "Not-belonging": Illness narratives of Mexican patients with ankylosing spondylitis. *Medical Anthropology: Cross-Cultural Studies in Health and Illness*, 35(5), 487–500. doi:10.1080/01459740.2012.716883.

Preston, L. (2014). The relational heart of focusing-oriented psychotherapy. In G. Madison (Ed.), *Theory and Practice of Focusing-Oriented Psychotherapy: Beyond the Talking Cure* (pp. 98–112). London: Jessica Kingsley Publishers.

Savage, L.B. (2013). Mindfulness: Narratives of living with pain. *Washington Association for Marriage and Family Therapy*, Fall, 8–9.

Scazzero, P. (2006). *Emotionally Healthy Spirituality: Unleash a Revolution in Your Life in Christ*. Nashville: Thomas Nelson. Retrieved from https://books.google.com/books?id=O2H4CwAAQBAJ&printsec=frontcover&dq=Emotionally+healthy+spirituality:+Unleash+a+revolution+in+your+life+in+Christ&hl=en&sa=X&ved=0ahUKEwi1-5mfn6bhAhVhi1QKHe2mAf8Q6AEIKjAA#v=onepage&q=Emotionally%20healthy%20spirituality%3A%20Unleash%20a%20revolution%20in%20your%20life%20in%20Christ&f=false.

Sinclair, D. (2010). The chronic pain patient and the doctor. *King County Medical Society*, March/April, 17–21.

Tang, N.K.Y., Shum, S.H., Leung, P.W.L., Chen, P.P., & Salkovskis, P.M. (2013). Mental defeat predicts distress and disability in Hong Kong Chinese with chronic pain. *Clinical Journal of Pain*, 29, 830–836. Retrieved from https://journals.lww.com/clinicalpain/Abstract/2013/09000/Mental_Defeat_Predicts_Distress_and_Disability_in.12.aspx.

Weingarten, K. (2012). Sorrow: A therapist's reflection on the inevitable and the unknowable. *Family Process*. doi:10.1111/j.1545–5300.2012.01412.x.

Weiser Cornell, A. (2013). *Focusing in Clinical Practice: The Essence of Change*. New York: W. W. Norton & Co. Retrieved from https://books.google.com/books?id=GXo2AAAAQBAJ&printsec=frontcover&dq=Focusing+in+clinical+practice:+The+essence+of+change&hl=en&sa=X&ved=0ahUKEwih6pTUoqbhAhWGLnwKHePIBTcQ6AEIKjAA#v=onepage&q=Focusing%20in%20clinical%20practice%3A%20The%20essence%20of%20change&f=false.

12

CHRONIC ILLNESS IN YOUTH

Cassady Kintner

"Don't say you understand, because you'll never know what I have to deal with every day," Anna screamed at her mother, Nancy. Anna had been silent for most of the session, arms folded with a look of anger coupled with exhaustion in her eyes. Cheeks flushed and tears streaming, she turned away as her mother desperately told her how frustrated and angry she felt when Anna "refused to take responsibility for her type 1 diabetes. She doesn't realize how much she hurts all of us when she doesn't take care of herself. It's selfish."

At the age of six, Anna was diagnosed with type 1 diabetes (T1D), a chronic condition in which the pancreas produces very little or no insulin. Insulin is a hormone that the body requires in order to assimilate glucose (sugar) into the cells and utilize it as energy. Now 17 years old, Anna had just been released from the hospital following diabetic ketoacidosis, a serious complication of T1D whereby the body goes into starvation mode and without sufficient insulin it begins to burn up its fat stores by producing ketones instead of the glucose necessary for energy. High levels of ketones can poison the body and lead to diabetic coma or even death. It was only after her seventh visit to the emergency room within a 12-month period for this serious complication that Anna's mother was able to get her to consider therapy. What actually got her in through the door, however, was the fact that I myself have had T1D for over 20 years.

There is a kind of instant credibility that I gain when I work with clients who have T1D because I know the frustration, anger, and defeat that come from both the mental and physical consequences of living with the disease. Twenty-four hours a day, seven days a week, patients with T1D must monitor their blood sugar and administer – either by pump or injection – the right amount of insulin, which varies constantly and is based on diet, exercise, stress, hormones, etc.

When they do not get the correct amount of insulin, they can become very sick (as Anna had), suffer organ damage, and even die. In addition, there is the pressure of knowing that too much insulin can result in sudden death.

My marriage and family therapy training has shown me the importance of using my own struggle to connect with others without judgment, and from a deep sense of empathy. ORCA has shown me that in addition to it being important to remain open and empathic to the suffering of others, it is critical to make sure that my own issues with the disease do not inhibit my ability to stay receptive and responsive within the context of my interpersonal relationships, including those with my clients. Furthermore, failure to do so may lead to burnout or compassion fatigue (Grauf-Grounds & Edwards, 2007).

ORCA also stresses the importance of staying out of the "expert" position, remaining curious about the client's own experiences and respectful of his or her own strengths, resources, and inner wisdom. Honoring those gifts from a place of truly wanting to know more about them will bring them into the light in a way that is both healing and empowering for the client. Even when I, too, have experienced something unique to T1D life that a client is telling me, it is crucial that I maintain cultural humility in that I make sure I am leaving space for the client's story to be different from my own as well as honoring his or her perceptions and takeaways.

Both my personal experience and professional training as a marriage and family therapist have made me a true believer in the power of systems thinking. Because we exist within the context of relationships, the physical and/or psychological welfare of those we care about can have a profound effect on our own well-being. This dynamic is exacerbated when chronic illness is involved because the state of one person's health is consistently in flux, if not threatened. I always say to my clients, "When one person gets diabetes, the whole family gets it too," and it is therefore imperative that the disease be addressed within the context of family therapy.

Nowhere does this statement ring truer than when I work with adolescents who have T1D. Like Anna, the adolescent who has diabetes is almost always the Identified Patient because parents tend towards the perspective that their child has a lack of appreciation for the severity of such an acute chronic illness. When a child becomes an adolescent, he or she is no longer a helpless baby to be cared for, and parents feel as though they are losing control. At our initial meeting, it was mostly Anna's mother who did the talking. She explained how Anna's health had begun to deteriorate as Anna entered middle school, when Anna began to take over more of the responsibility for managing her diabetes.

Adolescence is difficult because it is developmentally appropriate to begin individuating from one's parents by pushing for greater independence and responsibility and asking (or demanding) to be treated as an adult. This can intensify the pressure on an already strained parent-child relationship because successful diabetes management requires continued parental involvement and the gradual, often tumultuous process whereby the adolescent becomes the primary manager of his or her disease (Anderson, Svoren, & Laffel, 2007).

The *ORCA-Stance* is critical in these family sessions. Although I have experience as a caretaker and nurturer in several of my own relationships, I am not the parent of a child with T1D. I need to remain culturally humble and open in order to understand the terror that comes with knowing that I cannot always protect someone I love, nor have I ever been able to completely ensure their safety – whether from disease, buses, others meaning them harm or, perhaps the most difficult to hold, the knowledge that I cannot protect them from themselves. Even if this kind of thinking and risk-taking behavior is normal within the context of adolescent development, I need to understand that the stakes feel higher to parents because of those additional ramifications that may result from T1D, including hospitalization, long-term complications, and death.

At the same time, as a person living with T1D, I understand the desire to take ownership of my life and the feelings of being overwhelmed with the responsibilities that life with diabetes entails. I also know the crippling effect of the guilt that comes with the knowledge that my own health condition has an impact on others. A parent's feelings of terror and helplessness can be difficult to hold while simultaneously staying open and receptive to the fears of an adolescent who is facing his or her own challenges. On top of trying to stay afloat amid the normal physiological changes and social pressures of adolescence, an adolescent with T1D must also balance the intrusive and demanding responsibilities of having a chronic illness.

I must never belittle or scold a teenager for having fluctuating priorities, even when discussing something as serious as health, because working with a client from a stance that asserts "You know how serious this is. Why can't you just take care of yourself?" is not only unhelpful but damaging to the relationship. As difficult as it may be, it is imperative that I remain culturally humble in the face of what is actually normal teenage development. When an adolescent has a chronic medical condition, parents and practitioners alike can feel like there is an exponential rise in the stakes. This can lead to a focus on physical health at the expense of psychosocial well-being and an ORCA-Stance shutdown. In order to maintain cultural humility, I must make sure that I remain steadfastly open and genuinely curious about what it is like to be a child or teenager who is trying to maintain a more complex biopsychosocial balance that may not always fall in line with what others think it should be.

So how do I facilitate healing if the perspectives of the adolescent and the parent differ so greatly? If I cannot remain open to both parties, I cannot do effective systems work because I cannot recognize the ways in which each individual has contributed to the problem and how each can help with the solution. Anna's mother, Nancy, was not taking responsibility for her own feelings. She was simultaneously disempowering herself and putting her own worries and fears onto Anna, who already had her own issues with guilt to deal with. At the same time, Anna had become identified with her disease, and had begun to take on a victim mentality that had her pushing her mother away while simultaneously asking her for help. Both Anna and her mother possess a profound love for each other; otherwise they wouldn't have been so upset with one another. Many people with chronic illnesses have similar problems: they identify with their disease, they take on a victim mentality, and they push away the people who want to help. Their loved ones, like Nancy, get frustrated, especially if they feel that their beloved "sick person" is not taking the best care of him or herself.

It is a great honor to be allowed into people's lives. It is important to remain respectful of how they have come to be where they are, while holding the hope that not only can they get where they want to go, but that they already possess the resources to get there. We all have unique strengths, and many of our clients, particularly those who are chronically ill, come in to therapy having forgotten this. When we seek out and are respectful of our clients' inner wisdom, they can rediscover their compassion for others and themselves, and begin to heal.

As I showed respect for the struggle that both Anna and her mother were experiencing, they began to listen to and have compassion for each other. As I stayed open and curious about Anna's perspective and the challenges she faced, her mother was able to hear her daughter's pain despite her own fear and misgivings. Many of the families I work with will strive for "perfect" health at the expense of their relationships. For example, Nancy became so desperate and overwhelmed with the notion that Anna would continue to neglect her health that she became a self-proclaimed "nag" who only spoke to her daughter about insulin and blood sugar. They became enemies instead of teammates. However, as this mother and daughter remained open to the idea that chronic illness was not just a physical condition and stayed respectful of the psychosocial components of disease management, they began to tap into a strength that neither knew the other possessed. This strength would change their relationship with each other and the one they had with themselves.

Anna discovered that her mother could take a step back, and tend to her own needs. This was powerful because it modeled the importance of mindfulness and self-care, both of which had taken a backseat when Nancy became a mother. Having more balance in Anna's own life demonstrated several things that would be particularly important for a person living with a chronic illness – that it was okay to take care of herself first and foremost and the importance of cultivating relationships with others who understood her situation.

Anna dove deep into herself to find more empowering ways of defining herself outside of being a diabetic and found that there were other things about her that made her special. Anna looked at how her identity was tied into being a victim of her disease, and began exploring how she could feel cared for and validated in other ways that were not related to the condition of her health.

Ideas for Best Practice

- Use your personal experience to cultivate empathy, and be wary of taking the expert position. Respect your client's authority in his or her own life.
- Stay curious about your client's perspective and take care to not let your own issues cloud your ability to be open to your client.
- Remember that disease management is a biopsychosocial process for the whole family system. Patients and their families alike do not always know the importance of attending to their relationships and may struggle to stay open to the power and transformation that can take place through the simple act of listening to each other with compassion and respect.

References

Anderson, B.J., Svoren, B., & Laffel, L. (2007). Initiatives to promote effective self-care skills in children and adolescents with diabetes mellitus. *Disease Management & Health Outcomes*, 15(2), 101–108. Retrieved from https://link.springer.com/article/10.2165/00115677-200715020-00005.

Grauf-Grounds, C., & Edwards, S. (2007). A ritual to honor trauma: A training community's witness. *Journal of Systemic Therapies*, 26, 38–50. Retrieved from https://guilfordjournals.com/doi/pdf/10.1521/jsyt.2007.26.1.38?casa_token=Aa0ghlgbvvIAAAAA%3AgNCUN NVUyyggm61Thzge7UgT0qcXEfvTRiBHX4vn1wL_8gnwEkGoTZvVwJf4aMAIAyk R2mg&.

13

BODY SIZE AND HEALTH

Using the ORCA-Stance to Counteract Weight Discrimination

Emily Rich

You are about to see a new client for the first time, a female identified client named Sandra in her late twenties, struggling with anxiety, career stress, and relationship issues. On the phone, she mentions that she has been trying to find a partner for quite some time but has had little luck in the dating world and has felt quite lonely. She hopes that psychotherapy will be helpful in lowering and managing her anxiety and stress as well as supporting her in her singlehood and dating quest. When you step into the waiting room to greet Sandra, you notice she is in a larger body – what some might refer to as "obese." Perhaps you begin to form assumptions about this client: her health must be poor; she has a problem with emotional eating; her struggles in the dating world might be related to her body size; maybe she lacks self-discipline; she probably does not exercise; she probably does not eat well; she needs to lose weight; surely, one of her goals is to lose weight.

As you sit with her, you notice she has an immense amount of shame, and one of the very first topics she delves into is about her body size. She uses the word "should" again and again, especially in regard to her weight – "I know I should lose weight. I know I should exercise more. I know I should get my act together. I've tried to diet hundreds of times, but I always end up screwing it up and gaining the weight back. I guess I'm just lazy and lack self-discipline. If I were thinner, I wouldn't have such a hard time finding a partner. If I were thinner, I wouldn't feel so anxious. Maybe I just need someone to hold me accountable so that I follow through with what I should do in order to lose weight and be healthy."

What do you do? What do you think? Do you agree with Sandra's assessment of herself? Do you agree, even just a little, with the solution she proposes – that weight loss will help her? Do you consider being a part of this goal to "hold her accountable" in her weight loss efforts? Perhaps you can consider some alternative assessment points. Sandra's immediate launch into the "should" statements about her body size could be a coping skill she has developed and is her way of beating you to the punch, calling herself out for her "shameful" body size before you have a chance to make those painful judgments yourself. Her countless experiences of being shamed by health care providers have conditioned her to start the self-deprecation process before anyone else can, even when your initial phone conversation about reasons for seeking treatment had no mention about her body or weight at all. It's as if she instinctively dives into the topic of body dissatisfaction just to get it out of the way because she has learned that the topic will inevitably be brought up by her clinicians, regardless of her proposed goals or concerns.

What if her lengthy history of dieting actually demonstrates the presence of a fierce willpower and self-discipline, rather than a lack thereof? What if she is actually in fine physical health, despite her body size? Sure, maybe weight loss would help to decrease her anxiety, given that living in a larger body in a fat phobic culture means living in the face of continual rejection and ridicule. Similarly, a change in skin color might decrease a person of color's anxiety in an oppressive and White centric culture. But we would never tell a person of color that the solution to their oppression-induced anxiety is bleaching their skin and becoming a White person. The problem lies in the dominant culture's oppressive attitudes, not in the person's skin color. Similarly, what if the cause of someone having a problem like Sandra's lies in the culture, not in their higher body weight?

If thought about closely, and perhaps from a less traditional viewpoint, Sandra's story confronts us with a few important questions:

1. What are your biases, assumptions, or judgments that immediately arise when facing someone in a body size that is different from your own, or different from what is considered to be acceptable in our culture?
2. How does your own body size and relationship with your body impact the internal and external responses you have to someone like Sandra?
3. What do you do when you are faced with an issue that is greatly misunderstood and inaccurately represented in our culture? A situation in which decades of misinformation and stigmatization have existed and permeated our culture and health care system deeper than we are even aware?

Each of these challenging questions can be meaningfully addressed through the use of the *ORCA-Stance*. The use of curiosity and accountability, in particular, are helpful when dealing with this topic. They draw the therapist into a position of cultural humility, compassion, and grace toward both the client and the self, all of which are important pieces in dealing with this difficult and often unaddressed area of discrimination. This situation cannot be effectively addressed without the evaluation of the self-of-therapist. We must be curious about our own stories as well as those of our clients. We must be curious about the information we hold and the source from which we have acquired it. Furthermore, we must be accountable to the power we hold in the room. As clinicians, we are assigned some degree of authority when it comes to matters of health. This is especially true when it comes to weight and eating, not to mention the other potential elements that allot power to us, such as being in a smaller or average sized body, or of Caucasian descent, or both. Thin privilege is as real as White privilege and must be taken into consideration.

Weight stigma and fat phobia are pervasive in our culture but are often overlooked or unacknowledged because they are concealed by efforts to promote health. Since we are accountable to the power we hold as clinicians, we have a responsibility to be critical consumers of the information from which we operate, especially when it is information that drives our biases. In other words, we must exercise our curiosity around the information we have learned as we attempt to be accountable to the power we have. As such, perhaps it is helpful to begin with a brief overview of the research and information, or misinformation, which perpetuates the issue of weight stigma and fat phobia.

The demonization of fat and misconceptions about weight gain/weight loss are typically what drive the strongly held biases around body size. Two common misunderstandings about obesity are that it leads to a shorter lifespan and is the cause of a higher risk for disease. In addition, we have been taught to believe that our weight and size are within our control and can be easily manipulated; anyone is capable of losing weight and maintaining weight loss; and a maintenance of lower weight ranges would be beneficial, not only for the individual, but for the greater whole in terms of health care costs and health outcomes (Bacon & Aphramor, 2011).

Interestingly, in their in-depth evaluation of the existing research around obesity and health, Dr. Linda Bacon and Dr. Lucy Aphramor found many pieces of information contradicting that which is offered in the mainstream media and health care system (Bacon & Aphramor, 2011, 2014). For example, multiple studies have demonstrated that people who are "overweight" or "moderately obese" live just as long, and sometimes longer than, those who are identified as having a "normal weight" (Durazo-Arvizu, McGee, Cooper, Liao, & Luke, 1998; Flegal, Graubard, Williamson, & Gail, 2005, 2008; Troiano, Frongillo, Sobal, & Levitsky, 1996). Furthermore, research has shown that even obese people with diseases such as type 2 diabetes, hypertension, and cardiovascular disease have been shown to live longer than thin people with the same diseases (Barrett-Connor, 1985; Barrett-Connor & Khaw, 1985; Ernsberger & Haskew, 1987; Ernsberger & Koletsky, 1999; Kang et al., 2006; Lavie, Milani, & Ventura, 2007; Ross, Langer, & Barrett-Connor, 1997). The concern of dying young due to being overweight is unsubstantiated and oversimplified, yet it is a fear that countless individuals are haunted by and reminded of throughout their entire lives.

We are all familiar with the images in the media and the strongly worded news and magazine articles depicting obesity as an awful monster that "makes you more likely to have conditions including: heart disease, stroke, high blood pressure, diabetes, some cancers, gallbladder disease, osteoarthritis, gout, breathing problems," and more (WebMD, n.d.-a). Unfortunately, this unavoidable and fear-inducing material is missing a key piece of information: that *correlation is not causation* (Bacon & Aphramor, 2011). Just because fat and disease exist in one person, does not mean fat *caused* disease in that person. There are many factors involved when it comes to risk for disease aside from the existence of excess fat, yet the blame is continually placed on fat (and on the fat person, since it is presumed to be self-inflicted or self-perpetuated).

For example, weight cycling, the act of losing and regaining weight, a common symptom of dieting also known as "yo-yo dieting," has been shown to result in increased inflammation and to be associated with high blood pressure and worsened cardiovascular health (Strohacker & McFarlin, 2010). And who are the individuals most likely to experience repeated patterns of weight loss and weight gain? Obese individuals (Kruger, Galuska, Serdula, & Jones, 2004). They are more likely to attempt to lose weight through dieting/caloric restriction, as directed by their health care providers, and because diets rarely result in sustained weight loss, these people almost inevitably regain the weight they lost, plus some (Mann et al., 2007; National Institutes of Health, 1992). Sadly, they are then blamed for failing the diet when in reality the diet failed them.

Dieting has also been shown to increase stress, thus increasing cortisol levels, and this has been linked to an increased risk for development of disease (Tomiyama et al., 2010). The so-called "treatment" (dieting) for the "problem" of obesity actually makes the problem worse and damages people's health by causing greater stress and increased experiences of weight cycling. The diet-induced stress and weight cycling likely has much more to do with a person's health outcomes than does their body size.

Considering how little control we actually have over the size and shape of our bodies, given that there are several factors (e.g., genetics, developmental factors, age, and gender) that influence body size (Institute of Medicine Subcommittee on Military Weight Management, 2004), the encouragement of weight control and valuing thin body types is not only unhelpful, but can also be harmful. Placing a high level of value on thinness and demonizing fatness negatively impacts people in *all* body sizes, including thin people. It creates an overall sense of anxiety and fear around weight and has even been shown to promote eating disorder behaviors (Daníelsdóttir, Burgard, & Oliver-Pyatt, 2009). Those who are in thinner bodies may become terrified of gaining weight and therefore turn to unhealthy behaviors in order to maintain thinness, or may feel significant stress, depression, or anxiety if they actually experience weight gain. The issue of weight stigmatization and fat phobia is not just a fat person problem.

In order for eating disorders, the deadliest psychiatric disorder (NEDA, n.d.), to be properly addressed and treated, weight bias and fear of fat must be acknowledged and corrected, especially in our health care system. How can we expect someone to recover from anorexia and distance themselves from a fear of food and eating when we are simultaneously communicating that they need to gain weight but not too much weight? We are teaching them it is okay to gain weight, but only to a certain point because *fat is deadly* (which is the same message being communicated to them by their eating disorder). Our unaddressed weight stigma and fat phobia is colluding with their eating disorder!

Not only does unacknowledged weight bias impact the way providers see their patients or clients, but it also has the potential to impact the quality of care that people are receiving. Thin individuals might be deemed healthy even if they are not, while fat people might be deemed unhealthy and be over-treated when it is unnecessary. Even worse, a fat person's real health issues might be overlooked because of the provider's overemphasis on their weight (Wildman, 2008). The use of the body mass index – or BMI, a measurement of how one's height corresponds with one's weight (WebMD, n.d.-b) – as an indicator of health is negatively impacting the quality of health care being provided for both thin and fat people and is ultimately costing more money (Bacon & Aphramor, 2011). It continues, however, to be one of the most widely used measurements in our health care system. Never mind the fact that the development of the BMI tool was greatly influenced by pharmaceutical companies with the only weight loss drugs on the market at the time (Bacon & Aphramor, 2014), and consists of futilely assigned numbers and categories largely based on Caucasian populations (Kasten, 2018). At best, the tool is ineffective. At worst, the tool is harmful in the way it labels individuals as having a "deadly disease" without taking other data points or demographic information into account.

The anti-fat, pro-thin bias is prevalent among many health professionals (Schwartz, Chambliss, Brownell, Blair, & Billington, 2003) and some primary care providers have even admitted to having less respect for their obese patients. This lack of respect can impact the way they interact with these patients as well as how cared for the patients feel with their physicians (Phelan, 2015), often leading these patients to avoid seeking care in the future, including important preventive care (Alegria Drury & Louis, 2002). We, as clinicians, must do better.

Perhaps one of the most important issues left out of the conversation around obesity and disease risk is the topic of social determinants of health. For example, low income and marginalization are more strongly associated with the development of type 2 diabetes than weight, diet, or exercise habits (Raphael et al., 2010; Wamala, Lynch, & Horsten, 1999). Some examples of social determinants of health include the availability of and access to resources to meet daily needs (e.g., grocery stores, safe shelter, etc.); educational, financial, and occupational opportunities; health care services; high-quality education and training; transportation; public safety; social support, and more (Healthy People, n.d.). Imagine the level of stress, and the impact of that stress, that an individual or family faces when living in poverty and with reduced access to health care, food, and education.

The potential stress is even greater if they are a person-of-color or of some other minority group.

Case Study Revisited

Let's imagine that Sandra, the client mentioned earlier in this chapter, is not only a woman in a larger body, but is also a Black woman who grew up being raised by a single mother in poverty. Perhaps Sandra and her mother struggled to have a consistent supply of assorted groceries in the house; or perhaps Sandra never felt safe enough to play outside; or maybe Sandra never felt like she fit in with the group of predominantly White kids at her school being that she naturally had a curvier figure, darker skin, and curlier hair. Maybe Sandra's White primary care doctor focused in on Sandra's weight at a young age, recommending diets before she even reached her freshman year of high school. Sandra's weight becomes the problem to target instead of her safety, housing, food, or educational provisions. And, what about the stress of being discriminated against for being both Black *and* in a larger body? Dr. Linda Bacon and Dr. Melissa Fabello (2016) note that ill health is often tied more to the level of oppression that a person experiences than to their behaviors. This is further supported by the well-documented research on adverse childhood experiences (ACEs), which consistently demonstrates that elevated exposure to ACEs is associated with an increased likelihood of poor physical health, mental health, and substance use outcomes in early adulthood (Mersky, Topitzes, & Reynolds, 2013). Health outcomes are related to so much more than body size.

Looking through a systemic lens is crucial in being able to understand and provide support for clients and patients in larger bodies. The concepts of "historical unresolved grief" and "historical trauma" have been written about by Brave Heart and DeBruyn (1998) specifically in regard to American Indians. They explore the impact of previous generations' experiences of trauma and unresolved grief upon today's generation, noting symptoms like anxiety, impulsivity, depression, isolation, and higher death rates from cardiovascular diseases, suicide, and other types of violent death (Brave Heart & DeBruyn, 1998). In this way, we must look at the oppression a person is currently facing as well as the historical oppression that their ancestors may have faced when evaluating a person's health, knowing this has a major impact on one's body and overall well-being. Instead of perpetuating discrimination and oppression, let's critically evaluate the larger systemic issues as well as our own personal experiences that color our perception.

Ideas for Best Practice

- *Notice your own biases around health, weight, and body size.* What are some of the thoughts or attitudes that come up when you encounter a person in a larger body, or when the topics of fat, weight loss, weight gain, dieting, or health arise? Similarly, what are some of the thoughts or attitudes that come up when you encounter a person in a thinner body?

- *Reevaluate the knowledge you hold.* What information or misinformation is driving your judgments, assumptions, thoughts, or responses? Where did this information come from? Is the information correct? Do you need to revisit the research? Do you need to consult with someone in order to learn more?
- *Notice the privilege you may or may not hold, and practice cultural humility as you sit with those who are less privileged.* Do you have thin privilege? Does this privilege intersect with other privileges, such as White privilege, cisgender privilege, heterosexual privilege, or socioeconomic privilege? How might your client be feeling in the presence of your privilege? How might your privilege be showing up in session?
- *Be curious about your client's experience.* What is it like for your client to live in the body they have? What might they experience on a day-to-day basis? Is intersectionality a part of their experience? Do they experience oppression in more than one way? Do not make any assumptions about someone's health based on their body size or physical appearance. Curiosity needs to be present, regardless of the person's body size.
- *Be curious about your own experience.* What is it like for you to live in the body you have? Do you have judgments about yourself or your body? What kinds of attitudes did your family of origin hold around body size, health, and food? How has the culture influenced your perception of body size, health, and food? Have you been operating from misinformation? Have you unintentionally been participating in weight stigmatization and/or promoting fat phobia?
- *Create a safe, size-inclusive environment.* Be sure to make your waiting room and office a safe and comfortable place for people of all body sizes. Invest in chairs that don't have arms. Use terms like "larger body" instead of terms like "overweight" or "obese," which perpetuate the idea that a person's body size is diseased. The word "fat" is in the process of being reclaimed as a simple descriptor, rather than a negative and offensive word. Additionally, if you are personally involved in diets, fad cleanses/detoxes, food elimination challenges, or anything of the like, consider reevaluating your use of these questionable methods, and, at the very least, *do not* discuss this part of your life with your clients. Much harm is caused when clinicians of any kind mention their own current involvement in diets or weight loss efforts.

It is our responsibility to provide "inclusive, effective, and ethical care consistent with the evidence base" (Bacon & Aphramor, 2011, p. 9). The world needs more clinicians who operate from a size acceptance stance and reject the idea that weight is a central part of one's health. Instead, we need to use a systemic approach in seeing each person as a whole person, using curiosity to explore their story while being accountable for what we bring into the room. We have the opportunity to create a different experience for our clients by being clinicians who embody cultural humility when it comes to issues of health, body size, and eating.

References

Alegria Drury, C.A., & Louis, M. (2002). Exploring the association between body weight, stigma of obesity, and health care avoidance. *Journal of the American Academy of Nurse Practitioners*, 14, 554–561. Retrieved from https://onlinelibrary.wiley.com/doi/abs/10.1111/j.1745-7599.2002.tb00089.x.

Bacon, L., & Aphramor, L. (2011). Weight Science: Evaluating the evidence for a paradigm shift. *Nutrition Journal*, 10, 69. Retrieved from https://nutritionj.biomedcentral.com/articles/10.1186/1475-2891-10-9.

Bacon, L., & Aphramor, L. (2014). *Body Respect: What Conventional Health Books Get Wrong, Leave Out, and Just Plain Fail to Understand about Weight*. Dallas, TX: BenBella Books. Retrieved from https://books.google.com/books?id=Mqo3BAAAQBAJ&printsec=frontcover&dq=Body+respect:+What+conventional+health+books+get+wrong,+leave+out,+and+just+plain+fail+to+understand+about+weight.&hl=en&sa=X&ved=0ahUKEwiqmcOlxabhAhXRup4KHSAsCAMQ6AEIKjAA#v=onepage&q=Body%20respect%3A%20What%20conventional%20health%20books%20get%20wrong%2C%20leave%20out%2C%20and%20just%20plain%20fail%20to%20understand%20about%20weight.&f=false.

Barrett-Connor, E.L. (1985). Obesity, atherosclerosis and coronary artery disease. *Annals of Internal Medicine*, 103, 1010–1019. Retrieved from https://annals.org/aim/article-abstract/700208/obesity-atherosclerosis-coronary-artery-disease.

Barrett-Connor, E., & Khaw, K. (1985). Is hypertension more benign when associated with obesity? *Circulation*, 72, 53–60.

Brave Heart, M.H., & DeBruyn, L.M. (1998). The American Indian holocaust: Healing historical unresolved grief. *American Indian and Alaska Native Mental Health Research*, 8(2), 60–82. Retrieved from www.ucdenver.edu/academics/colleges/PublicHealth/research/centers/CAIANH/journal/Documents/Volume%208/8(2)_YellowHorseBraveHeart_American_Indian_Holocaust_60-82.pdf.

Daníelsdóttir, S., Burgard, D., & Oliver-Pyatt, W. (2009). AED guidelines for childhood obesity prevention programs. *Academy of Eating Disorders*. Retrieved from http://higherlogicdownload.s3.amazonaws.com/AEDWEB/05656ea0-59c9-4dd4-b832-07a3fea58f4c/UploadedImages/Press_Releases/POSITION-CHILDHOOD-PORTUGUESE.pdf.

Durazo-Arvizu, R., McGee, D., Cooper, R., Liao, Y., & Luke, A. (1998). Mortality and optimal body mass index in a sample of the US population. *American Journal of Epidemiology*, 147, 739–749.

Ernsberger, P., & Haskew, P. (1987). Health implications of obesity: An alternative view. *Journal of Obesity and Weight Regulation*, 9, 39–40. Retrieved from http://agris.fao.org/agris-search/search.do?recordID=US8851470.

Ernsberger, P., & Koletsky, R.J. (1999). Biomedical rationale for a wellness approach to obesity: An alternative to a focus on weight loss. *J Soc Issues*, 55, 221–260. Retrieved from www.researchgate.net/profile/Paul_Ernsberger/publication/229457469_Biomedic

al_Rationale_for_a_Wellness_Approach_to_Obesity_An_Alternative_to_a_focus_on_W eight_Loss/links/5a458a7d0f7e9ba868a93b76/Biomedical-Rationale-for-a-Wellness-Ap proach-to-Obesity-An-Alternative-to-a-focus-on-Weight-Loss.pdf.

Fabello, M.A., & Bacon, L. (2016). 11 reasons your phony "concern" for fat people's health has got to stop. *Everyday Feminism*. Retrieved from https://everydayfeminism. com/2016/01/concern-trolling-is-bullshit/.

Flegal, K.M., Graubard, B.I., Williamson, D.F., & Gail, M.H. (2005). Excess deaths associated with underweight, overweight, and obesity. *JAMA: Journal of the American Medical Association*, 293, 1861–1867. Retrieved from https://jamanetwork.com/journals/jama/ fullarticle/200731.

Flegal, K., Graubard, B., Williamson, D., & Gail, M. (2008). Supplement: Response to "can fat be fit." *Scientific American*, 297, 5–6.

Healthy People (n.d.). Social determinants of health. Retrieved from https://www.hea lthypeople.gov/2020/topics-objectives/topic/social-determinants of-health.

Institute of Medicine Subcommittee on Military Weight Management (2004). Factors that influence body weight. In *Weight Management: State of the Science and Opportunities for Military Programs*. Washington, DC: National Academies Press. Retrieved from www. ncbi.nlm.nih.gov/books/NBK221834/.

Kang, X. *et al.* (2006). Impact of body mass index on cardiac mortality in patients with known or suspected coronary artery disease undergoing myocardial perfusion single-photon emission computed tomography. *Journal of the American College of Cardiology*, 47, 1418–1426. Retrieved from www.onlinejacc.org/content/accj/47/7/1418.full.pdf.

Kasten, G. (2018). Listen … and speak: A discussion of weight bias, its intersections with homophobia, racism, and misogyny, and their impacts on health. *Canadian Journal of Dietetic Practice and Research*, 79, 133–138. Retrieved from https://dcjournal.ca/doi/pdfp lus/10.3148/cjdpr-2018-023.

Kruger, J., Galuska, D.A., Serdula, M.K., & Jones, D.A. (2004). Attempting to lose weight: Specific practices among U.S. adults. *American Journal of Preventative Medicine*, 26, 402–406. Retrieved from www.ajpmonline.org/article/S0749-3797(04)00028-5/fulltext.

Lavie, C.J., Milani, R.V., & Ventura, H.O. (2007). Obesity, heart disease, and favorable prognosis – truth or paradox? *American Journal of Medicine*, 120, 825–826. Retrieved from www.amjmed.com/article/S0002-9343(07)00725- 5/fulltext.

Mann, T., Tomiyama, A.J., Westling, E., Lew, A., Samuels, B., & Chatman, J. (2007). Medicare's search for effective obesity treatments: Diets are not the answer. *American Psychologist*, 62(3), 220–233. Retrieved from https://cloudfront.escholarship.org/dist/p rd/content/qt2811g3r3/qt2811g3r3.pdf.

Mersky, J.P., Topitzes, J., & Reynolds, A.J. (2013). Impacts of adverse childhood experiences on health, mental health, and substance use in early adulthood: A cohort study of an urban, minority sample in the U.S. *Child Abuse & Neglect*, 37(11), 917–925.

National Institutes of Health (1992). Methods for voluntary weight loss and control (Technology Assessment Conference Panel). *Annals of Internal Medicine*, 116, 942–949. Retrieved from www.ncbi.nlm.nih.gov/pmc/articles/PMC4090696/.

NEDA (n.d.). Statistics and research on eating disorders. Retrieved from www.nationalea tingdisorders.org/statistics-research-eating-disorders.

Phelan, S.M., Burgess, D.J., Yeazel, M.W., Hellerstedt, W.L., Griffin, J.M., & Ryn, M. (2015). Impact of weight bias and stigma on quality of care and outcomes for patients with obesity. *Obesity Reviews*, 16, 319–326. Retrieved from https://onlinelibrary.wiley. com/doi/full/10.1111/obr.12266.

Raphael, D., Lines, E., Bryant, T., Daiski, I., Pilkington, B., Dinca-Panaitescu, S., & Dinca-Panaitescu, M. (2010). *Type 2 Diabetes: Poverty, Priorities and Policy. The Social Determinants of the Incidence and Management of Type 2 Diabetes.* Toronto, ON: York University School of Health Policy and Management and School of Nursing.

Ross, C., Langer, R.D., & Barrett-Connor, E. (1997). Given diabetes, is fat better than thin? *Diabetes Care*, 20, 650–652. Retrieved from https://search.proquest.com/doc view/223040532?pq-origsite=gscholar.

Schwartz, M.B., Chambliss, H.O., Brownell, K.D., Blair, S.N., & Billington, C. (2003). Weight bias among health professionals specializing in obesity. *Obesity Research*, 11, 1033–1039. Retrieved from https://onlinelibrary.wiley.com/doi/full/10.1038/oby. 2003.142.

Strohacker, K., & McFarlin, B.K. (2010). Influence of obesity, physical inactivity, and weight cycling on chronic inflammation. *Frontiers in Bioscience (Elite Edition)*, 2, 98–104. Retrieved from https://europepmc.org/abstract/med/20036858.

Tomiyama, A.J., Mann, T., Vinas, D., Hunger, J.M., DeJager, J., & Taylor, S.E. (2010). Low calorie dieting increases cortisol. *Psychosomatic Medicine*, 42(4), 357–364. Retrieved from www.ncbi.nlm.nih.gov/pmc/articles/PMC2895000/.

Troiano, R., Frongillo, E., Jr., Sobal, J., & Levitsky, D. (1996). The relationship between body weight and mortality: A quantitative analysis of combined information from existing studies. *International Journal of Obesity and Related Metabolic Disorders*, 20, 63–75. Retrieved from https://europepmc.org/abstract/med/8788324.

Wamala, S., Lynch, J., & Horsten, M. (1999). Education and the metabolic syndrome in women. *Diabetes Care*, 22, 1999–2003. Retrieved from www.researchgate.net/profile/ Karin_Schenck-Gustafsson/publication/12713152_Education_and_the_metabolic_syndr ome_in_women/links/0deec51783df48f533000000/Education-and-the-metabolic-synd rome-in-women.pdf.

WebMD (n.d.-a). Health risks linked to obesity. Retrieved from www.webmd.com/diet/ obesity/obesity-health-risks#1.

WebMD (n.d.-b). Weight loss and body mass index. Retrieved from www.webmd. com/men/weightloss-bmi.

Wildman, R.P., Muntner, P., Reynolds, K., McGinn, A.P., Rajpathak, S., Wylie-Rosett, J., & Sowers, M.R. (2008). The obese without cardiometabolic risk factor clustering and the normal weight with cardiometabolic risk factor clustering: prevalence and correlates of 2 phenotypes among the US population (NHANES 1999–2004). *Archives of Internal Medicine*, 168, 1617–1624. Retrieved from https://jamanetwork.com/journals/jama internalmedicine/article-abstract/770362.

14

SEXUAL STRUGGLES

Tina Schermer Sellers

If you had to name the most reactive issue affecting relational health and parenting in America today, what would you say that it is? In a nutshell, I would say it is sex and intimacy ... how to do it, how to teach it, how to survive it, how to live it, and how to sustain it.

One day I got a call from a woman who said that she and her partner, Bruce, had been through four therapists and none of them had been very helpful. She had gotten my name from someone and was hoping I might be able to help them. Pam and Bruce (fictitious names) were in their forties and had been married for 15 years. They had four kids ranging in age from eight to 13. They described themselves as having a conservative Christian faith, very committed to their marriage and to working on their sexual life in a way that honored their faith. Pam and Bruce had both married as virgins, had enjoyed their sexual life, but over the majority of their marriage, she had been the high desire partner, sometimes feeling undesired by Bruce. Pam described that several years ago Bruce got very depressed and then confessed that he had a secret. He had, since his adolescence, sometimes masturbated with women's silk panties. Over the years since the disclosure, they had worked together to understand his fetish. Bruce didn't entirely understand his draw toward panties, all he knew is that it was calming and slightly arousing. In time, Bruce disclosed that what he really wanted was to wear women's panties under his pants and to bed.

When they came to see me, the primary problem Pam described was feeling like Bruce was more into the panties than he was into her. I carefully listened to understand how they expressed their care for each other, and how Pam expressed her desire for Bruce, how he responded to her, as well as how Pam engaged Bruce around the panty issue and how they had come to understand the role the panties played. We examined their meaning behind their marriage, their sexual relationship, the fetish, their faith, and their hopes for each of these things. Because of ORCA, my work as a sex therapist, and my years of working with people of faith, I was able to carefully let them define each of these components at play in their dance. I worked hard to understand them to the best of my ability, *from their perspective.*

The panties might be less threatening to Pam, provided she could feel wanted by Bruce. Over the course of five sessions, we were able to unpack that the fetish was not rejected by her; however, her anxiety was causing her to pursue him in a way that felt aggressive to him. This triggered him to withdraw and put up a wall, which is exactly what he had done as a child to protect himself from his father. When he did this, Pam felt rejected and abandoned. This triggered her early loss of a dear grandmother who had died of cancer before she could say goodbye. With even higher anxiety, any indication Bruce was giving attention to panties became a further indicator to her that he was leaving her − if only figuratively. Her anxiety would then begin to spin out of control.

As we were able to reveal the pattern, they began to shift in the way they responded to each other when they felt anxious. They learned to turn toward each other and say what they were feeling, what was going on for them, and what they needed. Very soon afterwards, Pam and Bruce began having more fun together. They made some modifications to their sex life and set some guidelines for the panties that felt fine for both of them.

From what Pam and Bruce said, what kept the previous therapists from working was an inability to clinically embrace ORCA − to really listen and hear their story before deciding what they needed to do. Fear or pre-conceived ideas about fetishes, conservative Christians, what treatment "should" look like, or what the diagnosis "really was" got in the way of true openness and curiosity, and it invited the other clinicians to jump to conclusions.

When working with individuals or couples around sexual issues, I have found it critical to embody an *ORCA-Stance.* Due to abstinence-only education and a crackdown from conservative influences in America, the vast majority of individuals raised in America over the last 40 years have had for the most part, inadequate sex education, whether from schools or from their physicians, even though parents would like help from professionals in talking to their kids about sex. This has meant that most people grow up in homes that are primarily silent around sex and sex education − often continuing the legacy of silence and shame. The vast amount of "education" comes from the media and culture, which provides its education packaged as bodies and people for sale and consumption. This combination of inadequate knowledge − coupled with an inaccurate highly marketed fantasy version of sexuality, people, and relationships − can tend to manifest as relational and sexual problems in actual lives and partnerships.

We know from research that male and female sexual dysfunction is prevalent at rates somewhere between 38 percent for men and 23 percent for women, and this can tend to increase with age. This data indicates to us, as therapists, that the majority of our clients will come to us with sexual issues and concerns. It is safe to assume they are likely ill-informed and uncomfortable talking about sexual issues, while at the same time desperate for help and deathly afraid of being judged or shamed. An ORCA-Stance is critical if space is to be created where a person can feel seen, known, accepted, and cared about. This first step in diminishing shame and silence is a critical component in creating a safe therapeutic space. Through demonstrating openness and curiosity from the ORCA-Stance, the therapist seeks to understand the lived experience and lived meaning of the sexual concerns and sexual goals of their client or couple. With cultural humility, the therapist asks permission, where appropriate, to provide information in order to dispel myths and empower the client with real knowledge about their body and the sexual process. Information is also given to normalize the experience of the client because so few people understand how typical their sexual experiences, thoughts, and desires are. If a particular sexual issue is wrapped within an emotional attachment, dance, or pattern of relating, the therapist helps the couple to untangle the issues so that they can see them more clearly, one from the other, and how and where they do and do not relate.

Ideas for Best Practice

- Sexuality is loaded – there is no way around it. Because of this, ORCA is a fabulous guide and a reminder to breathe, stay open, and listen – both within yourself and to your clients. Embracing cultural humility, many therapists recognize that they too did not receive adequate sexual health training in their graduate training and are obtaining post-graduate training in sexual health, sexual bias training, working with sexual minority populations, and treating sexual dysfunction. If you are being triggered, the best thing you can do is notice it and keep breathing, remain open and curious seeking to deeply understand the experience of your clients. Try to remember that the vast majority of people at their core want connection and pleasure and are trying their best to figure out how to get that amid a culture that provides little to no helpful instruction. Talk to a colleague or get supervision if the issue is triggering or something with which you are less familiar.
- Utilize the PLISSIT model – offer "P" – permission to discuss sexual issues. Remind your clients that therapy is a safe place to discuss topics of intimacy – connection and pleasure – and that you are a safe person to do this with. Give your clients "LI" – limited information – by providing *some* of the sex education that they likely need in order to understand their situation. So much of what is often creating difficulties for people is the misinformation they have obtained from the media and culture. Accurate sex education can help this. They may also need some "SS" – specific suggestions – from you about tasks they can try that can improve their connection and pleasure with each other. Often it is the "P-LI-SS" that people need more than the

"IT" – intensive therapy – when they come to see you because of how inadequate our culture is in providing comprehensive and healthy sexual information for our public – and how shame filled people are around their sexual lives.

- In addition to our clients feeling in the dark around sexuality, most therapists are too. Not only did we grow up in a culture that likely gave us very little sex education, most states only require one human sexuality course for state licensure as a psychotherapist. Most therapists receive an inadequate amount of training in the area of sexuality or exposure to their sexual biases. This requires a high level of cultural humility and inner attunement to counter transference. When triggered, it is ideal for a therapist to seek supervision from a certified American Association of Sexuality Educators, Counselors and Therapists (AASECT) supervisor. This allows for the therapist to attend to both person of the therapist and clinical development.

- In my fantasy world, I'd like to see all therapists add a few courses in clinical sexology to beef up their training in sexuality, as well as take a course exposing them to their sexual biases. This course is called a S.A.R. – sexual attitude reassessment – and it is offered all over the United States. Research demonstrates that therapists become competent to deal with sexuality and intimacy issues that their clients bring into therapy when they add *both* training and clinical supervision in clinical sexology. It is not enough for a therapist to be comfortable with the subject of sexuality – they must do extra training and supervision – or get dually trained as an AASECT certified sex therapist. To help our clients and to deal with one of the most pressing relational issues facing our communities today, embracing our awareness of sexuality needs to be in our clinical wheelhouse.

References

Kaiser Family Foundation (2007). *Sex Education in the US: Policy and Politics*. San Francisco, CA: KFF. Retrieved from www.kff.org/hivaids/sex-education-in-the-u-s-policy/.

Maheux, B., Haley, N., Rivard, M., & Gervais, A. (1999). Do physicians assess lifestyle health risks during general medical examinations? A survey of general practitioners and obstetrician-gynecologist in Quebec. *Journal of the Canadian Medical Association*, 160, 1830–1834. Retrieved from www.ncbi.nlm.nih.gov/pmc/articles/PMC1230436/pdf/cmaj_160_13_1830. pdf.

Marwick, C. (1999). Survey says patients expect little physician help on sex. *JAMA: Journal of the American Medical Association*, 281, 2173–2174. Retrieved from https://jamanetwork.com/journals/jama/article- abstract/1680225.

Mitchel, K., Jones, K., Welling, K., et al. (2016). Estimating the prevalence of sexual function problems: The impact of morbidity criteria. *Journal of Sex Research*, 53(8), 955–967.

National Public Radio/KaiserFamily Foundation/Harvard University (2004). *Sex Education in America: General Public/Parents Survey*. San Francisco, CA: KFF. Retrieved from www.kff.org/hivaids/poll-finding/sex-education-in-america-general-public-parents/.

15

SPIRITUAL STRUGGLES

Treading on Sacred Ground

William K. Collins

Jane came into my office confused and filled with fearful feelings close to panic. At 38, her husband had left her on her own in a small apartment, along with two children under the age of ten. It was hard for her to understand how her life had gotten to this point, or what a path to a satisfying future could look like. She had lost confidence in herself and her abilities. As we reviewed her life, she remembered her high school years as a lonely time, and a time when she had begun to doubt herself. She was both a straight-A student and just over six feet tall, and she remembered being perplexed about why boys had left her alone. She recalled a conversation with her mother at one point in her senior year, where she was wondering what was wrong with her. Her mother's comment had stuck with her: "maybe it will be different when you go to college." Unfortunately, this served to confirm her self-doubt about her gifts, as she thought "even my mother thinks there is something wrong with me!"

Curious, I asked her, "Jane, have you ever had a chance to ask your mother what she meant to say to you when she spoke those words? I wonder if she meant to say what you heard. I have learned that we often mistake the sense we make of another's words for something other than what they intended to say to us." She said no, but added that her mother was coming to visit this weekend to help with the kids, and that she might be able to ask her if she remembered.

The following week, Jane's mood was a little brighter when she came to see me. She had asked her mother if she remembered the conversation from 20 years before, and that her mother remembered it well. Jane asked her what she meant for her to hear, and her mother had told her that her heart was sinking as she listened to her daughter's pain, and that she wanted to say something encouraging. Her mother had sensed that Jane's strengths might be intimidating to the boys who went to school with her, and that she hoped those she met in college would be able to see her very positive qualities more clearly. All of this sounded new and unfamiliar to Jane, but as she reflected on the intent of her mother's words over the following days, she had begun to see herself in a different light. For her, her mother's more complete explanation had invited her into a way of seeing herself as loveable and capable, quite differently than she had been able to think of herself after her husband had left her. Sensing we had wandered into the sacred ground where a person begins to unpack their image of themselves, I remember feeling very glad I had thought to give voice to my curiosity.

The *ORCA-Stance* assists therapists to explore the role of spirituality and spiritual issues related to the presenting problems of therapy in at least three ways. First, the therapist using the ORCA-Stance is positioned to take an invitational stance that can consider the relevance of spirituality as part of the client's experience. Second, the values inherent in this process can provide a restraint for the therapist to fall into the risk of taking a convincing stance, helping them to maintain a boundary between their own values and the values that the client is interested in considering. Adopting a "not-knowing" approach (Anderson & Goolishian, 1992) positions a therapist to explore the client's culture humbly and emphasizes the curiosity that a therapist uses when they simply want to understand better. Third, using the ORCA-Stance – which focuses on practicing empathic responsiveness – allows the therapist to become attuned to the interaction and can explore the unique moment with the client.

The Invitational Stance of the Therapist

Often the therapeutic encounter engages a client to work on creative transformation because of their disappointment with the contemporary circumstances of their lives. They seem certain that something must change, though often they are not sure what that something is. Their therapeutic engagement with the therapist allows them to look "around" and "in-between" their presenting problems. Clients often see themselves at a crossroads.

In the "process thought" tradition that has its roots in the process philosophy of Alfred North Whitehead, an invitation toward a path of greater possibility is a part of every crossroads moment. Higher organisms, as Whitehead notes, originate novelty to match the novelty of the environment. "In a world in which all things flow, ongoing creative transformation is not only healthy, but necessary for survival" (as quoted by Epperly, 2011, p. 33). When clients are perplexed about the way things are, they are increasingly open to consider behavioral changes to address this.

Within the perspective of such a process theology, from moment to moment, the role of God is often described as inviting that individual to take the path of greatest possibility from this crossroads. This invitational action is repeated over and over again, so that whatever choice the individual makes at each crossroad, they are invited to embark from that point onto the path of greatest possibility that leads from that point.

God always calls us toward creative transformation. In our awakening to the grace of transformation, we begin a path of healing and sanctification, or spiritual transformation, in which tragedy and sin can be transformed into beauty of experience for others and ourselves.

(Epperly, 2011, p. 91)

This perspective offers the therapist utilizing an ORCA-Stance an image that is consistent with an improvisational invitational perspective. Isomorphically, the openness, respect, and curiosity of the therapist work within the possibility of the client's novel responses to consider which of the paths leading from the crossroads offer the greatest possibility to the client, precisely because the way ahead is not clear.

This stance allows the therapist to continually hold open the question: "From here, what path offers you the greatest possibilities, considering what you want most for your life?" By addressing the sacred in this way, the therapist remains respectfully open to all the possibilities that may be in line with the "heart's desire" of the client – even though the words which express such a desire may not yet have been created within the client's inner dialog or even in the therapeutic conversation. This question may be an invitation to "create the sacred" with the client.

A value within the spirit of ORCA is that the therapist comes to understand how those who they are talking with and listening to perceive their situation within the broader context of their lives. Not knowing the answers takes humility, especially cultural humility, so that the focus on emerging information can be maintained. In a sense, client and therapist are making a map together of a new territory not previously explored. By continually assessing the conversation and the needs of the client for the therapeutic process, the therapist conveys a sense of collaboration. It is expected that the therapist will check in with the client about the usefulness of these exploratory conversations, including asking explicitly if this way of talking about their situation is one that the client is interested in pursuing further.

Restraining the Zeal of the Therapist

The ORCA-Stance helps the therapist to invite client reflections about possibilities without inserting their own "good ideas" for the client's future path. Whitaker's one-liner, "If we can abandon our missionary zeal, we have less chance of being eaten by cannibals," has often acted as a caution for those therapists who are in possession of "good ideas" for their clients. As Michael White used to admonish therapists, it is easy to fall into a convincing position. He warned, "when therapists do assume primary authorship in this way, it is common to them to enter into a convincing mode" (White, 2007, p. 233). Whenever therapists seek to explore sacred ground with clients, their own "good ideas" for the client present a very different path than attempting to follow the path that the client prefers.

The "convincing position" is very much at odds with the ORCA-Stance that a therapist seeks to embody. Knowing what is good for or helpful to a client flows easily out of an expert position. With the aid of curiosity and cultural humility, the therapist's attention is shifted from a place within the therapist's head and toward questions about how the circumstances are being experienced by the client, and with the thoughts that the client has been brooding creatively about to discern what they might do to improve the situation, while respecting the values, both major and minor, that came into the room with the client.

The foundational ORCA-Stance allows the client and the therapist to explore their understandings of the sacred (i.e., the in-between). There may be parts of a client's life that connects them to the sacred when reviewing their current dilemma or problem. These areas can be discovered as the client seeks the help of a therapist in therapeutic conversations. All the values of the ORCA-Stance, but particularly the accountability to power, remind the therapist to explore these connections rather than follow their urges to provide the connections that they see – the ones that make the most sense within their own understandings of the world of the client.

Therapists embodying the ORCA-Stance report that they ask questions that begin with "I wonder if ..." or "Have you ever thought that ..." rather than engaging in attempts to convince.

Tuning in to the Reworking of Belief Systems in Therapeutic Conversations

If client and therapist are interested in understanding the role of spirituality in the circumstances of the client's life and its relevance to the work done in psychotherapy, Kenneth Pargament suggests helpful questions to consider with clients: "What do you hold sacred? and "Where do you currently stand in the search for the sacred?" (Pargament, 2007, p. 336). He also suggests that part of the therapist's role might be to explore the role of the client's use of their own existing spiritual resources: "In times of emotional distress, it is not uncommon for people to lose touch with the resources that normally sustain them in their lives." (Pargament, 2007, p. 241)

What signals to a therapist an opening into sacred ground? There are many clues to this sort of opening. In Emotion-Focused Therapy language, it might be called a "softening," namely when a previously hostile person accesses "softer" emotions and risks reaching out to someone else who is engaged and positive. It might be a comment like "I've never thought about this experience this way." This is a time when the respect and curiosity of the therapist comes forward to support a new exploration, particularly if there are signs of a shift in feeling.

When couples are exploring the barriers to vulnerability in their committed relationships, the therapist working with them to build trust and make emotional connections is a witness to their exploration of this sacred ground of relationship. In John Gottman's description of moments when partners are working together on attuning, to themselves and to each other, he speaks of the willingness to sacrifice for the relationship, sometimes putting his or her own needs on the back burner because the relationship matters most.

> When couples are trustworthy they send each other the message that they and the partnership are unique and irreplaceable. During couples' counseling, I call this "creating the sacred" because "sacred" and "sacrifice" have the same root – both words originated in early religious practices that involved sacrifice as a form of worship.
>
> *(Gottman & Silver, 2012, p. 14)*

The connections they are making are facilitating the process of becoming fully human and fully alive. For ORCA-informed therapists who describe these special moments of therapeutic conversations to colleagues, quite commonly there is an explicit recognition and acknowledgment that what they are witnessing is a spiritual struggle for the partners, letting go of one experience of relationship to discover a richer deeper connection with each other.

In the spirit identified by Pargament and Gottman, several pathways into sacred ground are noted in clinical work, stemming from an array of different clinical theories. In each of them the foundation of the ORCA-Stance helps the therapist to pace with the discovery of new valuable perspectives.

In another situation, a client might need help slowing down. As Leslie Greenberg (2002) writes: "To enter a state of feeling, so very different from a state of thinking or acting, you need to be able to slow down. To feel is a slow process" (p. 132). Curiosity and respect are particularly helpful to the therapist in requesting a client to move more slowly.

Case Study

In a first session a young woman who was prompted to enter therapy after a romantic break-up was telling me "I'm not feeling right about myself without the missing relationship." She felt tears coming to her eyes as she talked about how she missed the friendship she had with her partner. Crying was something she had not wanted to do, for reasons she was unable to identify. But when she cried, slowing down a bit with my encouragement allowed her to feel what she was feeling – "just let yourself feel this feeling." Values of openness, respect for, and curiosity about the experience guided me in taking this position, slowing down the process to make room for the feeling. At the beginning of the following session, she reported being more in touch with her joy throughout the week and wondered how the expression of the sadness, which she was feeling, had made that possible. Her own curiosity allowed her to enter into the previously unwanted feelings. In the weeks that followed, she was often "surprised by sadness," and made a connection that living with this sadness was part of preparing to be ready for other relationships. Allowing the sadness to contribute was a part of her participation in a creative transformation of her circumstances.

For the therapist who is exploring the kinds of transformations that might emerge from the set of circumstances that brought their client into therapy, inquiries shaped by ORCA values are foundational tools. One important question they might ask is: "What are you noticing about yourself as you experience this unfamiliar ground?" Exploring the "in-between" might also come in the moment when a therapist offers a reframing of a situation, for example in the situation above: "Might it be that when you noticed that unwanted sadness, a part of you was doing work to come to terms with what you have lost – sort of gathering yourself, so that you are ready once again to move on?" The Pixar film – *Inside Out* – offers a contemporary example of transformation resulting from experiencing with an open perspective a previously unwanted or unvalued way of experiencing life events.

When the therapist wants to include the spiritual values of the client and explore the shifting ways in which each client is making sense of their life experiences, the ORCA values help the therapist to become more comfortable with slowing down, opening up, creating space for other perspectives, for the wondered about, and for adjustments to the frame in which experience is being held. With an attitude of cultural humility, the therapist is tracking the client's articulation of the sense of their circumstances that is emerging, and asking questions that seek to create secure connections between the existing cultural content and new values that are brought forth in the transformation, as well as to explore the dissonances that appear.

The work remains improvisational because conversations do not follow a predictable path and openings to spiritual conversations may occur when they are least expected. It is also invitational because of the therapist's respect for the client's ideas, and the expectation that the conversations will be useful to the client as they consider the crossroads that made therapy a good idea for them. In such a stance, space is left for a creative transformation as the client works with their experience within the therapeutic conversation.

Ideas for Best Practice

- Become aware of what drives you away from curiosity. It will often be necessary to find your way back to the path you have wandered away from.
- Even as you attune all your senses to "softening" in the therapy process, slow down and seek to explore these shifts in process.

References

Anderson, H., & Goolishian, H. (1992). The client is the expert: A not-knowing approach to therapy. In S. McNamee & K.J. Gergen (Eds.), *Inquiries in Social Construction: Therapy as Social Construction* (pp. 25–39). Thousand Oaks, CA: SAGE.

Epperly, B.G. (2011). *Process Theology: A Guide for the Perplexed*. New York: Bloomsbury. Retrieved from https://books.google.com/books?id=uQAUfKwVNGcC&printsec=fro ntcover&dq=Process+Theology:+A+Guide+for+the+Perplexed&hl=en&sa=X&ved=0a hUKEwiXnO77o6bhAhVKj1QKHXLXBUsQ6AEIKjAA#v=onepage&q=Process%20 Theology%3A%20A%20Guide%20for%20the%20Perplexed&f=false.

Gottman, J., & Silver, N. (2012). *What Makes Love Last? How to Build Trust and Avoid Betrayal*. New York: Simon and Schuster. Retrieved from https://books.google.com/ books?id=GQ2oAAAAQBAJ&printsec=frontcover&dq=What+makes+love+last?+Ho w+to+build+trust+and+avoid+betrayal&hl=en&sa=X&ved=0ahUKEwj29a2IpKbhAh UM658KHazCAqIQ6AEIKjAA#v=onepage&q=What%20makes%20love%20last%3F% 20How%20to%20build%20trust%20and%20avoid%20betrayal&f=false.

Greenberg, L.S. (2002). *Emotion-Focused Therapy: Coaching Clients to Work through Their Feelings*. Washington, DC: American Psychological Association.

Pargament, K. (2007). *Spiritually Integrated Psychotherapy: Understanding and Addressing the Sacred*. New York: Guilford Press. Retrieved from https://books.google.com/books? id=q_dFyOx4UrcC&printsec=frontcover&dq=Spiritually+integrated+psychotherapy:+ understanding+and+addressing+the+%09sacred.&hl=en&sa=X&ved=0ahUKEwjtwuun pKbhAhUK7J8KHb1QC4oQ6AEIKjAA#v=onepage&q=Spiritually%20integrated%20 psychotherapy%3A%20understanding%20and%20addressing%20the%20%09sacred.&f=fa lse.

White, M. (2007). *Maps of Narrative Practice*. New York: Norton. Retrieved from https:// books.google.com/books?id=qDdoLhCr7PgC&printsec=frontcover&dq=Maps+of+nar rative+practice&hl=en&sa=X&ved=0ahUKEwjaz-G1pKbhAhVpsFQKHS46BBoQ6AE IKjAA#v=onepage&q=Maps%20of%20narrative%20practice&f=false.

Whitehead, A.N. (1978). *Process and Reality* (Rev. Edn.) New York: The Free Press.

16

CHILDREN

Lahela Isaacson and Kyle Isaacson

One of my most vivid memories of working as a new clinician took place in the third-floor office of a community mental health center where I worked with children. In this large room, I met with Alice for play therapy, which included drawing, fantasy, and other interventions neatly articulated in my treatment plan. Each evening as we met, however, a train rolled past the building, heavy and loud and unapologetic, and as it did Alice would bound towards the window, climbing boxes and furniture to catch a glimpse of it. She would call out, "Train!" Fastidious and anxious as I was, I took this to be a significant interruption of what would otherwise prove to be an auspicious treatment regimen, in which my efforts would yield in Alice the therapeutic growth we all wanted for her. I tried to ignore the train or to redirect from the presence of the train, but it was to no avail, because, as I later realized, these efforts constituted an urging for Alice to enter into my life world on my terms. I would not have phrased it as such at the time, but what Alice's consistent enthusiasm ultimately revealed to me was that therapy is not something clinicians do to their clients, but rather something that therapists do with their clients. In order to truly connect with Alice, I needed to enter into her world, a world in which trains are worth celebrating.

Openness, respect, curiosity, and accountability to power – the *ORCA-Stance* – helped me to eventually do that. These principles provide a foundation for therapy in which clinicians, new and experienced, may more richly and effectively engage their clients who are children. An exploration of these principles of cultural humility in the context of working with children will more fully illuminate how this is possible.

Openness

When working with children, openness is the posture that sets the context for all other principles that follow. Respect, curiosity, and accountability to power find their expression in an initial posture of openness that makes space for the therapeutic relationship in all of its possibilities. With children, openness begins with openness to this child, in this place, for this session.

Openness to this child, in this place, for this session acknowledges the uniqueness of each client as you encounter with her/him the realities of the present. No two children are alike, and while developmental trajectories may follow a roughly similar course, openness to the idiographic nature of the developmental journey recognizes not only the unique needs of clients but their humanity as well. In her novel *Gilead*, Robinson (2004) states, "Any human face is a claim on you" (p. 66). The humanity of the Other captures you in its individuality. It is possible, however, to close oneself off to this claim, to deny it by glossing over the challenge that their unique existence might make to you or your anticipations of what your mutual encounter might be. The temptation exists to fit children into the realities of the treatment plans or modalities therapists might wish to use with them, rather than fitting the therapeutic strategies into the realities of the child's world. This requires cultural humility from the therapist because it challenges the universalizing, and thus oppressive, tendencies of any theory or system, even those designed for healing and growth. Put differently, openness to this child, in this place, for this session invites the therapist into a learned ignorance about the unique lifeworld of each young client that ultimately permits intervention in service of the child as they are encountered over time. Scalzo (2010) puts it well in his book on therapy with children when he states,

> In meeting a child at a particular time, in a particular way, with a certain therapist, something new has been created which cannot be transposed and objectified into a seminal moment of the process. Each encounter is unique and special, and reveals something of the child *in that moment*. Upon meeting them again in a different time or place, this is, to all intents and purposes, not the same child.
>
> *(p. 18, emphasis added)*

Openness is the foundational posture that permits this kind of generative encounter.

In addition to the vulnerability invited by openness to this child, in this place, at this time, a second vulnerability is revealed, which is openness to one's own experiences that arise in working with children. Patterson, Williams, Grauf-Grounds, & Chamow (1998) characterize self-reflection as an important developmental task for clinicians. The posture of openness, fundamental in the ORCA-Stance, is foundational to self-reflection, and is thus integral to the initiation of that competence. Openness to one's own experiences when working with children enables therapists to identify the dynamics they tend to co-create with others and to see how one's personal experiences as a child influence their work with clients in that stage of life. It also enables them to experience the emotions that arise in their work with children and use those emotions to inform their practice in ways that might benefit the client.

Finally, openness sets the stage for one to navigate therapy with children as a dynamic and fluid process. Therapy possesses these characteristics regardless of the age of the client, but children face particular realities that are unique to the early stages of life. These include, among others, a lower position of power in family and social systems, accelerated physical and emotional development compared to later stages in life, and advancing cognitive abilities. These particularities interact in such a way that openness to fluidity while maintaining predictability in therapy with children constitutes an essential feature of the work.

Taken together, these three forms of openness form a space in which respect, curiosity, and accountability to power can find richer expression. In other words, the final three postures refine what takes place in the therapeutic space that has been opened so that children receive excellent therapeutic engagement.

Respect

A respectful therapist is one who meets the child at their developmental level and joins them in their world. In therapy with children, this often means playing symbolically. A child's symbolic world acts as a safe space in which to express and resolve emotional experiences and experiment with new ideas and ways of being (Landreth, 2002; Greenspan, Wieder, & Simons, 1998). Respect allows adults to acknowledge the reality of the unreal (fantasy/play) in the lives of children. In fact, play therapy is built around this concept (Landreth, 2002). When a therapist creates a safe play space where all emotions are heard and welcomed, respect is established. Respect, as evidenced by this radical form of acceptance, is a key aspect of child-centered play therapy as outlined by Landreth (2002).

> This attitude [of the therapist toward self and child] is characterized by an acceptance of herself and of the child and a deep and abiding belief in the capacity of the child to be responsible for himself in the process of exercising self-direction resulting in more positive behaviors ... The objective of the therapist is to create a climate in which the child feels free to be fully who she is at the moment in the shared experience of learning about self and each other. Out of a deep respect for the child the therapist gives full, complete, and undivided attention to the child.
>
> (p. 105)

One manifestation of respect referred to by Greenspan, Wieder, & Simons (1998) as "following a child's lead" is key to developing communication and therefore promoting social-emotional development (p. 124). Following a child's lead includes respecting the child by waiting and watching in order to determine what the child's interests and intentions are within the play or therapeutic interaction, and then joining the child in those interests.

Respect also makes space for the child client to develop in their own way and at their own pace. When respect is incorporated into the therapeutic process, the therapist allows the child to grow and develop without an expected timeline or direction. "Thus the relationship with the child is a continual prizing of his uniqueness and an empathic experiencing of the moment-by-moment living out of his world at a pace of unfolding determined by the inner direction of the emerging child" (Landreth, 2002, p. 78).

Curiosity

Curiosity is the enemy of assumption. It challenges a priori notions about what a client might need, want, or experience, and instead posits a collaborative therapeutic space in which an encounter might occur. One of the more profound mechanisms of curiosity operates around the notion of individual differences, which is outlined in particular writings concerned with children with special needs (Greenspan, Wieder, & Simons 1998; Greenspan & Wieder, 2006).

Individual differences constitute those unique aspects of people that differentiate them according to a substantive individuality. Greenspan, Wieder, & Simons (1998) identify four aspects of individual differences: "(1) how the child reacts to sensations, processes information, plans actions, and sequences behavior and thoughts; (2) the level of functional emotional, social, and intellectual capacities; (3) typical and necessary interaction patterns; and (4) family patterns" (p. 11). These individual differences surface in developmental trajectories and affect the meanings made from one's environment and experiences. Individual differences are illuminative for all clients, but are especially so with children, suggesting that the posture of curiosity holds particular importance in drawing out the full individuality of each young person. Of course, every therapist knows what it is like to be a child. Although often minimized, a profound solidarity exists between all adults and all children in that unlike other demographic identifiers, all therapists were once children. Drawing on this fact may induce empathy, but it is curiosity that enables each client to be the child that they are, over and against any other narrative that might subjugate them. Staying curious helps therapists to listen more closely to, and to make space for individual differences.

Finally, in addition to enriching engagement with the client, curiosity also serves to expand one's awareness of the various forms and trajectories that therapy with children might assume. Curiosity allows the therapist to think creatively about what could be included in therapy. While engaging the life-world of a client who loves trains might require openness and respect, imagining how one might enfold affection for trains into a coherent treatment plan requires curiosity.

Accountability to Power

When discussing power, and one's accountability to it when working with children, the first consideration is the low level of agency children wield in their environments. Children live in a world of adults. They are subject to the decisions and preferences of adults, and exercise less control over their own lives in everything from eating to relationships. This often impacts the number of decisions they are invited to participate in making, as well as the authority of their voiced choices. In situations when the power is distributed with such inequity, attention to the dynamics of power and how they impact therapeutic progress is paramount.

A therapist's job in responding to power dynamics in therapy with children is to respect their experiences, input, preferences, choices, and activities as necessary and influential. It might also mean respecting their developmental needs by honoring their youth in instances of parentification or neglect. In either case, a few principles related to the posture of accountability to power in the ORCA-Stance help to set a therapeutic foundation that promotes ethicality and insight. First, a clinician can exhibit accountability to power by informing child clients in developmentally appropriate ways about the nature of their power in the therapeutic situation. In a way, this constitutes providing informed consent to the child in a manner that invites engagement while providing a clear description of the process in which the child is about to participate. This honors both their status as children in their systems, while also empowering them from the start to operate as agentic individuals.

A second action therapists can take that honors the power dynamics in therapy is to invite clients who are children into decision-making as much as possible. Asking children for input on decisions related to therapy does not mean treating them like adults, but rather is a way of honoring them and their voice as vital to the health of the systems of which they are a part. As Landreth (2002) puts it, "This attitude of commitment respects children's right to make choices and recognizes the capacity of children to make choices that are both maturely satisfying to them and ultimately acceptable to society" (p. 105). Relatedly, it implicitly affirms that having power and voice are necessary to healthy human functioning across the lifespan. As a powerful person, the therapist can empower children by inquiring about their preferences, ideas, and opinions as decisions are made about their lives.

A third expression of accountability to power is to support the voice of the child as a valid member in the various systems of which the child is a part (Lund, Zimmerman, & Haddock, 2002). This is related to the first two actions, but extends them to broader domains of experience beyond decision-making and information. Taking this posture with children sometimes means aligning with them and advocating for them when other stakeholders might press for conformity to existing structures. For example, parents might bring their child to therapy when in reality their symptoms express broader dysfunction in the family and marriage. As low-agency persons in the family, the child is easiest to commit to treatment, and treating them without honoring their voiced experience colludes with the parents in perpetuating dysfunction. This comes at a great cost, including children's self-perception, ability to trust experience, and sense of impact on the world around them. In other words, accountability to power sets the foundation for the clinician to honor the children who are their clients while also avoiding the perpetuation of dysfunctional power dynamics. If the child is either too powerful or powerless, accountability to power sets a frame in which the therapist may promote a thoughtful and propitious therapeutic engagement.

Case Study

The ORCA-Stance principles have proven themselves invaluable in our clinical work with children as shown in the following case of Ainsley, a four-year-old girl diagnosed with autism spectrum disorder. When treatment began, Ainsley was withdrawn in relationships and experiencing tantrums multiple times a day that included banging her head on hard surfaces and biting herself and others. Ainsley's parents were divorced, and she and her older sibling lived with each parent for equal amounts of time. Treatment consisted of a combination of in-home dyadic parent-child and family sessions using a DIR®/Floortime® (a registered parenting program) framework. The clinician adopted a parent coaching model in which the parents were supported in tailoring their way of interacting to fit Ainsley's needs, thus addressing the power differential and empowering Ainsley by following her lead during sessions.

An attitude of openness to this child in this moment and curiosity about her specific individual differences led to a consultation with an occupational therapist. During this consultation Ainsley's individual differences were assessed and it was noted that she had strengths in visual processing and challenges in auditory processing. She was sensory-seeking in her proprioceptive system (input to joints and muscles) and sensitive to auditory and tactile input. The clinician and parents held a curious stance and spent much time guessing and imagining what it might feel like to have Ainsley's specific individual differences. They imagined that the world felt too loud and sounds were jumbled and hard to separate from one another. Clothes were agitating and gestures of physical affection were often uncomfortable. In response to Ainsley's individual differences and relational environment, the clinician limited their use of verbal language and instead increased their gestural communication. Out of respect, the therapist believed that Ainsley (and her family) were doing the best they could with what they had, which especially helped to illuminate Ainsley's functional intent and the sensory experiences behind her "disruptive and harming" behaviors. When the environment became loud and Ainsley began to withdraw and bang her head, the therapist invited her parents to join her on the floor, cover their own ears and say, "It's so loud Ainsley."

Ainsley had a well-developed vocabulary but was not necessarily using language meaningfully. She often scripted from books or movies during moments of heightened emotion. An attitude of openness helped the therapist to stay engaged with Ainsley in her scripting and join her in playing out her favorite scripted scenes. Curiosity made space for the therapist to listen closely to the emotional tone of the script and use it as a clue for what Ainsley might be feeling. Ainsley's parents were coached to narrate her feelings as they played out the script with her. This intervention led to many moments of connection between parent and child. Out of respect for Ainsley, the therapist held several foundational beliefs during intervention. The therapist assumed Ainsley's competence and watched closely for intentionality, even when it was hard to recognize. By tailoring treatment to Ainsley's unique sensory profile, individual differences, and relationships with family, the clinician and the family were able to promote Ainsley's development and increase relational connectedness over several years of treatment.

Ideas for Best Practice

In regards to taking seriously the foundational aspects of therapy, Wampold and Budge (2012) state, "Simply said, the real relationship is therapeutic because it is a real relationship with an important and significant other who is invested in the patient's well being" (p. 611). As a comprehensive set of postural principles for therapists working with children, the ORCA-Stance sets a rich and expansive frame for the development of a real relationship with child clients. A few key ideas help to promote this kind of best practice when using the ORCA-Stance to enrich one's work with children.

- Openness and respect are the foundation for perspective-taking, which is key to not making assumptions with clients who are children.
- Children's emotions, experiences, and symbolic worlds are revealed and validated through the four postures of the ORCA-Stance.
- Identifying and addressing power dynamics in the system is integral to establishing healing spaces for children, which is necessary for positive therapeutic outcomes.

References

Greenspan, S.I., & Wieder, S. (2006). *Engaging Autism: Using the Floortime Approach to Help Children Relate, Communicate, and Think*. Boston, MA: Da Capo Lifelong Books. Retrieved from https://books.google.com/books?hl=en&lr=&id=1yUqcJzopjAC&oi= fnd&pg=PR9&dq=Engaging+autism:+Using+the+Floortime+approach+to+help+%09c hildren+relate,+communicate,+and+think&ots=1_g6p53dWd&sig=CRADPRJzVn24c huitvErAH8GRNM#v=onepage&q=Engaging%20autism%3A%20Using%20the%20Flo

ortime%20approach%20to%20help%20%09children%20relate%2C%20communicate%2C%20and%20think&f=false.

Greenspan, S.I., Wieder, S., & Simons, R. (1998). *The Child with Special Needs: Encouraging Intellectual and Emotional Growth*. Reading, MA: Addison-Wesley/Addison Wesley Longman. Retrieved from https://psycnet.apa.org/record/1997-36853-000.

Landreth, G.L. (2002). *Play Therapy: The Art of Relationship*. (2nd edn.) New York: Brunner-Routledge. Retrieved from https://books.google.com/books?id=W9zy5Ajcrq4C&printsec=frontcover&dq=Play+therapy:+The+art+of+relationship&hl=en&sa=X&ved=0ahUKEwiLsPHcvaXhAhXFqp4KHWXhC4MQ6AEIKjAA#v=onepage&q=Play%20therapy%3A%20The%20art%20of%20relationship&f=false.

Lund, L.K., Zimmerman, T.S., & Haddock, S.A. (2002). The theory, structure, and techniques for the inclusion of children in family therapy: A literature review. *Journal of Marital and Family Therapy*, 28(4), 445–454. doi:10.1111/j.1752-0606.2002.tb00369.x.

Patterson, J., Williams, L., Grauf-Grounds, C., & Chamow, L. (1998). *Essential Skills in Family Therapy: From the First Interview to Termination*. New York: Guilford Press.

Robinson, M. (2004). *Gilead: A Novel*. New York: Picador. Retrieved from https://books.google.com/books?id=ERVAPnnF3gcC&printsec=frontcover&dq=Gilead&hl=en&sa=X&ved=0ahUKEwi-4oCHvqXhAhXDuZ4KHb0ZA9YQ6AEIKjAA#v=onepage&q=Gilead&f=false.

Scalzo, C. (2010). *Therapy with Children: An Existential Perspective*. London: Karnac Books. Retrieved from https://books.google.com/books?id=giZTDwAAQBAJ&printsec=frontcover&dq=Therapy+with+children:+An+existential+perspective&hl=en&sa=X&ved=0ahUKEwjakM6qvqXhAhXRop4KHQyxBGUQ6AEIKjAA#v=onepage&q=Therapy%20with%20children%3A%20An20existential%20perspective&f=false.

Wampold, B.E., & Budge, S.L. (2012). The 2011 Leona Tyler award address: The relationship – and its relationship to the common and specific factors of therapy. *The Counseling Psychologist*, 40, 601–623. doi:10.1177/0011000011432709.

17

TWEENS

Clinical Praxis for Pre-Adolescents

Shannon West

> So often we want to help the people we love fix their problems. We want to show them how to solve a dilemma, resolve a conflict, or get rid of painful emotions. But in order to give them what they need most of all, which is to make them feel felt and connected with us, we need to not do these well-intended things first and instead simply be present.
>
> *(Siegel, 2014, p. 218)*

In a culture growing and changing as quickly as its young people, it's getting harder to differentiate between age-defining adolescents and the tween boys and girls fast approaching on their heels. In the presence of rapid developmental and cultural change for pre-adolescents, the value of a timeless and transcendent therapeutic framework is a significant asset to both professional scholarship and applied practice. Embodiment of the *ORCA-Stance* bestows a powerful skillset of transforming clinical conversation and relationships, enriching the therapeutic process, and enhancing its success (Grauf-Grounds, Edwards, MacDonald, Quek, & Sellers, 2009).

According to the National Institute of Health, puberty onset is arriving earlier than in previous years and no longer necessarily coincides with adolescent brain development (Greenspan & Deardorff, 2014). Especially true for girls, puberty and sexual maturation often arrive before children hit double digits in age (Siegel, 2014). As a result, pre-adolescent years are marked with a spectrum of experiences ranging from the simplicity of childhood play to the complexity of pubescent transformation. In addition, budding brain development introduces growth and maturation, impacting a youth's thinking and reasoning and ways of relating to others. Early years are marked with novelty-seeking, increased emotional intensity, and creative exploration (Siegel, 2014). In construction, pre-teens are learning to control emotions and impulses, organize tasks, set goals and priorities, strategize and problem-solve, empathize with others, and demonstrate insight and sound judgment (Greenspan & Deardorff, 2014).

These years of rapid development create a powerful context for pre-adolescent confusion, stress, and challenged emotional coping. As a result, self-esteem often declines for both genders, as does confidence and skill in social and emotional realms. Youth approaching these years are likely to experience increased emotional intensity and awakened experimentation, as life now becomes a "social game" in which he/she is a new and full participant (Gurian, 2002). Likewise, tweens and their parents also enter a new "game-changing" season as they redefine parent/child relationships and renegotiate the rules and boundaries of their adjusting familial system (Preto, 1999).

Because these formative years are often the catalyst for tweens and their families first seeking therapy, a therapist's ability to kindly greet this developmental period and offer a relational space of companionship in this "game" is a poignant invitation. In this context, clinicians can be encouraged by pre-adolescent desire to be meaningfully involved in family therapy (Stith, Rosen, McCollum, Coleman, & Herman, 1996) and by a positive shift in adolescent expectancies and experiences of therapy over the past 30 years (Stewart, Steele, & Roberts, 2014). As discerned in such findings, it is of particular importance that therapists create a receptive and inviting experience for a tween entering therapy, thus enhancing comfort, minimizing attrition, and increasing clinical effectiveness. Embodying cultural humility, the principles of the ORCA-Stance accomplish and cultivate this praxis and legacy.

A clinician's cultural humility and openness to the tween experience is paramount to pre-adolescents welcoming the therapeutic relationship, especially for youth beginning therapy for the first time. Entering new territory together, a clinician has the crucial role of modeling well the unique capacity and boundaries of the therapeutic relationship. With readiness to receive and respond to one another, it is expected that a young person will seek to build a rapport with her/his therapist by asking the therapist to be open about their life, sharing information about their world alongside the practice of asking questions. *What information are you comfortable sharing in this way? What domains do you feel open or closed to discussing together?* The especially inquisitive nature of a pre-adolescent provides an ideal context to exemplify the openness of the ORCA-Stance by acknowledging and practicing the ways in which interpersonal impact is present within the clinical relationship and in social contexts beyond.

Among the avenues to impart openness is the exploration of internalized messages for youth, particularly pertaining to developing notions of masculinity and/or femininity and sexuality. Both genders are often given mixed messages about these vital domains.

> Many boys report that, by the onset of puberty, they have been taught little or nothing about masculinity, dating, sex, and sexuality. Even more

distressing, they feel they have no one who can understand what's happening to them and with whom they can discuss their feelings about the changes in their bodies.

(Pollack, 1998, p. 153)

This expression is not only exclusive to boys; many girls echo these sentiments of challenge and burden. The invitation of openness to explore these domains have the potential for both girls and boys to feel significantly more prepared to receive, understand, and navigate the intensely delicate complexity of these tween years.

For all pre-adolescent youth, and in all domains, this invitation is the successful hallmark of therapy. However, it's important to acknowledge that by the time they reach adolescence, boys have largely learned to deny emotional need and/or disguise or avoid their feelings, and are at greater risk of depression and suicide (Kindlon & Thompson, 1999). As a result, a clinician's thoughtful ability to foster a culture of openness with young men offers a uniquely safe environment where boys can bring themselves into conversation with another about their emotional world – free from messages encouraging anything but a genuine, unapologetic sense of self.

Therapeutic respect marks the second attribute of the ORCA-Stance, perceiving and honoring the value of each youthful life. Often these pre-adolescent years are marked by dismissive messages about a young person's circumstances and emotional experiences. "He's just becoming a teenager," or "she's acting this way because it's a teenage thing," often diminish a tween's ability to feel respected in the uniqueness of their life. It is from a culturally humble stance of honoring the fullness of the tween world carried upon their shoulders that clinicians can offer the greatest context of therapeutic support, conveying messages of worth and dignity belonging justly to each young life.

Pre-adolescent youth are often riddled with both internal and external questions about this young life: their identity, their place in the community, and their role in society. In the presence of peer and familial relationships, tweens search for their own space in which to belong and contribute. When clinicians engage in the full belief of their young client's unique and valuable identity in the world, these contributions to his/her development are compelling as they unfold in the unique microcosm of therapy. When a youthful client receives the respect he/she is inherently due, there is the infinite possibility that he/she will transfer such respect and dignity to additional contexts and relationships, leaving a significant legacy throughout the remainder of his/her esteemed life.

Today's youthful generation is particularly worthy of respectful consideration. Given current contexts of cultural over-stimulation and hyper-stress, alongside increased technology exposure and declining familial engagement, we're witnessing one of the most stressed generations we've yet encountered (Gurian, 2002). While overwhelmed, they're also a generation navigating with remarkable skill and endurance – deserving our most genuine respect. A therapeutic posture of resisting simplistic or "thin" conclusions (White, 2007) about pre-adolescent travelers allows us to engage with greater respect without generalizing or marginalizing the journey of the tween in our care. *How are you moved toward deeper reflection and/or newfound respect for today's generation of youth?*

The rise of internet use and the insidiousness of cyber-bullying have become infectious for many pre-adolescents. While research findings remain varied, consensus indicates that approximately one in four youth have been victims of cyber-bullying, while one in six youth have been responsible for such bullying (Patchin & Hinduja, 2012). Our culture is still assessing and waging war on these unprecedented and unparalleled messages presented online. It's vital, therefore, that therapists not only offer unwavering cultural humility and clinical respect but also thoughtfully engage in combating potential messages of disrespect that the client is resisting in both their off-line and online tween world.

Engaging this world well invites us to explore the array of messages of tween culture and the social constructs surrounding them. The ability to practice thoughtful curiosity in this engagement is an offer to join clients in their youthful theater of wondering aloud and reflecting within about the details of their lives and the messages they have encountered. Posturing curiosity without imposing a need to fix or change is largely unprecedented in the lives of young people intertwined in systems often seeking concrete remedies and resolutions for the challenges of youth. Bestowing the clinical principles of the ORCA-Stance grants an exceptional alternative. The culturally humble practice of authentic curiosity casts aside pre-conceived notions of a pre-adolescent's journey, resisting messages of potential stereotypes in the presence of a tween's story.

After several sessions, 12-year-old Jamie spoke about her interest in a particular social media site that has a reputation for being utilized among teen girls who often post essays and images about depression, self-harm, and suicide – experiences Jamie had also encountered. Knowing this information, it was tempting to rush to assumption and judgment about Jamie's experience with this site. Alternatively, questions of curiosity stirred new understanding: "*I notice you 'light up' when you talk about spending time online. Can you tell me more about what you're finding there? What posts are you enjoying most? Are there other people in your life who share in these conversations?*"

Jamie's internet use revealed newfound passion for discovering blogs and commentaries about social justice, global events, and notions of feminism. A social media site largely marked by reputation of concern was in fact a life-giving portal for pre-adolescent exploration and identity development. Curiosity uncovered the isolation Jamie felt in her life since this particular website was the only place where these spaces of interest were engaged. In the absence of bringing her passions and interest into her larger world, depression had flourished. Pausing with curiosity birthed understanding and launched new clinical direction.

When we cease curiosity, we stifle clinical possibilities and inspired conversation. We also risk the dangers of adopting an expertise or knowledge that is often incorrect. This risk is especially poignant during the pre-adolescent years when tweens are teetering between the two worlds of childhood and the launch of adolescence. Youth on the heels of adolescence are moving from intense childlike interest in the world around them toward the tween intensity of feelings within them. They are swimming among the fondness for childhood and the newness of social dynamics, desiring connection, sexual attraction, identity, decision-making, discernment about substance use, and how to navigate the influence of peers. They are also beginning to wrestle with abstract concepts of mortality, the meaning of their own life, aspects of spirituality, and spaces of personal identity (Siegel, 2014). As tweens transition from the concrete thoughts of childhood to these greater abstract domains of youth, therapeutic conversation will be richer for the way in which curiosity seeks to explore the road between these two realms.

Among the dual worlds youth straddle are those pleading for curiosity in spaces of gender identity and sexual expression. It is of immense value to deconstruct both overt and covert internalized narratives about gender and sexuality in the life of a tween. In the particular presence of increasing technology use, young people are more exposed to both accidental and intentional sexualized images than ever before in our history. The software of such content and the hardware it's being viewed on are impacting both brain and social development in ways not yet fully known (Greenspan & Deardorff, 2014). In the absence of assumption and with the readiness to be surprised, there's tremendous value in exploring the intricate aspects of how this new technological frontier has certainly impacted and touched a young person's life.

Foundational to this practice of curiosity within the ORCA-Stance is the freedom from "fixing" the details of a person's life (Grauf-Grounds et al., 2009). While we may join in a tween's desire to create a more preferred experience in their life, emulating curiosity without expectation of resolution allows for a clinical context where a young person is offered a space to exist just as they are in the world. During days of personal ambivalence and self-doubt encountering an environment where tweens can wonder aloud and process the inner workings of their life without pressure to do otherwise is a remarkable and rare endowment during these age-defining years.

In the presence of therapeutic privilege in the life of a pre-adolescent comes therapeutic power in equal esteem. Since the tween years are often the first experience a young person has with therapy, it's especially crucial that clinicians honor their accountability to the therapeutic impact they have in the life of a young client. When a young person enters therapy, he/she is not only the recipient of a therapeutic relationship; he/she also enters a relationship with an adult, perceived to be one of trust as well as social power, influence, and esteem. *What demonstrations of both acknowledged and unrecognized social power will you bring into the life of a youth?*

A clinician's acknowledgment of such power and professional authority is paramount in working with pre-adolescents. It is especially crucial to maintain legal and ethical responsibilities and to discuss them with tween clients. This involves clarifying the therapeutic role, responsibilities, and boundaries of a therapeutic relationship, not always understood by a young person. *How might you engage in developmentally congruent conversations about these dynamics of professional power? In your role, are there aspects of accountability easier or more difficult to reconcile and own?*

In specific regard to mental health diagnosis in a young person's life, given that shifts in emotion and identity become more stable for an adolescent across time, it is particularly important that clinicians be cautious in pathologizing a youthful life. While being accountable to the considerations of the health care system in which clinicians practice, therapists must also recognize that caring for a tween demands seeing their development and coping as an unfolding process. Accountability to power requires providers to be mindful that diagnostic definition may be inaccurate in the presence of current developmental processes and/or unfolding contextual information.

One of the most challenging domains of accountability in working with tweens is maintaining clinician differentiation within a pre-adolescent's familial or social system. Given a young person's growing cognitive and emotional development, his/her perspective may require expansion to include a greater understanding of perception. Encouraging parental participation and collaborating with others in a pre-adolescent's life is not only beneficial to the therapeutic process but is often necessary in practicing accountability to the profession. A skillful clinician is wise to assist a young person in their endeavor to differentiate, remaining mindful of the ways a young person may represent their parents (or others in authority) as figures worthy to rebel against. The goal for families during this season is to balance a young person's rising decisions alongside parental regulation and concern (Siegel, 2014). The task for every accountable therapist is to represent both perspectives well while preserving family ties.

When attending to therapeutic accountability during patients' tween years, each clinician must be aware of the age of therapeutic consent in respective states as it relates to privilege of confidentiality and the ability to establish treatment goals in addition to and/or apart from parental desires for therapy or family participation. In specific respect to confidentiality, therapists working with tweens may encounter both the legal and ethical mandate of reporting sexual activity and/or child pornography. This is especially true amid working with a generation of youth engaged in technology use and maybe on the precipice of virtual or in-flesh sexual activity.

While the principles and practices of the ORCA-Stance are clinical assets to all therapeutic encounters, they can be especially meaningful when working with youth and families of unique, marginalized, and/or vulnerable circumstances. Incorporating the values of the ORCA-Stance is particularly helpful when working with pre-adolescents bringing experiences of foster care or adoption, racial, transracial or bi-cultural identity and family contexts, cultural adjustment dynamics, immigrant journeys, secondary language experiences, and/or those representing either economic extremes of poverty or affluence. Those engaging in conversations about gender and/or sexual identity will also appreciate the cultural humility of the ORCA-Stance in therapeutic relationships.

Case Study

Eleven-year-old Collynn began therapy after becoming secretive with her parents, lying where honesty had once thrived. In session, Collynn shared that she recently had her first kiss with a classmate. This was a new experience in Collynn's life and she wasn't sure how her parents would respond. Over time, one secret led to another until a dishonest pattern ensued. Collynn had a convinced perspective of her parents not being supportive – yet struggled to articulate how these conclusions came to be strong.

Personified openness to hearing more about Collynn's experience conveyed both clinical comfort and permission in discussing Collynn's relationship with a peer and newfound expressions of attraction and affection. *"Collynn, thank you for sharing with me. I know telling someone about a first kiss can be very special. What was it like to kiss someone for the first time? What did it feel like to you? Are there friends you've been able to share this experience with? What does it feel like for us to talk about it?"*

Instead of dismissing the significance of Collynn's first kiss and budding relationship, therapeutic respect validated the complex and tender path Collynn has been traveling. *"Collynn, sometimes decisions we make about relationships and kissing or sex can be challenging to make. How did you decide you wanted to have your first kiss? What helped you make this decision? I'm wondering – was this one of the first big decisions you didn't talk about with your parents? What has that been like for you?"*

Engaging with genuine curiosity to understand more fully Collynn's experience affirmed therapeutic interest in knowing more about the journey Collynn has been navigating with both peer and parental relationships. *"Have you imagined sharing this news with your parents? What do you think they might say? How do you hope they might react if they knew more? What has it been like for you to keep this moment to yourself? What has it been like carrying this secret in your life, and in your family?"*

Rather than simply align with Collynn's initial story of her parents being harsh and unapproachable, accountability to therapeutic power invited family conversation. Together, Collynn joined with her parents in learning about their own experience of liking people in school and having their first kisses. In the presence of parental disclosure, Collynn was then able to share her own story and its role in her family's encounter with secrecy. Fostering collaboration rather than remaining isolated in a pre-adolescent perspective brought new understandings for both Collynn and her parents.

Ideas for Best Practice

We can be assured that clinical work reflecting the postures and practices of the ORCA-Stance offers a greater experience in the world than solely taking place within the confines of therapy. As an aspiring young adult, partner and/or parent, a tween touched by the ORCA-Stance will be enriched by a therapeutic foundation and clinical legacy far transcending these fleeting and formative years. In the spirit of such significance, the following suggestions are intended to highlight this meaningful work:

- Consider the unique developmental context of the tween era and the complex intersections present in clinical encounters. Seek to both engage and model experiences embodying respect for these distinctive years.
- Cultivate tween conversations with cultural humility and genuine readiness to learn. Set aside pre-supposition and allow pre-adolescent perspectives to guide clinical work together and inspire remarkable, curious questions.
- Create a trusted and welcoming relational space to which the young patient is likely to return. If a youth's formative experience in therapy is regarded as safe and transformative, he/she is likely to fondly pursue therapeutic conversations in the future and across a lifetime.

References

Grauf-Grounds, C., Edwards, S., MacDonald, D., Quek, K.M., & Schermer Sellers, T. (2009). Developing graduate curricula faithful to professional training and a Christian worldview. *Christian Higher Education*, 8, 1–17. Retrieved from www.tandfonline.com/doi/pdf/10.1080/15363750802134931?casa_token=ojkYdVRY9cAAAAAA:59p_v81Fg Idqai7-jFDuEnVm-ukEwerb6sY_W5gLSiWe_yr2VAY3NSrpK_fktyoRKud1R1Lvg.

Greenspan, L., & Deardorff, J. (2014). *The New Puberty: How to Navigate Early Development in Today's Girls*. New York: Rodale. Retrieved from https://books.google.com/books?i d=WfhZBAAAQBAJ&printsec=frontcover&dq=The+new+puberty:+How+to+naviga te+early+development+in+%09today%E2%80%99s+girls.&hl=en&sa=X&ved=0ahUKE wiu1djTxqXhAhXqhVQKHWOCA6IQ6AEIKjAA#v=onepage&q=The%20new%20p uberty%3A%20How%20to%20navigate%20early%20development%20in%20%09today% E2%80%99s%20girls.&f=false.

Gurian, M. (2002). *The Wonder of Girls: Understanding the Hidden Nature of Our Daughters*. New York: Atria Books. https://books.google.com/books?id=IvAB2jXkkXgC&printse c=frontcover&dq=The+wonder+of+girls:+Understanding+the+hidden+nature+of+our +daughters&hl=en&sa=X&ved=0ahUKEwjKxY3exqXhAhUD7FQKHdL2CDoQ6AE IKjAA#v=onepage&q=The%20wonder%20of%20girls%3A%20Understanding%20the% 20hidden%20nature%20of%20our%20daughters&f=false.

Kindlon, D., & Thompson, M. (1999). *Raising Cain: Protecting the Emotional Life of Boys*. New York: Ballantine Books. Retrieved from https://books.google.com/books?id= 2D0OQAGV96kC&printsec=frontcover&dq=Raising+Cain:+Protecting+the+emotion al+life+of+boys&hl=en&sa=X&ved=0ahUKEwj40ILtxqXhAhUCG3wKHf6FAsMQ6

AEIKjAA#v=onepage&q=Raising%20Cain%3A%20Protecting%20the%20emotional%2
0life%20of%20boys&f=false.

Patchin, J.W., & Hinduja, S. (2012). *Cyberbullying Prevention and Response: Expert Perspectives.* New York: Routledge. Retrieved from https://books.google.com/books?id=br2sA gAAQBAJ&printsec=frontcover&dq=Cyberbullying+prevention+and+response:+Expe rt+perspectives&hl=en&sa=X&ved=0ahUKEwjDzL72xqXhAhUPGnwKHXvRAyoQ6 AEIKjAA#v=onepage&q=Cyberbullying%20prevention%20and%20response%3A%20E xpert%20perspectives&f=false.

Pollack, W. (1998). *Real Boys: Rescuing Our Sons from the Myth of Boyhood.* New York: Henry Holt and Company.

Preto, N. (1999). Transformation of the family system during adolescence. In B. Carter & M. McGoldrick (Eds.), *The Expanded Family Life Cycle* (3rd edn.) Boston, MA: Allyn & Bacon. Retrieved from https://play.google.com/store/books/details?id=ba_zCAAAQ BAJ&rdid=book-ba_zCAAAQBAJ&rdot=1&source=gbs_atb.

Siegel, D. (2014). *Brainstorm: The Power and Purpose of the Teenage Brain.* New York: Penguin Group. Retrieved from https://books.google.com/books?id=SOi4yca7FSsC& printsec=frontcover&dq=Brainstorm:+The+power+and+purpose+of+the+teenage+br ain&hl=en&sa=X&ved=0ahUKEwi0ypfAx6XhAhWDnp4KHfxnB2YQ6AEIKjAA#v= onepage&q=Brainstorm%3A%20The%20power%20and%20purpose%20of%20the%20te enage%20brain &f=false.

Stewart, P., Steele, M., & Roberts, M. (2014). What happens in therapy? Adolescents' expectations and perceptions of psychotherapy. *Journal of Child and Family Studies*, 23, 1–9. Retrieved from https://link.springer.com/article/10.1007/s10826- 012-9680-3.

Stith, S., Rosen, K., McCollum, E., Coleman, J., & Herman, S. (1996). The voices of children: Preadolescent children's experiences in family therapy. *Journal of Marital and Family Therapy*, 22, 69–86. Retrieved from https://search.proquest.com/docview/2209 41805?pq-origsite=gscholar.

White, M. (2007). *Maps of Narrative Practice.* New York: W.W. Norton & Company. Retrieved from https://books.google.com/books?id=qDdoLhCr7PgC&printsec=frontc over&dq=Maps+of+narrative+practice.&hl=en&sa=X&ved=0ahUKEwiU26zix6XhAh XGrJ4KHZI1ArIQ6AEIKjAA#v=onepage&q=Maps%20of%20narrative%20practice.&f =false.

18

ADOLESCENTS AND THEIR FAMILIES

Scott Edwards

> John, a high school senior close to graduation, paused as he reflected on his relationship with his parents. When he spoke, he firmly and definitively stated, "Once I go to college, I will never go back home to visit them."

When listening to a statement like this from an adolescent, most adults may have thoughts or respond with attempts to instruct, teach, correct, fix, or challenge. Often, when listening and sitting with adolescents, we can easily reflect on our own experiences as a resource yet lose perspective due to any lingering reactivity or unresolved struggles from those experiences. The period of adolescence is continually being shaped by an ever-changing context and culture.

Adolescent Culture

Statements made by adolescents can be intense, reactive, and extreme without much thought or understanding of their long-term impact. Difference is a hallmark during this life cycle stage. Working with families where one or more individuals is an adolescent has its own particular cultural context. There are ample resources for exploring the setting of the adolescent – whether conceptualizing adolescent coping (Frydenberg, 2008), working with difficult adolescents and their families (Selekman, 2005), and/or facilitating effective session activities and handouts (Sori, Hecker, & Bachenberg, 2016). Understanding the context of the adolescent within their family will also involve attending to the family processes of individuation, differentiation, and launching from the immediate and extended families.

Developing a posture of cultural humility with the adolescent, other family members, and the family system is an important and foundational process when working with adolescents and their families. Useful questions that may assist slowing down and exploring the adolescent's cultural setting may include:

- What surfaces for adults (parents and therapists) when reflecting on their own experiences with their personal adolescent culture?
- What comes up when adults (parents and therapists) identify experiences and aspects of the current adolescent culture?
- What comes up when adolescents reflect on their own experiences with their current adolescent culture?
- What are typical differences that arise between adolescents and adults within the family? Within the culture? Within the therapy context (adolescent, parent, therapist)?

Exploring these questions with adolescents and families may help to develop cultural humility in ways that foster understanding and connection with each other. Embodying the *ORCA-Stance* is a powerful posture of practicing this cultural humbleness with adolescents.

The ORCA-Stance

A therapist embodying an ORCA-Stance has a different way of reflecting and being in the moment with clients, attempting to embody openness, respectfulness, curiosity, and accountability to power. Through the culturally humble posture of the ORCA-Stance, therapists are able to empathize, understand, connect, and come alongside others during this developmental time of exploration, affective intensity, and identity formation impacting the family system.

Openness

Openness may be useful in coming alongside adolescents as one receives and responds to what is shared without judgement, while also being open to being impacted by them and them by you. Adolescents in the midst of their *current* adolescent culture will – by the very nature of adolescence – definitely be different from the therapist and their experiences. Creating a therapeutic context filled with grace, which invites personal stories that have not previously been shared, facilitates an open witnessing of their adolescent experiences and their sense of self as it is developing. Exploring, brainstorming, and being open to differences invites genuineness and a context of healing.

Respect

Respect is an aspect of the ORCA-Stance in which one honors and responds to others as unique, worthy, and valuable individuals. Honoring each person's voice, perspectives, and experiences – especially in the midst of the emotional intensity, identity formation, and differences that are distinctive within adolescence – respects the adolescent as a unique and worthy individual. Respect is an interpersonal process which exists, occurs, and is experienced within and between others – it is not something to be earned, given, or received. When you are truly respectful about the choices and thoughts of an individual and the impact they may have in their relationship contexts, then you open windows to the space between others and the meaning within those and extended family relationships.

Curiosity

Curiosity may be useful in wondering out loud and inside about another's sense of self and their relationship contexts without the need to instruct, direct, and/or correct. When we are curious and open to the determinations and choices of adolescents without assuming the need to fix anything, we are more likely to get a sense of their experiences, self, and relationships.

Although each of the interrelated aspects of the ORCA-Stance are relevant and meaningful in sitting with adolescents and their families, I find the practice of curiosity to be an aspect that is easily overlooked; yet when embodied curiosity infuses the session with humility and supports the interplay between the other aspects of the ORCA-Stance.

Accountability to Power

With the posture of the ORCA-Stance, accountability to power (specifically social power) necessitates the therapist to be responsible for their impact on the relationship, both as a person and as a professional. Attending to social constructs, assumptions, and implications of power, gender, ethnicity, socioeconomic status, and age impact the therapeutic relationship with the adolescent. The therapist, as an adult, has a social role of authority over the adolescent with various spoken and unspoken expectations for behavior, consequences, and power struggles with others. The process of intentionally attending and being accountable to power within the relationship facilitates the interpersonal and humble process of power within and through the relationship rather than power over another.

Case Study

When hearing statements similar to John's from adolescents, I am initially filled with a sense of curiosity. Reflecting in the moment on how to respond to John, rather than direct my focus to identifying an applicable resource or tool for engaging, I slowed down and opened myself to embodying curiosity. With curiosity at the forefront of my mind and heart, I wondered what it might be like if John's statement were to come to fruition. What might be the impact on him?

His family system? His family members? What might some of the meanings and consequences of this type of decision have for John? His family? In the short term? In the long term? Has John shared this with family members? What if John's statement has more meaning within his family system than just his relationships with his parents and sibling? Has the family previously experienced the cut-off of relationships? Presently? Curious of his parents' experiences of launching processes within their families of origin, I respectfully reflected back to John, "*Once you go to college, you may decide to change your mind or not change your mind, or even change your mind after you change your mind.*"

My response was grounded in the ORCA-Stance, embodying humility, as I took a one-down position with John, acknowledging that he would be making his own choices (respect) while simultaneously wondering out loud (curious) about all the choices available to him, even those not yet considered (openness). The embodiment of the ORCA-Stance alongside John provided him with an opportunity to voice his desire (accountability to power) to share his stance with his parents to start off the next session. John – not me in my role as therapist – began the next session with his parents, "*Once I go to college, I will never go back home to visit you.*"

With heightened intensity in the room, John added, "*When I leave for school, I am in control of our emotional relationship for the next four years.*" Interestingly, his father responded, "*No, you are in control of our emotional relationship from here on out, for the rest of your life.*" My intentional practice of curiosity at the forefront of an ORCA-Stance, rather than attempts to mediate, control, shape, suggest, or fix aspects of their relationships, allowed this family to access their own resources, experiences, and wisdom as they grew in connection.

I humbly wondered out loud with the family, "How did it come to be that dad did not have a power struggle with John about who was in control? About who was in control of John's life? How might mom/dad experience you, John, when you choose not to return? Any thoughts of other losses you all have experienced?" My curiosities continued, "I wonder what this may also be about – seems like it is something more than just the space between you and your dad?"

The intentional practice of the ORCA-Stance led by curiosity with each individual, their relationships, and their larger family system provided an opportunity and invited the father to enter into a relationship with his adolescent son and family differently. The father voiced significant losses that he himself had experienced – the suicides of his own father and sister within the space of a year when at the same age as John is now when he went off to college. The way in which I came alongside this family system in therapy opened up space for the father also to consider the impact of his choice to isolate and cut himself off from his family for several days when upset. Themes of grief, cut-off, and loss were identified on numerous levels of the family system. The practice of cultural humility, led by curiosity at the forefront of the ORCA-Stance, opened up space for this adolescent and his family system to explore deep and meaning-filled connections amid their larger family system within the challenges of their present transition. They were able to access their own experiences, resources, relationships, and beings to begin growing and changing how they relate with each other.

Ideas for Best Practice

I have found several practices which naturally embody the ORCA-Stance in ways that may be useful in working alongside adolescents and their families. Although the content of the work with adolescents and their families is always contextual, below are practices I find myself commonly using with adolescents which embody the ORCA-Stance:

- *Problem wonderings*: During initial sessions I join with adolescent family systems wondering (curiosity) about the presenting problem with the adolescent, "What did you bring your parent(s) in to work on?" This question challenges the definition and frame of the presenting problem (accountability), honors the adolescent's voice and perspective (respect), and infuses the therapeutic relationship with playfulness (curiosity, openness). All too often adolescents and their families develop thin and constrained conclusions about their struggles. Humbly practicing problem wonderings within the family may open a space for families to become curious themselves and reflect on their situation differently. Expanding the context for problem wonderings, I commonly wonder out loud about where problems may be located, "What if what is occurring, although impacting you and your parents, has little to do with you? Has little to do with your parents? Has little to do with your relationship? Exists outside of everyone and only in spaces between you?"
- *Usefulness*: My clients, supervisees, and students share a common experience of my wondering of how I may be *useful with* them as opposed to being *helpful to* them. I wonder out loud (curiosity, openness), throughout and at the end of each session, about the usefulness of conversations, perspectives, and change that I attempt to facilitate rather than assuming that my role is to be helpful to them (accountability, respect). Embodying a stance of being useful with practices cultural humility, as one can come alongside in a one-down position (as opposed to being helpful to, which punctuates a top-down stance that tends to limit possibilities).
- *Family growth*: The period of adolescence is a time of the family life stage in which the adolescent and caretaker(s) are shifting stances of independence/dependence while remaining connected. Adolescents and families may be unaware that their patterns in reaction to each other actually limit the family's potential for growth. When I obtain a genogram during the initial sessions in working with families, I wonder, "Which aspects of your family of origin would you like to pass down to your kid(s)? Which aspects of your

family or origin do you not want to pass down, and which would you like to pass down instead? Which of the aspects that you are passing down do you want to maintain?" (curiosity, openness, respect). Embodying family growth curiosities at the time of this life span developmental stage plants seeds of perspective. I commonly pose questions such as "With the [x] years left in your home, are there values or qualities you would like your child to learn/pass down – whether they are able to express and follow through with them or not?" "What does it mean to become an adult in your family? A man in your family? A woman in your family?" "What cultural influences are impacting your relationship and expectations?" "What values and skills do you want your child to know in the next few years before they launch?" This practice of cultural humility explores the process and meaning of parenting to prepare for the future versus parenting to protect in the moment (Parry & Doan, 1994), and it plants seeds for adolescents and their families in exploring possibilities for their future.

- *Expanding responses*: When brainstorming potential solutions with adolescents, one of the first suggestions made by the adolescent is usually the same response that resulted in the problem. For example, exploring potential choices when one experiences anger, the adolescent may respond by offering suggestions such as to yell, fight, or hit someone. An initial response from an adult or therapist may be to correct the idea or judge the response and classify it as more of the same, or even assume that the client is resistant. However, when embodying cultural humility with an adolescent, I find myself usually stating, "Yeah, that's one solution. That is one way to approach it" (openness, respect) and then wonder (curiosity), "I'm curious what might be some other ways to approach it." I will often ask, "What other choices may be useful for you in the short and/or long term?" Embodying cultural humility may also result in other expanding responses such as "I have some thoughts, if you are interested, let me know" (accountability). This invites the adolescent into connection in the midst of differences with many possibilities for consideration.

- *Therapist not-knowing*: I am not all-knowing. It is not uncommon for me to wonder out loud (curiosity) about my not-knowing in a humble and humorous way. Clients hear, "I like to think I am a Jedi knight from *Star Wars*, know the future, and know all the great questions to ask. However, I'm not. I wonder what questions you wish I would have asked you? Your parents? And are there any questions that you're glad I did not ask?" This practice creates a relational posture embodying cultural humility, allowing clients to access their own wisdom and resources (respect). Another therapist not-knowing practice which I commonly use is role reversal with adolescents (accountability, respect, openness). Especially when feeling stuck, I playfully assume the role of the client and the client assumes the role of the therapist. This experiential practice begins by switching chairs in the therapy room followed my curiosities of: "Thanks for meeting with me. You know, even though I have [name strengths and resources of the client], I find myself stuck in [summarize the current problem/context]. I just don't know. I wonder if you have any thoughts that can be useful for me?" This experiential practice embodies all aspects of the ORCA-Stance by allowing the adolescent to access their own wisdom and abilities with wondering about him or herself from a different perspective without the need to fix anything.

References

Freedman, J., & Combs, G. (1996). *Narrative Therapy: The Social Construction of Preferred Realities*. New York: Norton. Retrieved from https://books.google.com/books?id=cE9 NHan9a2IC&printsec=frontcover&dq=Na rrative+Therapy:+The+social+construction +of+preferred+%09realities.&hl=en&sa=X&ved=0ahUKEwjQ2vWlyKXhAhUHqp4K HYp3CQIQ6AEIKjAA#v=onepage&q=Narrative%20Therapy%3A%20The%20social% 20construction%20of%20preferre d%20%09realities.&f=false.

Frydenberg, E. (2008). *Adolescent Coping: Advances in Theory, Research, and Practice*. New York: Routledge. Retrieved from https://books.google.com/books?id=YGl9AgAAQB AJ&printsec=frontcover&dq=Adolescent+coping:+Advances+in+theory,+research,+an d+practice.&hl=en&sa=X&ved=0ahUKEwjplP6tyKXhAhXEtp4KHeFdDv0Q6AEILjA B#v=onepage&q=Adolescent%20coping%3A%20Advances%20in%20theory%2C%20re search%2C%20 and%20practice.&f=false.

Parry, A., & Doan, R.E. (1994). *Story Re-visions: Narrative Therapy in the Postmodern World*. New York: Guilford Press. Retrieved from https://books.google.com/books?id=thax7 XM_IpYC&printsec=frontcover&dq=Story+re-visions:+Narrative+Therapy+in+the+po stmodern+world&hl=en&sa=X&ved=0ahUKEwj_vIC7yKXhAhUVvJ4KHfOqC70Q6 AEIKjAA#v=onepage&q=Story%20re-visions%3A%20Narrative%20Therapy%20in%20 the%20postmodern%20world&f =false.

Selekman, M.D. (2005). *Pathways to Change: Brief Therapy with Difficult Adolescents* (2nd edn.). New York: Guilford Press. Retrieved from https://books.google.com/books?id=dSvqC QAAQBAJ&printsec=frontcover&dq=Pathways+to+change:+Brief+Therapy+with+dif ficult+adolescents&hl=en&sa=X&ved=0ahUKEwjRw6PFyKXhAhXJs54KHZ9AAyM Q6AEIKjAA#v=onepage&q=Pathways%20to%20change%3A%20Brief%20Therapy%20 with%20difficult%20adolesc ents&f=false.

Sori, C.F., Hecker, L.L., & Bachenberg, M.E. (Eds.) (2016). *The Therapist's Notebook for Children and Adolescents: Homework, Handouts, and Activities for Use in Psychotherapy* (2nd edn.). New York: Routledge. Retrieved from CgAAQBAJ&printsec=frontcover&dq=The+t herapist%E2%80%99s+notebook+for+children+%09and+adolescents:+Homework,+ha ndouts,+and+activities+for+use+in+psychotherapy&hl=en&sa=X&ved=0ahUKEwiQ2 NfQyKXhAhWGpZ4KHegrDuAQ6AEIKjAA#v=onepage&q=The%20therapist%E2% 80%99s%20notebook%20for%20children%20%09and%20adolescents%3A%20Homewor k%2C%20handouts%2C%20and%20activities%20for%20use%20in%20psychotherapy&f= false.

19

COUPLES

Shawn Whitney

I just concluded a phone conversation with a woman who describes her marriage as good, yet desires it to be better. She characterized both her and her husband as preoccupied with raising children and work in and outside the home. Her sense is their communication could improve. My sense is their connection could improve.

Many couples, regardless of their life stage, could improve their connection with each other. Most partners experience connection in spurts (e.g., date night, navigating a crisis together, cuddling on the couch), yet we are wired for ongoing connection with our partners. This discrepancy often triggers questions like, "Is this as good as it gets?" or statements like "You aren't the same person I married." Regardless of the conclusions we draw, the truth is we desire ongoing connection with others.

To clarify, when I say "connection" I am referring to emotional, intellectual, physical, sexual, and spiritual connection. When accomplished, these dimensions of connection allow us to experience intimacy. It is intimacy that is critical to the development of friendship (Gottman & Silver, 2015) and ongoing relationship satisfaction. In her book *Hold Me Tight: Seven Conversations for a Lifetime of Love*, Sue Johnson discusses the importance of emotional connection. "What couples and therapists too often do not see is that most fights are really *protests* over emotional disconnection", she says (Johnson, 2011, p. 30, emphasis in the original). The longer and more disconnected we are from our partner, the quicker we are to criticize, be contemptuous, get defensive, and stonewall the other (see Four Horsemen of the Apocalypse, Gottman & Silver, 2015). So, an important task for couples is to create a culture of connection which requires humility and intentionality.

Why Do Couples Seek Therapy?

Couples typically initiate therapy because one or both partners are not open (or are closed) in some way. While many people begin an intimate relationship with a desire to be open with their partner, patterns of distance often develop over time. Past histories, shame, secrecy, pain, and resentment seem to perpetuate these distancing patterns. When the distance becomes too much to ignore, one of the partners usually calls on a therapist for assistance in addressing the patterns.

Mary and John started couples therapy with me at her request. She had stated in our initial phone conversation that John has an anger problem and she recently moved out because of it. Although he did not want her to move out, Mary reported that John understood and that he was motivated to work on their marriage. Watching them sitting on opposite ends of the couch describing each other's faults, it became increasingly clear that John's short-fused anger and Mary's biting criticism were being fueled by an absence of emotional safety and connection in their relationship.

Openness

In the initial stages of treatment, partners often identify what it is safe to be open about (e.g., communication issues). Essential to the growth of a relationship is our ability to be open with our partner. Gottman & Silver (2015) identified willingness to be influenced by your partner as a key component to healthy relationships. Moreover, I view accepting influence as a necessary step in becoming more open to your partner.

Openness is a posture that is typically maintained when our empathic need to be cared for is attended to by our partner. When this profound need is not met, we tend to distance ourselves from our partner in subtle and overt ways. In order to effectively address/challenge the distancing behaviors, we need to help couples to identify these behaviors and simultaneously model for them openness and acceptance.

Establishing an environment of acceptance is a vital step in the development of openness. When the therapist can extend acceptance to both partners, the culture in the room shifts. When partners can extend acceptance to each other, the culture in their relationship shifts. The reason for this is that acceptance increases safety. This sense of safety often translates into greater openness. Greater openness consistently leads to an increased understanding of our partner and ourselves.

Various in-session exercises (and eventually between-session exercises) that address openness can gradually shift partners to increasingly open postures (e.g., giver-receiver exercises in a non-judgmental environment that increase openness over time). These take a great deal of practice and patience. The giver identifies something they can tolerably risk sharing, while the receiver actively listens and validates the giver. When it appears that both partners are able to operate in both roles, then the amount of risk taken increases over time. Normalizing the challenges associated with being vulnerable and identifying the appropriate pace at which the exercises are facilitated are the therapist's tasks.

Respect

In popular culture, there are songs and catchphrases about the importance of respect. While respect seems to be a cultural value, we appear more focused on demanding it instead of earning it. The downside of demanding something from someone is that they are often resistant to obliging, and this is often where partners get stuck. "You need to respect me because ..." or "I don't have to do anything I don't want to!" This locking of horns serves as another distancing behavior in partner relationships.

Take Linda and Sam, for example. Linda is a full-time mother of four children and Sam is a full-time employee with a local technology company. Over the past few years, both have felt increasingly disconnected from, and not appreciated by, their partner. One evening Linda asked Sam if he could pick their oldest child up from martial arts practice while she got dinner ready. "I just got home from a long day at work and I still have work to do. You need to respect that," Sam said in a defensive tone as Linda was already starting to walk away from him. Unfortunately, this particular interaction continued with yelling, slamming doors, and ultimately hurt feelings for both. Like Linda and Sam, many couples' normal interactions become significant conflicts when one (or both) partner(s) feel disrespected. In recounting this interaction, Linda said, "I'm not trying to disrespect him. I just want to feel like both of our needs are important." This strikes me as a great definition of respect.

A wise mentor of mine once said that couples often engage in "competition for respect." In a sense, each partner believes that their way is the better way of doing life. Unless both partners can accept each other's influence, the ability to mutually respect one another and develop a "we-ness" in their relationship is virtually impossible. That is precisely why fostering a culture of respect in therapy is critical to the expansion of intimacy between partners.

In my experience, therapists can foster a culture of respect by embodying and encouraging couples to practice civility in their interactions with one another. Sadly, civil conversations and debates have become somewhat of a lost art in modern culture. It seems that we have replaced listening and thoughtful responses with loud and unchanging monologues. Instead of allowing partners to raise their voices and dig in their heels, hold them accountable to practicing civility – taking turns talking and listening, expressing curiosity, validating different perspectives, and seeking greater understanding. When we can expand our ability to be civil, a culture of respect can be realized.

Curiosity

Do you remember wondering about things and how they work when you were a child? While most therapists continue to ask questions in our adult life, we often grow out of our natural curiosity as we transition to adulthood. My sense is that openness and playfulness fuel curiosity – two postures children often excel at. As we grow up, it seems that many of us become less open and playful, which cripples our tendency toward being curious. What makes this shift problematic is the impact that decreased curiosity has on intimate partner relationships. Assuming that curiosity is a primary vehicle for increasing intimacy, therapists need to get partners back to asking each other questions/studying each other – much like when they were in the honeymoon phase of their relationship.

Gottman & Silver (2015) refer to "emotionally intelligent couples" as partners who are "intimately familiar with each other's world" (p. 54). According to Gottman & Silver (2015) these *love maps* are the part of the brain where we store information about our partner's life. The process of "love mapping" requires curiosity and, in turn, enhances our connection to our partner. A male client recently said, "If I thought about my wife as much as football, we'd have a great marriage!" Although this was an off-the-cuff comment delivered with some sarcasm, he's probably right. He added up the hours he's involved with football in some way and it exceeded 45 hours per week! This is in addition to his full-time job. Just think of the jolt his marriage would experience if he redirected his curiosity for football to his wife.

I encourage therapists to facilitate and assign exercises to couples that foster curiosity. There are numerous books and materials available to the public that pose questions and provide activities intended to increase curiosity about and connection with their partner. In addition to the perspectives taken within the *ORCA-Stance*, Gottman & Silver's *Seven Principles for Making Marriage Work* is one such resource for couples. For therapists, getting trained as a Gottman Certified Therapist, an Emotionally Focused Therapist, a Psychobiological Approach to Couple Therapy provider, and/or a Certified Sex Therapist will provide framework for effective couples therapy.

Regardless of what exercises you choose, the hope is that they can help people to rediscover their natural/innate tendency to be curious. The results of this rediscovery can rekindle infatuation, enable couples to get current on each other, and even operate with fewer assumptions. Clients report that when their partner is curious about them, they feel cared for, valued, seen, and known. One client, Jane, said, "His genuine interest in me makes me want to be vulnerable and intimate with him." Jane's comment illustrates the power of curiosity.

Many couples are quick to tell me that they understand the benefits of curiosity, yet want to know how to be curious in a meaningful way. Just as personalities differ, so does the expression of curiosity. However, here are five key elements to embodying curiosity with your partner:

1.   Foster a desire to know your partner.

   • Chances are you were curious at one time. *Re*-fostering this curiosity is important. It's also important to remind yourself that your partner has changed over time, just like you.

2.   Actively listen.

   • This requires taking headphones off, putting your phone down, not watching television, etc. Basically, removing any potential distractions so that your mind, body, and soul can be active in listening to your partner. Curiosity is truly a full-body experience.

3.   Practice being non-judgmental.

   • Many of us are good at making assumptions and judgments about other people. The problem is that most judgments are made before we know the whole story. As a result, our judgments can often be ill-informed and critical.
   • Since criticism kills curiosity, we must help couples to not judge and instead embody humility when attempting to understand their partner.

4.   Ask open-ended questions.

   • We rarely gain deeper understanding about someone from them saying yes or no (the typical response to a close-ended question). So, asking questions that elicit more response than a one-word answer typically results in learning more about our partner.

5.   Model vulnerability.

   • Brene Brown (2012) has discovered in her research that being vulnerable transforms your life. She says, "Rather than sitting on the sidelines and hurling judgment and advice, we must dare to show up and let ourselves be seen" (p. 2).
   • The key is not waiting for your partner to show vulnerability, it is modeling it with the hope that it will be contagious.

When partners are able to be genuinely curious, the likelihood of increased connection rises. While a posture of curiosity does take consistent effort, it is the benefits that outweigh the costs.

Accountability to Power

Power, the fourth aspect of the ORCA model, is viewed as the leverage and influence we possess in the social and relational contexts we operate within. In many regions of the world, including the United States, your biological sex largely influences the amount of power you possess (i.e., being male means that you have more social power). However, social power goes beyond gender.

Take Lisa and Jeff for example. Lisa is a schoolteacher and Jeff is a grocery store clerk. Although she has more formal education than he does, they report that he has the last say in decision-making. He is Caucasian and she is African American. She makes more money than him, while he is in leadership at their church. As this couple illustrates, we all possess some amount of power in our lives. Often, we possess more power in one context (gender) and less power in another (education). This often results in unequal balances in social and relational power that can create tensions and resentments, even separation and divorce.

Lisa and Jeff also illustrate the distinction between "power over" versus "power with." *Power over* is using the leverage and influence we possess for our benefit and/or the detriment of others. In this case, Lisa and Jeff are attempting to embody *power with* by using their influence to share power with each other. In order to increase partners' awareness of power, I recommend doing an assessment of power dynamics in their relationship (e.g., who makes decisions about major purchases?). Then tailor in-session activities and homework assignments to increase their ability to name, shift, and maintain power in ways that honor their partnership.

Case Study

Kate and Tim are a Caucasian couple in their thirties, who initiated couples therapy to address intimacy issues in their relationship. They are a blended family with two children from Tim's first marriage and one child together. Kate is a full-time stay at home mother while Tim owns and operates a business with offices in multiple states. They both report a high level of commitment to their relationship yet acknowledge lower levels of satisfaction at the time of intake. Their treatment goals include personal growth, increasing intimacy, and addressing their brokenness together.

Why Do Couples Seek Therapy, Revisited?

When asked why they are seeking couples therapy at this time, Kate reports that they are unable to solve their issues and problems on their own. In addition, she expressed a desire to save their relationship rather than throw it away. Similarly, Tim reflected that learning, growing, and saving their relationship is important to him. Tim also stressed that he wants to be a better person and, more than any-thing, to make Kate happy. When hearing Tim share, a brief smile flashed across Kate's face. "It turns out we both don't know how to do this," she added.

Like so many couples, Kate and Tim report lacking tools to navigate their relationship in healthy ways. They acknowledge that commitment alone is not enough to sustain a meaningful relationship. That is why their wisdom to engage in couple's therapy is right on target. Acquiring new tools in therapy increases the probability that their relationship satisfaction could eventually mirror their commitment to the relationship.

Ideas for Best Practices Applied to the Case Study

I commonly introduce the ORCA-Stance to couples during the initial phase of treatment as a "way of being." In other words, it becomes a road map for navigating conversations and connections in their relationship. ORCA-informed exercises in-session reinforce new ways of being with their partner. One such exercise was inviting Kate and Tim to embody openness.

Openness Applied

Standing back to back, I asked Kate and Tim to use their arms to represent openness. Then I had them turn toward each other to reveal their postures. Kate and Tim found it humorous that they both had their arms outstretched to their sides. While they held their postures, I asked them to reflect on how they're feeling in the moment. Tim spoke first and shared that it signals acceptance, which is significant for him. "On a day to day basis, I search for acceptance," he explained. Kate shared that she felt vulnerable, accepted, and safe. "For me, the most open we've been with each other is in therapy," Kate said.

After Kate and Tim dropped their arms and returned to the couch, we discussed how they could embody more openness in their relationship. Kate felt that practicing empathy would increase openness, while Tim thought that more honesty and communication would foster openness. Both of them were correct about key elements of openness and also areas of growth in their relationship. Often ORCA-informed exercises expand understanding about our partner and ourselves.

Respect Applied

I invited Kate and Tim to reflect on the nature of respect in their relationship. Kate grew up internalizing male-centric messages about respect. She shared, "I always felt it was: you were supposed to respect the man. I never thought about it as: I also deserve respect." Kate reported that she is drawn to and desires mutual respect in their relationship. I reflected that she was describing the empowering concept of *power with*.

Tim followed Kate's reflections with "I had a very convoluted anxiety about the way [respect] was supposed to go." He shared that respect has always come with authority, that power and leadership demand respect. I reflected that this hierarchical view of respect seems to promote *power over* postures. During his reflections Tim expressed gratitude to Kate that "you fighting *with* me in this [relationship], instead of me fighting *against* you, has made a difference." The key element here seems to be their commitment to "with."

Curiosity Applied

I posed the question, "What does curiosity feel like?" to Kate and Tim. Both responded with words like valued, seen, openness, no assumptions, and genuine care. Suffice it to say, Kate and Tim notice and appreciate curiosity. As for their relationship, Kate shared, "There's a fear along with the curiosity about what we might find. As you become more comfortable with each other, you start to assume you know what you need to know. Like, there's nothing new to know here." However, Kate went on to reflect on the role that curiosity plays in intimacy. "You can't have honesty, vulnerability, and transparency without curiosity," she said.

Tim expressed, "I have a genuine curiosity about you, but we only do the things I like to do. I want to understand what you like and want to do." It is important to note that Kate expressed discomfort with Tim's desire to know her more fully. Since we were reflecting in-session, I was able to facilitate additional processing around Kate's discomfort. "I'm scared what he might see!" Kate said. To which Tim replied, "You don't look for something you don't want to see. And I want to see you." Tim was astute to identify that curiosity expands what we see.

Additionally, like others I have worked with, Kate reflected that "I haven't been curious about myself in I don't know how long? Instead of being curious, we avoid." It's true that the common strategy of avoidance stifles our capacity for curiosity. It also seems true that many of us grow out of curiosity and grow into avoidance in our adult lives. To their credit, Kate and Tim are committed to the emotional heavy lifting curiosity requires.

Accountability to Power Applied

Kate and Tim consented to participating in an experiential exercise designed to identify privilege. I placed an object in the middle of the room and had them stand on opposite sides of the room facing it and each other. I posed a variety of closed-ended questions to them and if they could answer "yes" they could take a step toward the object. For example, "Did you graduate from high school?" "Are you employed?" "Are you a male?" "Do you identify as Caucasian?" "Are you housing secure?" etc. After posing the last question, Tim found himself standing next to the object. While Kate was two steps away from Tim, as they stood in the middle of my office, Tim broke the silence by saying, "This is uncomfortable." His honest reflection proved to be the backdrop for our conversation about power.

I invited Tim to share about his discomfort, to which he responded, "I don't want to view myself as privileged; it's not how I feel. I feel like I dug out of my upbringing." Knowing his family of origin experience, I can confirm that Tim has worked hard to become a successful business owner. Yet his ability to answer "yes" for the vast majority of questions means that Tim possesses power others do not. "Now there is a big sense that what I say and do has an impact on Kate and the kids," he reflected.

Kate shared that she has not been accountable to her power in the past. "I didn't understand the amount of responsibility that comes with the power I have. I value it more now and don't want to use it in an abusive way with anybody." Kate also reflected that "accountability is not our strong suit." Going forward, she desires the type of relationship with Tim that is mindful of power. "I don't want to hurt people, especially my family," she said. My sense is that Kate and Tim are pointed in the right direction regarding their relationship with power. The reason for this is that power becomes increasingly difficult to abuse when you are committed to being accountable to it.

It is true that intimate connection with your partner takes consistent effort. However, the ORCA-Stance provides scaffolding for couples around how to experience and maintain meaningful connection with their partner. Whether as a professional therapist or intimate partner, my hope is that you can pursue and embody openness, respect, curiosity, and accountability to power in the relationships you participate in. Personally, I have found the ORCA-Stance to be an effective model for fostering a culture of connection that extends beyond cultural humility. My hope is that you will discover the same.

References

Brown, C.B. (2012). *Daring Greatly: How the Courage to be Vulnerable Transforms the Way We Live, Love, Parent, and Lead*. New York: Avery. Retrieved from https://books.google.com/books?id=2JFADwAAQBAJ&printsec=frontcover&dq=Daring+greatly:+How+the+courage+to+be+vulnerable+transforms+the+way+we+live,+love,+parent,+and+lead&hl=en&sa=X&ved=0ahUKEwieheaHyaXhAhVXvZ4KHcnAAjMQ6AEIKjAA#v=onepage&q=Daring%20greatly%3A%20How%20the%20courage%20to%20be%20vulnerable%20transforms%20the%20way%20we%20live%2C%20love%2C%20parent%2C%20and%20lead&f=false.

Gottman, J.M., & Silver, N. (2015). *The Seven Principles for Making Marriage Work*. New York: Harmony Books. Retrieved from https://books.google.com/books?id=8IWOxW1VEIYC&printsec=frontcover&dq=The+seven+principles+for+making+marriage+work&hl=en&sa=X&ved=0ahUKEwio96KUyaXhAhWNjp4KHUzVBrkQ6AEIKjAA#v=onepage&q=The%20seven%20principles%20for%20making%20marriage%20work&f=false.

Johnson, S. (2011). *Hold Me Tight: Seven Conversations for a Lifetime of Love*. New York: Little Brown & Co. Retrieved from https://play.google.com/store/books/details?id=jPLaqKhumPQC&rdid=book-jPLaqKhumPQC&rdot=1&source=gbs_atb&pcampaignid=books_booksearch_atb.

20

DIVORCING AND STEPFAMILIES

Gerry Presar

A man who carries a cat by the tail learns something he can learn in no other way.
(Mark Twain)

The major life disruption of divorce simultaneously impacts key factors of emotional well-being, including identity, social status, self-worth, role in family, social support systems, and financial security. Individuals undergoing this upheaval must somehow find equilibrium even as the fabric of their lives is being torn apart.

For remarried couples the challenges can be equally formidable. Litigious ex-spouses, divergent parenting styles, loyalty binds, and clashing family cultures are but a few of the difficulties that confront these clients. In the midst of this tumult, the couple must somehow find a way to nurture their relationship even as the demands of forming a new family system continually press down upon them.

Faced with the complexity and raw emotion that often accompanies working with these populations, as therapists we are challenged to provide structure and guidance that is in alignment with the client's culture and various other factors informing their worldview. The *ORCA-Stance* helps to serve this purpose by positioning us in the dual role of guide and fellow explorer as we join with our clients in a collaborative effort to map the treacherous territory at hand and find a way through the wilderness.

Divorce: Drastic Change and Disruption

Clients seeking therapy for divorce are often psychologically bruised and battered from a prolonged and ultimately unsuccessful attempt to save their marriage. Engaged in a grand struggle – frequently the most supreme challenge yet encountered in their lives – they often find themselves lost in the grip of uncertainty, fear, shame, and loneliness.

When working with this population I find that focusing on the ORCA elements of respect and accountability are particularly helpful in establishing and deepening my connection with clients experiencing divorce. From this joined place I can be most fully present to the impact of their stories marked by examples of their integrity, strength, and courage. As I listen, reflect, and inquire from an attitude of respect and vigilance toward accountability to the power differential in the room, an environment of acceptance and safety is created wherein vulnerable issues can be explored, unencumbered by fear judgment.

As my clients' basic need to be known and validated is being met, the therapeutic relationship deepens. When I share how I am moved by the courage and strength they exhibit during times of crisis, I am holding up a therapeutic mirror in which they can see a reflection unbound to the existing narrative of failure and self-blame. From this broadened perspective, they can begin to view the end of their marriage with greater objectivity and an increased capacity for self-compassion.

Carl, a 50-year-old man recovering from a contentious divorce came to my office embittered and depressed. He never imagined that his life would come to this dark place. The gut-churning interactions with his ex-wife subsided for a time after the divorce was final, but that relative calm had recently given way to escalating conflict around co-parenting. Once the embodiment of self-confidence, Carl found himself battling depression as he struggled to accept and effectively deal with his life circumstances. Family and friends were supportive at first, but this empathy was soon replaced by unsolicited opinions about what he needs to do "to get on with his life".

It was difficult for Carl to open up in therapy at first. He had seen friends go through divorce with apparent ease, yet he was struggling. To Carl, seeking therapy was an admission of defeat; further evidence that he was weak and broken. Immersed in shame, he saw himself as a complete failure, making it difficult for him to envision the possibility of deriving personal growth from this dreadful experience.

As our work progressed, it became evident that Carl's shame was preventing him from exploring the respective parts that he and his wife played in contributing to the demise of their marriage. Recognizing Carl's isolation in his shame, I weighed whether to share some of my personal experience with divorce in order to foster an environment where he could feel deeply known and accepted (Barrett & Berman, 2001). As I considered self-disclosure, I was also mindful of keeping it relevant to his experience. If he perceived it to be ill-fitted to the topic at hand, he could end up feeling trivialized and misunderstood (Roberts, 2005). Sharing personal stories related to events not yet fully processed would run the risk of burdening Carl with the need to protect me (Audet & Everall, 2010) Also on my mind was accountability and the power differential in the therapeutic relationship. Did Carl hold me up in his mind as someone who had somehow transcended human vulnerability and frailty?

In light of these considerations, I took time before our next session to reflect on what would be helpful for Carl to know about me as well as what I was comfortable in disclosing. The next time I met with Carl, I shared something of my own experience of grappling with feelings of shame and failure following my divorce some years earlier. Upon learning that I too had wrestled with some of the very same issues and emotions he was experiencing, Carl was comforted that his experience was normal given the gravity of the situation. In addition to any insight gained as a result of my self-disclosure, the therapeutic alliance was strengthened as Carl came to know that I truly understood and cared about what he was going through.

The first issue addressed in the course of our work was Carl's occasional angry outbursts during encounters with his ex-wife. After these emotional eruptions, he would descend into a pit of shame knowing that such behavior is harmful to his children. To Carl, this difficulty in maintaining emotional equilibrium was yet another example of his failure as a human being.

Looking through the lens of respect for Carl's experience, I was able to see his pain as a reflection of his deep desire to be a loving father and cooperative co-parent. Reframing the situation by pointing out that the pain he felt after "losing it" was a sign of how deeply devoted he was to the well-being of his children helped Carl to broaden his perspective and access self-compassion as he strove to change his behavior.

During our work together we explored numerous examples of strength, whereas previously Carl had only been able to see weakness. As Carl began to recognize these qualities within him, he came to realize that he was doing the best he could under very difficult circumstances. With this growing self-acceptance came a new openness to encounter the pain of loss.

My work with Carl exemplifies the lack of cultural recognition for the grief experienced by men going through divorce (Baum, 2004). By happenstance, I was aided by the fact that we were of similar ages, raised in the same culture, and had direct experience with divorce. I had firsthand experience with the less-than-stellar job American culture does in supporting men in grief. A different therapist without these areas of experiential overlap could have addressed this deficit by seeking supervision, doing research, and embracing an attitude of cultural humility while operating from the ORCA-Stance.

When he first entered therapy, Carl was stuck, with little awareness that such a thing as a grieving process even existed. As Carl opened up to his experience and allowed himself to enter into the grieving process, he gained clarity about the parts that both he and his ex-wife played in creating the emotional distance that eventually brought their marriage to an end.

Remarriage/Blended Families: Where Cultures Collide

By the time therapy is sought, blended family couples are often overwhelmed by their circumstances and discouraged with a life they had not envisioned (Visher & Visher, 1993). They seek to understand the forces at play and identify possible ways in which they can more effectively respond to relentless stressors, many of which are beyond their control.

Part of the struggle for therapists and clients alike is that norms applicable to traditional nuclear families do not always apply to blended families (Bray, 1998). A prominent reason for poor therapeutic outcomes as cited by blended family clients is "feeling like the therapist just doesn't get it" by mistakenly applying nuclear family norms in therapy (Visher & Visher, 1996). For example, a lack of love between stepparent and stepchild is not necessarily indicative of pathology, whereas this would be much more cause for concern in a nuclear family where bonds between parent and child have formed since birth.

When the process of remarriage involves children, a new dimension of complexity is introduced. The disparate backgrounds of each family member shape the formation of a new entity – the blended family. The challenge of establishing a new family system is compounded further still when the parents come from different cultures, bringing with them internalized norms around roles and behavior.

As I work with this population, I seek to balance my knowledge of best practices related to blended family formation with sensitivity to the perspective of each member of the couple. Staying anchored in the ORCA elements of openness and curiosity helps me to stay aligned with their experience as we do the delicate work of unpacking the dynamics affecting their family. When I am operating from an attitude of openness and curiosity, I am more fully available to see the world through my client's eyes. At the same time, a climate of safety is being established as I gently explore, bear witness, and validate the experience of each partner. The normalization that comes with this process of uncovering and validating each person's experience helps each partner to see the struggle of the other and to move toward a more collaborative position.

Case Study

Joe and Laurie stood at the altar basking in the warmth of love with hands entwined and eyes locked in an adoring, but nervous gaze. Standing beside them, bearing witness to this momentous occasion, were their children from previous marriages.

The couple entering my office 18 months later bore scant semblance to their formerly enraptured selves. Battle weary and demoralized, they desperately sought refuge from the chaos engulfing their lives. In unpacking their history, I learned that they had met each other shortly after their respective divorces were final. Joe, who had moved to the United States from Kenya 17 years ago, brought a ten-year-old daughter to the new marriage. Laurie, born and raised in the same town in which they now reside, brought a nine-year-old son. Laurie's ex-husband was largely cooperative; however, Joe's ex-wife, with her combative communications and rigid interpretation of the parenting plan, had proven to be a central challenge for the couple.

Over the preceding year, Laurie had grown weary of Joe's perpetual conflicts with his ex-wife. Joe felt misunderstood, caught between the demands of two wives, one past and one present. His behavior alternated between protesting with angry outbursts and withdrawing to his "man cave" in the garage. Parenting also proved to be more difficult than anticipated. Joe's identification as a "strict disciplinarian" was at odds with Laurie's permissive parenting style.

The couple also couldn't agree on the authority that Joe should exert with his stepson. Joe was insistent on having equal authority over both children informed by his belief that rules – his rules – should be consistent for all the kids in the household. Laurie was equally adamant that each partner should parent their own child in their own way. Amid the tensions in the marital relationship, Laurie drew closer to her son, which Joe perceived as undermining his authority in the family by taking sides against him. Laurie experienced Joe's behavior toward her son as inflexible and unloving, leading to her withdrawal fueled by a seething resentment.

Among other issues faced by the nascent family was Laurie's struggle in forming a relationship with her stepdaughter who has repeatedly rejected Laurie's bids for connection. The kids got along fairly well initially, but several months and one honeymoon period later, areas of conflict expanded to a new battleground – the shared bathroom. Adding to the difficulty the couple faced in integrating their family was the unequal custody arrangement whereby Joe's daughter lived in the household over 90 percent of the time, while Laurie's son was in the house every other weekend thereby leaving him feeling like an outsider.

As I sat with Joe and Laurie, I could viscerally sense the chasm separating them as they leaned against their respective ends of the couch. The unproductive conversations that had been increasingly escalating into fights had taken their toll.

It soon became apparent to me that the most immediate sticking point was the fact that Joe was insisting on full discipline with his stepson before establishing a relationship with him – a common misstep in blended family formation (Papernow, 2013). The more Joe pressed for respect and obedience, the more his stepson resisted. When I pointed out this dynamic, accompanied by a little psycho-educational information about how it interfered with the process of forming their new family system, Joe seemed duly impressed. However, with each passing week the dynamics between Joe and his stepson appeared to be getting worse. It seemed that Joe wasn't particularly interested in putting into practice the behavioral changes discussed in therapy.

Upon reflecting on the possible reasons for my being stuck, I discovered to my great chagrin that my ego had a hand on the steering wheel. In reaction to Joe not properly drinking from the cup of my wisdom by altering his behavior, I was doubling down on the advice. This humbling realization led me to consider what else I had overlooked. I didn't have to look far. Even though it seemed like I had been thorough in unpacking each partner's position, I realized that I had failed to adequately address how the norms of Joe's cultural origins might be informing his position.

Our next session found me in touch with a sense of cultural humility to help to guide the conversation. We began with a check-in during which I exercised accountability by sharing my concern that I had been overly eager in setting the pace of our work together – and in so doing, had fallen out of therapeutic alignment. I also normalized their difficulty in making behavioral changes before the important influence of culture and emotion was better explored and understood.

With this realignment in place, I learned that Joe's outward cooperativeness during previous sessions didn't accurately reflect his position. In fact, he was feeling somewhat guarded and suspicious, informed in part by his culturally instilled belief that values are mainly learned in the context of family (McGoldrick, 2005). Advice from someone outside the family (me) was difficult for Joe to accept. With this information in head and heart, I redoubled my efforts to build a collaborative relationship with the couple. In addressing this block, we agreed that Joe would try to be more forthcoming with any concerns and that I would provide scaffolding by checking in with him more often during session.

As our work continued, we discovered that Joe's stringent demands for compliance from his stepson was largely influenced by two factors: his culturally informed assumption that he should be the head of the household and a desire to be accepted and respected by his stepson. We also looked at the family-of-origin and culture influences that informed Laurie's expectations of a marriage that functioned more as an egalitarian partnership.

Over time, Laurie came to see the that Joe's behavior came from a place of passion toward fulfilling his internalized cultural role as a strong leader of the family. Joe was able to grasp that Laurie was not intentionally trying to undermine him in her bids to attain equality in the relationship. Once they were able to step back from seeing the other as an adversary, the door opened to begin work toward navigating their differences and accommodating each other's needs.

Ideas for Best Practice

- Utilize self-disclosure judiciously. Be mindful of the common traps of making disclosures that are too frequent, elaborate, or dissimilar to the client's experience. Avoid sharing personal information that is unprocessed.

- Avoid assuming that traditional nuclear family norms are applicable to blended families. For example, the absence of love between stepparent and stepchild isn't necessarily indicative of a problem. Connect with the client's experience before reaching for interventions.
- Suspect misalignment with client if interventions don't appear to be effective. Consider which element of ORCA might need shoring up. For example, operating from curiosity and respect toward a client's culture aids in making internalized norms explicit so that they can be integrated into the therapeutic conversation.
- Practice periodically checking in with yourself throughout each session to discern if aligning with ORCA or cultural humility would aid in gathering information or enhancing alignment with your client. Doing this on a regular basis will facilitate it becoming second nature in your work.

References

Audet, C.T., & Everall, R.D. (2010). Therapist self-disclosure and the therapeutic relationship: A phenomenological study from the client perspective. *British Journal of Guidance & Counselling*, 38(3), 327–342. Retrieved from https://pdfs.semanticscholar.org/5abb/0a38289547a5d1db4851f9cf08a29206e9b0.pdf.

Barrett, M.S., & Berman, J.S. (2001). Is psychotherapy more effective when therapists disclose information about themselves? *Journal of Counseling and Clinical Psychology*, 69(4), 598–603. Retrieved from https://psycnet.apa.org/record/2001- 18163-002.

Baum, N. (2004). On helping divorced men to mourn their losses. *American Journal of Psychotherapy*, 58(2), 174–185. Retrieved from https://psychotherapy.psychiatryonline.org/doi/pdf/10.1176/appi.psychotherapy.2004.58.2.174.

Bray, J.H. (1998). *Stepfamilies: Love, Marriage, and Parenting in the First Decade*. New York: Broadway Books. Retrieved from https://books.google.com/books?id=2XN0ZaTBznAC&printsec=frontcover&dq=Stepfamilies:+Love,+Marriage,+and+Parenting+in+the+First+Decade&hl=en&sa=X&ved=0ahUKEwjWj7zhl6bhAhVCM3wKHUtvDsgQ6AEIKjAA#v=onepage&q=Stepfamilies%3A%20Love%2C%20Marriage%2C%20and%20Parenting%20in%20t he%20First%20Decade&f=false.

McGoldrick, M., Giordano, J., & Nydia, G.-P. (2005). *Ethnicity & Family Therapy* (3rd edn.). New York: Guilford Publications. Retrieved from https://books.google.com/books?id=6Al1kB_6GyMC&printsec=frontcover&dq=Ethnicity+%26+Family+Therapy&hl=en&sa=X&ved=0ahUKEwje5ZaMmKbhAhXnjlQKHT3IAm8Q6AEIKjAA#v=onepage&q=Ethnicity%20%26%20Family%20Thera py&f=false.

Papernow, P.L. (2013). *Surviving and Thriving in Stepfamily Relationships: What Works and What Doesn't*. New York: Routledge. Retrieved from https://books.google.com/books?id=WzfO2aMXthcC&printsec=frontcover&dq=Surviving+and+Thriving+in+Stepfamily+Relationships:+What+Works+and+%09What+Doesn%E2%80%99t.&hl=en&sa=X&ved=0ahUKEwiuxb6znKbhAhWWoJ4KHfeEDEcQ6AEILDAA#v=onepage&q=Surviving%20and%20Thriving%20in%20Stepfamily%20Relationships%3A%20What%20Works%20and%20%09What%20Doesn%E2%80%99t.&f=false.

Roberts, J. (2005). Transparency and Self-Disclosure in Family Therapy: Dangers and Possibilities. *Family Process*, 44(1), 45–63. Retrieved from https://onlinelibrary.wiley.com/doi/pdf/10.1111/j.1545-5300.2005.00041.x.

Visher, E.B., & Visher, J.S. (1993). *Stepfamilies: Myths and Realities*. New York: Citadel Press. Retrieved from https://books.google.com/books?id=wVz695SACj8C&printsec=frontcover&dq=Stepfamilies:+Myths+and+Realities.&hl=en&sa=X&ved=0ahUKEwiA1uugnabhAhXJhVQKHVUHDQIQ6AEIKjAA#v=onepage&q&f=false.

Visher, E.B., & Visher, J.S. (1996). *Therapy with Stepfamilies*. New York: Brunner Mazel. Retrieved from https://books.google.com/books?id=0WFCpJmapCAC&printsec=frontcover&dq=Therapy+with+Stepfamilies&hl=en&sa=X&ved=0ahUKEwiXvufFnabhAhWJiFQKHfbwCRcQ6AEIKjAA#v=onepage&q=Therapy%20with%20Stepfamilies&f=false.

SECTION III

Contextual Applications

In this section we apply the ORCA-Stance to a range of contexts. Chapters 21–23 note how we have been influenced by this Stance within our personal lives, Chapters 24–27 document how we intentionally provide clinical training from this perspective, and Chapters 28–31 explore a few ways that the ORCA-Stance can be applied beyond the boundaries of university mental health training setting. Finally, Chapter 32 invites the reader to apply a culturally humble perspective into their own contexts.

21

APPLYING THE ORCA-STANCE TO PARENTING

Hee-Sun Cheon and Don MacDonald

Imagine it is your interview day. Dressed in your best suit, you are prepared to impress the interviewers with the perfect answers. You meet with a group of four interviewers. The interview is running so smoothly; you feel like you're flying to the finish line. You share a bit about yourself, including your family and kids. At that moment, one senior interviewer warmly addresses you and asks, "What have your kids taught you?" The question catches you off guard, because you definitely did not prepare for it.

This was my personal (Hee-Sun Cheon) experience while being interviewed for a faculty position at Seattle Pacific University. This question helped me to realize that not only was I a provider to my kids, but also that I was in a position to receive and learn from them. This awareness brought a novel perspective on parenting, and placed the sense of gratitude at the center of developing relationships with my kids. Now, I would like to invite you to answer the same question that I was asked, as I co-author this chapter with Don MacDonald who, by the way, was the senior interviewer in the story above.

The ORCA-Stance in Parenting Younger Children (Hee-Sun Cheon)

The families I have worked with in clinical settings have patiently taught me many profound lessons over the years. First, they taught me that no matter how dysfunctional, critical, or bizarre their reactive behaviors, families acted out of an irreducible desire for love, connection, and belonging. Some were driven by the intention to protect their family members from pain, worry, or fear. Once my clients and I get to the core of their inner experiences and desires, we often encounter their deeply seated love for one another. As Attachment

Theory and research have taught us, our reactive behaviors are just the tip of the iceberg.

Second, I observed that families were doing their best to communicate their love within the given resources, often resulting in rigid patterns of interactions; this tallies with the observations made by Satir (1988) as one of the pioneers of marriage and family therapy. Those observations confirmed my belief in human beings' hard-wired need for connection and belonging, but made me feel compassion towards their intense pain and suffering – despite their love and good intentions. The issue here was that they were loving and reaching out to their loved ones in a one-directional way, lacking the reciprocal connection that Hughes (2009) explained as "the intersubjective process." When the process of reciprocal connection and influence are not present, our kids often feel unheard, unseen, and unloved. Out of these clinical observations, I came to realize that love that falls short of reciprocal connection and influence is incomplete. As a parent, my priorities have been rearranged. I need to stay connected to my kids, and open to hear their words, verbal and nonverbal, honing my wholehearted ability to see beyond their behaviors.

One of the careless mistakes we make as caring and good-intentioned parents is assuming that we know our kids. We do not always know what they are thinking, cannot know how they are experiencing an event, and should not assume "what's in their best interest." The moment we assume, we are most likely to be insensitive and disrespectful to our children. I have met many parents who say, "I gave birth to my kids. They are like an extension of myself. I know them." But my question is, "Do we really?"

As the mother of two kids, aged 13 and four, the ORCA-Stance has helped me to mature my parental love in two distinct ways. First, ORCA helps to slow me down in the heated and/or hasty moments of making assumptions and judgments – the two most unwelcomed visitors in parenting. The false assumption of "I know my kids" fuels my brakeless judgment train, leaving it difficult to suspend that judgment. When relying on ORCA, I find a better sense of peace and comfort, believing that there would be more than what I can ascertain in my kids' behaviors. It helps to encourage my desire to understand my kids better – from their perspective.

Second, the ORCA-Stance reminds me to stay open to my kids' words and remain curious to explore their unspoken desires and internal experiences. It helps me to navigate their possible motives through non-judgmental curiosity and increase my flexibility to be influenced by what they have to offer me. In so doing, my children experience receiving respect, eventually learning to extend respect to their parents and others as well.

It was a bright, sunny day in the summer. People were laughing and enjoying the rare occasion of a big family gathering. Adults were busy grilling BBQ while catching up with one another and little kids were running around and riding bicycles. The relaxing family reunion was cut short when my three-year-old son

Eugene started screaming at his cousin who was playing with the bicycle. I knew he was waiting for his turn, and immediately assumed that his sudden screaming had something to do with the bicycle. Sure enough, Eugene got everybody's attention and I knew the spotlight was on me and I needed to perform some miraculous disciplinary action.

If you have experienced something similar to this, you would easily relate to my experience. I felt hugely embarrassed, upset, and even shameful. When those emotions seize us, we are often too quick to judge our kids, mainly based on their behaviors and our interpretation of their actions. However, I adjusted my impulse with a sense of curiosity. Realizing that I had never seen Eugene that upset before, I was intrigued to hear him out. So instead of disciplining his behaviors right away, I decided to separate him from the scene and simply asked what had happened. Struggling to find the words, Eugene looked up tearfully. "Mommy," he said with the most concerned and determined look on his face, "she was standing on top of the bicycle and that's not safe." He was really worried about his cousin's safety but did not have the language to communicate the perceived urgency, so he reverted to the tools he possessed: screaming. If I had not gotten curious and respected his intention, I would have easily ignored his consideration, and missed a precious moment of connection and validation.

Accountability to Power in Parenting Kids

I have decided to separate accountability to power from the other principles of the ORCA-Stance because of the power this principle has and the toll we have to pay when we are not embodying it as a part of our stance. But more importantly, mature parental love demands us to consider the power we have over our kids.

Parenting is an endless rebalancing act. The moment we feel like we have conquered it, it slaps us right back in the face. It humbles us. We are challenged to embrace it with our whole soul, mind, and heart because we are parents regardless of our mood, good or bad. Parenting does not cease to exist for our convenience. Perhaps the most precious lesson my kids have taught me is to appreciate the co-existing contradictions of life (Siegel, 2011). This seemingly unnatural and incomprehensible truth of life is best captured in parenting. Think about your children. They can be the most loving and caring creatures one minute, then, very hateful and self-centered beings the next. At times, this is presented as an incomprehensible challenge to some parents, and even confusion and despair to others. If we are not attuned to our own inner noises, fears, or shame, we can easily get lost in the endless rebalancing dynamical interaction that is parenting. Being fully mindful of our power as parents and going slowly with the other three principles – openness, respect, and curiosity – helps to tame our inner challenges and to stay connected with our kids even at the peak of messiness.

The ORCA-Stance with Grown Children (Don MacDonald)

Children grow up. That is, those who survive the risks that are part of childhood (e.g., severe illness) and adolescence (e.g., drug addiction, car accidents) become adults who may be more or less prepared to help to raise the next generation and to lead productive lives. A deceptive aspect of developmental stage theories such as Erik Erikson's (1980) is that growth occurs in qualitatively different chunks of life – childhood, adolescence, and adulthood – in its most simplified form. Instead, the various dimensions of development ebb and flow unevenly, blending into external and internal growing that manifest themselves in unique individuals who operate in multiple contexts that also change (Berger, 2014; Carter, McGoldrick, & Garcia-Preto, 2011). An implication of this flow is that applications of ORCA with children and adolescents also work with adult children, only adjusted to their increasing maturity.

The three sons that my wife and I have, by the time they reached their mid-twenties like many in North America, were starting on a career path, living more or less independently, and engaging in one or more serious dating relationships (Berger, 2014). One was even a parent by this time. Regardless of lifestyle, they were making big, potentially life-changing decisions and making these choices with or (frequently) without parental input. Significantly different from childhood and adolescence, then, we as parents move from active guidance and insistence on certain conduct (e.g., "No, the curfew I gave you was my actual expectation, not a suggestion") to consulting and learning how to be more patient with the choices and timing of our sons and daughters.

The five of us also noticed a shift from a parent-child relationship to more of an adult-adult relationship. This shift is possible in part by neural and cognitive maturation. That is, the young adult's brain and executive decision-making capabilities start reaching full maturity by the mid-to-late twenties (Siegel, 2012). While having such capabilities did not insure that our sons would make sound decisions, the potential for doing so existed. As discussed in the previous section on ORCA with children and adolescents, this potential interacted with the world around them, including our family relationships, to help to hone their judgment and skills for making mature life decisions (Fulmer, 2011; Titelman, 1987). ORCA is a stance that helped my wife and I to relate more smoothly with our sons and, hopefully, pass on the stance to the next generation. Two of our three sons are now married and are parents. Both seem to apply ORCA principles in their partnering and parenting, although neither could explicitly define the four aspects if prompted.

Openness shows up in being willing to acknowledge and at least attempt to understand issues in ours and our children's lives. The adjustment for a parent with a young adult would have been more challenging if we as parents were accustomed to closely monitoring and guiding our children's decisions up through adolescence; being willing to step back and hear about experiences, behaviors, feelings, and ideas that felt foreign to us was at times difficult, but we intentionally tried anyhow. Of course, the amount of parental involvement operates on a continuum. A 20-something relative recently said, "My parents were hippies who tried to control very little of my life. I learned early on that I had to make decisions for myself." At the other end of the continuum lies the example of very high-achieving parents who informed their two teenagers that their future professions were to be in law or medicine; one child duly became a lawyer and the other a doctor. The relative's example is one of extreme openness, while the latter suggests extreme lack of openness. I would like to think that the parenting efforts of my spouse and I were more in the middle.

Our sons have many choices to make, review, and remake: lifestyle choices such as music and piercings, dietary issues (such as becoming vegan), friendships, employment, and living conditions. Often the range of choices differed from their parents' choices, including some radical divergences. In order to optimize our relationships and communications, it was vital for all of us to be open to learning about and considering these decisions. It was unnecessary to agree, although this would make life easier. Rather, it was a matter of engaging in dialogue, sharing views and anticipated consequences, then letting it go. After all, consequences are great teachers (Patterson, 1977) and we all can learn vital life lessons from them. As a parent, what I feared, of course, was that some consequences were more serious than others. For example, rushing into an early marriage, a subsequent divorce, and single parenthood is a harsher consequence than the pain of dating someone, deciding that he or she is not a long-term partner prospect, and breaking up. Nevertheless, openness to discussing the pros and cons of early marriage, plus sharing love and support for this child we loved, was preferable to attempts to strong-arm him into doing what we thought was best. It is very much like Carl Rogers' (1951) concept of unconditional positive regard: we may disagree yet each of us seeks to understand and accept the other for who they are intrinsically.

Respect overlaps with openness insofar as it also entails unconditional positive regard. I seek to be open to a son partly due to my respect for his intrinsic worth. Thus, someone has value simply because they exist. By respecting my adult child, I acknowledge, at least on a metacognitive level, his specialness. Philosopher Emmanuel Levinas (1969) spoke about this notion of upholding the sacred value of the Other by recognizing the presence and worth of the Other before recognizing himself. This valuing applies to family life as well as psychotherapy (Sayre, 2015).

Respect appears in numerous large and subtle ways in parent-child relationships. Supporting an adult child in a big life decision with which I disagree (e.g., choice of a spouse or partner, choice of work) is one example. None of my three children went into the same line of employment as my wife and I (both university professors), although I had secretly hoped that at least one would. I experienced some regret that none of them wanted the career that their mother and I find so rewarding. Even so, neither of us lobbied for our children to follow our lead; we supported the very different occupational directions that they selected, and all three are content and productive in their chosen lines of work.

More ways of subtly showing respect or lack of it include numerous nonverbal and para-verbal actions. Rolling the eyes, breaking eye contact, turning away from someone, grunts of displeasure are instances of expressing disrespect in rather subdued yet still noticeable ways (Ivey, Ivey, & Zalaquett, 2014). The underlying message of large-to-subtle disrespect runs along the lines of, "You, my child, are failing to please me as you should and likely in the process of ruining your life at the same time." However, indicators of respect express, "I might disagree with you or not understand you, but I trust your judgment and want to help as best I can."

Curiosity entails an active interest in being a learner about someone else. In terms of being a parent, curiosity involves gradually shedding parental authority, guidance, and expertise. The expertise part for us was informed by both of our children's parents holding doctorates in psychology, including a lot of study and experience in developmental issues and family life. Nevertheless, our children's excitement about a first-grade project, their disappointment about a dating relationship gone wrong, their decision to move across the country were important to them at the time and important for us to engage in inquiry. As with openness and respect, our agreement was not required. Rather, the process entailed seeking information and personal preferences about choices, with no stated agenda as to what our adult child ought to seek.

As an example, the process of inquiry and then letting go became clear to my wife and me when one of our children decided to move to the opposite coast to court and eventually marry the love of his life. That move meant that we would miss time with him, his wife, and contact with their children, but the choice was vital to him. We sought an explanation from him about this choice, he provided one, we helped to transport him and his possessions, and we still offer the support that we can. We tried to remain curious when seeking to understand his rationale. Even though we wish that he and his bride lived closer to us, we remain interested and inquisitive about their lives thousands of miles away and about what is important to them as individuals and as a family.

Accountability to power recognizes the effects that parents have on their children and attempt to have those effects be as beneficial as possible. Yes, parents are powerful influences on the lives of their child or children (Berger, 2014). We as parents do not determine the directions of our sons' lives yet we have important influences on them. Accountability is part of family polity. Recognizing what we advocate, lobby for, or coerce is important, since our child cannot help but be influenced by such forces (Carter, McGoldrick, & Garcia-Preto, 2011). Hence, it is important that we recognize the importance of our influence and seek to exert or mollify it appropriately so as to contribute to our sons' growth.

With our adult sons, our influences are less than when they were young, since we encourage their independence rather than their enmeshment (Bowen, 1978).

Even so, parental wishes and aspirations never cease to affect adult children's decisions and actions. I knew, for example, that my parents disapproved of some of the ways that my wife and I raised our children (e.g., no corporeal punishment). Neither of them said anything about their disapproval for a number of years. On one telephone call, though, my mother eventually said, "You know your father and I have never tried to interfere with how our children raised their children …" At that point, realizing the "but" that was coming next, I responded, "And you know, mom, I cannot tell you how grateful I am to you for taking that position." The conversation pivoted at that point. At some level, my mother and I knew that accountability for raising our children was the job of my wife and me, not my parents or her parents, and we adopt the same position regarding our sons and their wives as parents.

Conclusion

Active parenting is a lifelong commitment. While particulars of parenting change as offspring grow and the circumstances of their lives change, the ORCA-Stance continues to hold us in humility with gratitude for the sacred lessons we have learned while parenting our kids. So even in the lowest valley or hastiest moments of parenting, we humbly encourage you to slow down and ask yourself this very question, "What have my kid(s) taught me?"

References

Anderson, H., & Gehart, D. (2007). *Collaborative Therapy: Relationships and Conversations that Make a Aifference*. New York: Routledge. Retrieved from https://books.google.com /books?id=ct9ONlDG3dIC&printsec=frontcover&dq=Collaborative+therapy:+Relatio nships+and+conversations+that+make+a+difference.&hl=en&sa=X&ved=0ahUKEwi1 gZurzabhAhWMEnwKHffNDEEQ6AEIKjAA#v=onepage&q=Collaborative%20therap y%3A%20Relationships%20and%20conversations%20that%20make%20a%20difference.& f=false.

Berger, K. (2014). *The Developing Person through the Lifespan* (7th edn.). New York: Worth.

Bowen, M. (1978). *Family Therapy in Clinical Practice*. Northvale, NJ: Aronson. Retrieved from https://books.google.com/books?id=4g7PdF6oW6EC&printsec=frontcover&dq= Family+therapy+in+clinical+practice&hl=en&sa=X&ved=0ahUKEwjOo_S8zabhAhWL wcQHHXjBARkQ6AEIKjAA#v=onepage&q=Family%20therapy%20in%20clinical%2 0practice&f=false.

Carter, B., McGoldrick, M., & Garcia-Preto, N. (2011). *The Expanded Family Life Cycle* (4th edn.). Upper Saddle River, NJ: Prentice-Hall. Retrieved from https://play.google. com/store/books/details?id=ba_zCAAAQBAJ&rdid=book-ba_zCAAAQBAJ&rdot=1& source=gbs_atb.

Erikson, E. (1980). *Identity and the Life Cycle*. New York: W.W. Norton. Retrieved from https://books.google.com/books?id=mNTECQAAQBAJ&printsec=frontcover&dq=Id entity+and+the+life+cycle&hl=en&sa=X&ved=0ahUKEwiAqsTazabhAhVJjVQKHfu5 CmEQ6AEIKjAA#v=onepage&q=Identity%20and%20the%20life%20cycle&f=false.

Fulmer, R. (2011). Becoming an adult: Leaving home and staying connected. In B. Carter, M. McGoldrick, & N. Garcia-Preto (Eds.). *The Expanded Family Life Cycle* (4th edn.). Upper Saddle River, NJ: Prentice-Hall. Retrieved from https://play.google.com/store/books/details?id=ba_zCAAAQBAJ&rdid=book-ba_zCAAAQBAJ&rdot=1&source=gbs_atb.

Hughes, D. (2009). *Attachment-Focused Parenting: Effective Strategies to Care for Children.* New York: W.W. Norton. Retrieved from https://books.google.com/books?id=e95hgXLSwp IC&printsec=frontcover&dq=Attachment-focused+parenting:+Effective+strategies+to+c are+for++children.&hl=en&sa=X&ved=0ahUKEwiK8eTwzabhAhVIslQKHY2LAC0Q 6AEIKjAA#v=onepage&q=Attachment-focused%20parenting%3A%20Effective%20strat egies%20to%20care%20for%20 %20children.&f=false.

Ivey, A.E., Ivey, M.B., & Zalaquett, C.P. (2014). *Intentional Interviewing and Counseling* (8th edn.). Belmont, CA: Brooks/Cole. Retrieved from https://books.google.com/books?id=YeM WAAAAQBAJ&printsec=frontcover&dq=.+Intentional+interviewing+and+counseling &hl=en&sa=X&ved=0ahUKEwiCxKX7zabhAhWKrVQKHQYlAYUQ6AEIKjAA#v =onepage&q=.%20Intentional%20interviewing%20and%20counseling&f=false.

Levinas, E. (1969). *Totality and Infinity.* Pittsburgh, PA: Duquesne University. Retrieved from https://books.google.com/books?id=7oDPBgAAQBAJ&printsec=frontcover&dq= Totality+and+infinity.&hl=en&sa=X&ved=0ahUKEwjHmtqDzqbhAhVpsVQKHXJOD iIQ6AEIKjAA#v=onepage&q=Totality%20and%20infinity.&f=false.

Patterson, G.R. (1977). *Living with Children* (rev. edn.). Champaign, IL: Research Press.

Rogers, C.R. (1951). *Client-Centered Therapy.* Boston, MA: Houghton-Mifflin.

Satir, V. (1988). *The New Peoplemaking.* Mountain View, CA: Science and Behavior Books.

Sayre, G.G. (2015). Toward a therapy for the Other. In K.C. Krycka, G. Kunz, & G.G. Sayre (Eds.). *Psychotherapy for the Other: Levinas and the Face-to-Face Relationship.* Pittsburgh, PA: Duquesne University. Retrieved from https://www.tandfonline.com/doi/abs/10.1080/13642530500087187.

Siegel, D.J. (2011). *Mindsight: The New Science of Personal Transformation.* New York: Bantam Books Trade Paperbacks. Retrieved from https://books.google.com/books?id= wSEA_qHzbH0C&printsec=frontcover&dq=.+Mindsight:+The+new+science+of+per sonal+transformation.&hl=en&sa=X&ved=0ahUKEwiHrIzMzqbhAhWFCnwKHSleD _gQ6AEIKjAA#v=onepage&q=.%20Mindsight%3A%20The%20new%20science%20of %20personal%20transformation.& f=false.

Siegel, D.J. (2012). *The Developing Mind: How Relationships and the Brain Interact to Shape Who We Are* (2nd edn.). New York: Guilford. Retrieved from https://books.google.co m/books?id=lF-BA_cdEO0C&printsec=frontcover&dq=The+developing+mind:+How +relationships+and+the+brain+interact+to+shape+who+%09we+are&hl=en&sa=X&v ed=0ahUKEwi-uO3XzqbhAhUIHnwKHYj2AQAQ6AEIKjAA#v=onepage&q=The% 20developing%20mind%3A%20How%20relationships%20and%20the%20brain%20intera ct%20to%20shape%20who%20%09we%20are&f=false.

Sue, D.W., & Sue, D. (2012). *Counseling the Culturally Diverse* (6th edn.). Hoboken, NJ: John Wiley & Sons. Retrieved from https://books.google.com/books?id=OjDvvsJmm 9gC&printsec=frontcover&dq=Counseling+the+culturally+diverse&hl=en&sa=X&ved =0ahUKEwjjm5Lkzqbh AhWiMHwKHVp-CosQ6AEIMTAB#v=onepage&q=Counse ling%20the%20culturally%20diverse&f=false.

Titelman, P. (1987). The therapist's own family. In P. Titelman (Ed.). *The Therapist's Own Family: Toward the Differentiation of Self.* Northvale, NJ: Jason Aronson.

22

REFLECTIONS ON GROWING UP IN AN ORCA HOUSEHOLD

Tina Schermer Sellers, Chloe Sellers and Christian Sellers

If a child lives with criticism, he learns to condemn.
If a child lives with hostility, he learns to fight.
If a child lives with fear, he learns to be apprehensive.
If a child lives with pity, he learns to feel sorry for himself.
If a child lives with ridicule, he learns to be shy.
If a child lives with jealousy, he learns to feel guilt.

BUT

If a child lives with tolerance, he learns to be patient.
If a child lives with encouragement, he learns to be confident.
If a child lives with praise, he learns to be appreciative.
If a child lives with acceptance, he learns to love.
If a child lives with honesty, he learns what truth is.
If a child lives with fairness, he learns justice.
If a child lives with security, he learns to have faith in himself and those about him.
If a child lives with friendliness, he learns the world is a nice place in which to live.

(Children Learn What They Live (1959) Dorothy L Law)

Reflections from a Mom

When I was a little girl we had a cloth wall hanging in our family room that I remember noticing every day. The words are quoted above. As I got older and could read my letters, I would use it to practice reading out loud. As time passed the meaning hidden in the sentences began to sink into my six-year-old heart. I remember many times saying to myself, "That wall hanging is right! I am going to try and be *that* kind of parent someday." Deep down in the depths of my little soul, being a good parent became, and continued to be, my highest aspiration – higher than getting my doctorate, becoming a family therapist, starting programs, writing articles or books.

I began graduate school when my son was two and finished when my daughter was three weeks old. That following year, I then began teaching in the very same program, and on the very same campus my son had learned to ride his bike. To say my children grew up on that campus is no understatement – they literally did.

One of the things I have always loved about our marriage and family therapy program, and why I felt so honored to teach in it, was its focus on the person of the therapist and the faculty's role as mentors to our students. There has always been a deep investment not just in crafting good clinicians, but also in helping these students become people of even greater integrity and vision. In many ways, our teaching philosophy grew naturally from the roots of my parenting – and I was living them both every day. Like contrasting threads in a canvas, my life at school and my life at home depended upon their color, chaos, and texture like threads purposefully creating what could not be created without the tension of the other.

Over the years, kids came to school and students came to the house. Students became colleagues, and we both watched each other's children grow. In 1996, during a faculty strategic planning and visioning meeting, we began discussing our core values. I remember it was a lively meeting with each of us building on the others' ideas. As we put words on a whiteboard – respect, curiosity, openness, accountability to power – like magic ORCA emerged. Given how interwoven my professional and personal vocations were, delineating our program values made even more visible my motherhood manifesto. I held myself to a higher standard of demonstrating each of these values with my children – even in the nitty gritty of our busy lives. That following year, adding a layer of complexity to this call to arms, with kids aged 11 and six, I began the journey of single parenting.

The Litmus Test

I am writing this 20 years after that visionary meeting. That two-year-old boy is now 29, married and managing his own business. The infant I nursed as I received my graduate degree is now 25, a graduate of the same university, and now pursuing post-graduate studies. In the intervening years as a single parent, we raised each other, me attempting to live out ORCA while juggling sometimes three jobs and two busy children.

As the faculty contemplated writing this book, I wondered what *my children* would say about how these principles were or were not experienced in *their home* growing up? What would be *their evaluation* of my parenting? Of our life together? Listening to the wisdom of children and teens over the years has taught me that often *their experience* is not exactly that of their parents. And certainly the vantage point of the parent is significantly different than that of a child or teen.

So, even though the kids and I talk often, I was not exactly sure what they would say. Had the manifesto which I had intended that they should experience actually been absorbed? Or had it been simply a case of vastly different worlds colliding? Knowing their penchant for brutal honesty, I was fairly certain of what I would hear, should I dare to ask. Whatever it would be, knowing them like I did, I knew they would be my litmus test. Has this been an ORCA household or something else?

So, with that in mind, I asked Christian and Chloe if they would let me interview them about their experience of growing up in our home. How did they, or indeed did they, experience openness, curiosity, respect, and account-ability to power? I was curious about the stories that might emerge as they talked together, and as I listened. Being five years apart in age, in many ways they had different childhoods. Chloe was entering first grade and Christian sixth grade when their dad and I split up – very different developmental phases. Up until that point, I had worked part-time as an adjunct professor with a small private prac-tice, but that next year I accepted a full-time teaching position in our program. Thankfully it still afforded me a lot of flexibility compared to most full-time jobs. Despite their age difference, Christian and Chloe have always had a special bond. After the divorce, however, they leaned on each other in new ways – of course we all did. We leaned into our life together.

A Conversation between a Mom and her Young Adult Children

Openness

TINA: Christian and Chloe, talk with me a bit about how you did or did not experience openness in our family growing up? By openness, I mean, my ability to be open to new ideas, yours and others.

CHRISTIAN: I definitely think one of your fundamental personal rules was open-ness. I always felt like considering another's perspectives was critically important. I have consistent memories of you saying, "How do you think your sister feels when you do or say that?" or "Why do you think they did that?" That was pretty consistent. Openness was an important part and you used it in helping us in problem solving and in managing conflict. Helping us understand another's point of view.

CHLOE: Yeah, I have a few stories that pop into my head. One is going to the Solstice Parade (www.fremontfair.com/) at a really young age. The whole feeling behind it was very open. It was not "these people look a particular way" and "those people don't." It was an appreciation of taking in multiple body types and ethnicities. Taking in everything. It was just about seeing it, appreciating it, and just being in it. Later in life, I remember you taking me to the Capitol in Olympia when they were marching on Gay Rights and I was 14. It was constantly "What situations can my children benefit from in terms of seeing other people's perspectives and other people's struggles?" I feel like we were put in a lot more situations than most children to take in a lot of people's lifestyles and ways of being, so by the time I was old enough to form my own opinions, it made sense to me. I had already experienced so much in such a non-threatening, open and accepting way."

TINA: What about openness to your perspectives, when your ideas were different than mine. How did you experience my openness or lack of openness there?

CHLOE: I think that is something I have struggled with. I think openness to other people's ways of life was definitely there, but in certain situations I think it is hard to bring that into the world of parent and child because you are also worried about our well-being and safety. For example, with piercings and tattoos. That is something that has continually been an issue. I can see your openness with other people, but not an openness with us – or specifically with me. But other than that, I think there has been a lot of conversation. When something came up that wasn't necessarily something we agreed on, there was always open communication, where we could have whatever conversation was needed. But when it came to our well-being, there's been conflict in terms of openness to a different generation's way of seeing things, or a different way of being in the world than you are used to.

CHRISTIAN: I think Chloe and I handle this kind of thing differently. Something that comes to mind is when you were urging me to go to college. You said, "Go check out SPU [Seattle Pacific University]." With me at least, I didn't think it was any more than you wanting to be sure that I pursued it, and at least understood my options. You didn't want me to just go off whatever my young brain desires. But anything past that, I think I didn't open the door to conversation. If I knew it was something you disagreed with, but I felt strongly about, I didn't feel it was something that you needed to know about. This was not just with you, though, I did this with everyone. I realize now, there are all sorts of flaws with this – it was more my method.

It is hard for me to come up with memories about how you urged openness in the family in conflict situations. Nothing comes to mind that goes beyond the situation where I was heard and you were heard, but then you pressed the issue further in some kind of unproductive way. If I heard you and you heard me, then at least we are communicating and now the decision rested on me. I don't think I or we went past that mark. In this way, I think openness was intrinsic to our family life.

TINA: I want to make sure I understand. Once you felt like I understood your perspective and you understood my concerns, there was an understanding that the ultimate decision rested on you. Is that what you are saying?

Whether it was covert or overt, you did not seek my advice beyond that point and I did not press the issue. Is that right?

CHRISTIAN: Yeah. That is what I am saying. I think the only time I would open the door beyond that point is if I was wanting your approval, but I don't think that was something I really sought much of the time. I think I just thought I knew what was best.

TINA: It is interesting to listen to you say that because what pops in my head is that is so much the way I thought when I was a teenager. There was a point at which I just made my decisions.

CHRISTIAN: Yeah, you took into council the people whose opinions you trusted and then you made your decisions. And if they gave a new point that I hadn't considered, I'd consider it. If their opinion wasn't close to what I had considered, I'd move forward.

TINA: I completely understand. As you know I had a dad whose opinion I respected. But I had my own opinion, stubbornness and desire to make my own decisions. And fortunately, my dad respected that and let that be okay too.

CHLOE: I feel like I am all emotion and all sensitivity. If you tell me you are embarrassed to take me somewhere, I have to figure out this whole approval thing or I am going to lose my mind.

CHRISTIAN: That seems like that has been the struggle with you and mom.

CHLOE: Yeah, and I think you've made this point before. You and I got so close it makes not getting approval really, really hard.

CHRISTIAN: Like you are wronging the team.

CHLOE: In all fairness, you have said some really hurtful things when you did not want me to get a tattoo or piercing. So, you *are* saying I am wronging the team and I do take that to heart. So, I do think that has definitely been a struggle.

CHRISTIAN: Partnerships are complex.

TINA AND CHLOE: They are, they are.

Respect

TINA: So, respect. Feeling valued; feeling like *who you are* is valued. I remember having this belief when I was a child when I would think about someday being a parent. I believed children fundamentally deserved to feel valued and respected at whatever age they were. How did you, or did you feel this growing up in our home?

CHLOE: I remember so clearly the idea "You are acting your job description." That is what is in my head. Even when I was being the worst, you would say that. Christian and I could be having a conflict and it would be seen as normal for ages five and ten. You would say, "Chloe, you need to understand that this is how your brother sees things, and Christian, you need to understand that your sister doesn't have the capacity to do that." I feel like it was always, "You are doing exactly what I would expect for your age and you need to meet this other person in the place where they are." That is still the way I think when I see kids that are only a couple of years younger than I am. I think, "They are acting their job description." Especially when I watch people lose their minds, and give a kid so much crap. Like when you have a parent saying, "My 16-year-old is smoking weed. We need to send them to rehab. I think, "Slow down! They are being 16! Just watch their patterning and behavior." It is respecting exactly who and where they are in their life. I feel like that was such a normal and helpful part of our family life.

CHRISTIAN: Yeah, I always felt respected. It was overall a respectful environment. We were educated when our perspective was shallow and it was done in a respectful manner. I am trying to think of when it would have been the most difficult to be the most respectful in our family. I think about the harder times, like when you guys were splitting up. I feel like respect was still the number one attempt. For example, we were given the dialogue that problems between you and Pop were to travel between you and Pop. We were told that we kids don't ever have to be the go-betweens. Or being told that you and Pop were not to say mean things about each other in front of us. I remember thinking, "Oh, that is something I should know about." Then, I had what I needed when either one of you was saying something hurtful, or whatever, I had the dialogue. I felt we were given a lot of tools so we knew when we were being respected, and how we were being disrespected, so we could communicate that. I felt that *even that* was respectful. I felt like I had good dialogue and good tools because of you.

CHLOE: I feel like we were given a lot of agency in our lives. Even though we were young, we were given the chance to speak our minds about exactly how we were feeling and express what we felt. And whatever that was, it was taken and respected. So, in a situation as big as the divorce of two partnered people, to take into account what a seven-year-old is saying and thinking – in my opinion that is respect to the nth degree. I felt like you demonstrated to me, "You can stand up for yourself in this situation. You can say when something is not OK or when it is, and we will listen and believe you." That kind of agency in your own life at that young age is not usually seen. It is usually, we are going to deal with our crap and you kids "are going to get the 'teeny tiny kids story': "your parents just aren't happy anymore and you can't possibly understand." Instead, it was like "This is what is happening and I want you to have the space to speak exactly your truth about it." I think that is above and beyond anything I know from any of my friends who went through similar situations.

Curiosity

How do you think about your childhood regarding curiosity? By curiosity I mean the difference between someone imposing their ideas upon you and someone really seeking to understand your ideas, your ways of knowing, your experience – while suspending their assumptions and meanings in such a way that they ask questions that help you to clarify your own ways of knowing. How do you think of your childhood with regard to curiosity? Was that emulated? If so, how? Any stories?

CHRISTIAN: I think we are all very curious people. I think we were all in pursuit of what we were passionate about at the time. I think you instilled in us, and Pop and Grandpoop [maternal grandfather], instilled in us the power of listening, so our curiosity was crafted in a manner where we wanted to know what other people knew. So, while I was discovering things on my own, I was also interested in what others were discovering too. I think curiosity was really healthy in our family. It was a core value of our family. I remember sayings like, "Curiosity is important," "The power is in the question, not in the answer," "No one has ever learned anything with their mouth open." All of those sayings I learned as a kid, and all have only proven more and more useful as I have grown. I attribute my curiosity 100 percent to being fertilized in my family.

CHLOE: I totally agree. That was one of the skills I learned – to be curious about other people. When I think about how it was shown to me, one of the stories I remember was from when I was 12 and I was questioning my sexuality. I remember talking to you and Christian and you both responded with so many questions. And I was 12! You know, your hormones are raging, who knows what I was thinking? Who knew if this was going to be a phase or what? But both of you were so open and so curious to the experience I was having as a 12-year-old female. I think for most other parents, their own stuff would have gotten in the way of them being able to be curious. This was a big turning point for me. I was so aware that you both were seeking to know me. With a different parent, I might not have been able to be known at all in this really confusing place.

Part of curiosity is really seeking to know someone. And you Mom, and you Christian, you were only 16 or 17 years old, and to really know my experience in that moment, and how you could be a part of it, was so meaningful to me. So, when I think of curiosity, this is the story that comes to mind. It could have been treated so different. It could have been treated like, "She is a hormonal 12-year-old in a phase," and instead I felt like I was really seen and known at home with both of you.

Accountability to Power

TINA: The next value is accountability to power. What we mean by this is the person in power has an awareness that their power can easily trump the situation and they are mindful of this. They don't abuse that power. They hold themselves accountable to the effect of that power. So, even though they might not feel like they have power, they recognize that they have been given power by their position in reference to another person, and because of this they are mindful of the influence of that power. So, given this definition, and my role as your mom in our family, when you think about your childhood, how do you think power was managed in my relationship with you when you were growing up?

CHRISTIAN: I think for someone to hold their power over you, to prove their power, they have to have more ego and pridefulness than you have. So, what comes to mind is not so much how you used your power, but the lessons you taught me when it came to Chloe. I remember so many times growing up where you reminded me I was more powerful than Chloe, and that I could very easily be unfair. You would also help me see this with friends because I was generally bigger than most of my friends. I still think about this a lot, because I think I have more ego and pride, and I can tell that I enjoy power somewhat. I still think about those lessons, and find myself evaluating when is power OK and when is it crossing the line. When is it a good choice to use power to achieve something and when is it taking advantage of someone who has lesser power or skills? When I think about actual lessons or conversations with you, I can think of several flashes of times where you would say "You have more power than Chloe does" or "You are being disrespectful because of the position you are in."

CHLOE: I have a similar experience to Christian. Because when I try to put you in that place of misusing power, it just isn't even there. I never felt like you were using your power. It was kind of like the openness, respect, and curiosity meant we both knew our own power and our own strengths, and you really helped us develop that and played to that. So, when I think of accountability to power, I think of how those lessons now help me to recognize when power is being used against me out in the world. Some of the biggest lessons in my young adult life have been when I have been too trusting and I have experienced someone misusing their power. But when this has happened, I have felt very equipped to process those situations and categorize them in my head, and realize this is where power was misused. I feel like all of these things, openness, respect, curiosity, and accountability to power have all led to the tools in my tool kit to assess a situation and deal with a situation in a healthy way. So even now, as a woman, I can recognize when someone higher up in a company – a male or someone else – is misusing their power, I am much more aware of it than I would have been otherwise. It is not so much images and pictures and stories from my childhood, it's how learning about all of those things have equipped me now to be able to recognize power and know my own strength in it.

CHRISTIAN: I would agree. Non-gender related, I feel like power is such a fun game for me and something I pay some attention to now. Like when someone is making a power move. I think about why they are making it, are they conscious of it or not? This makes a difference to how I react or not, or how long I let time play it out before I play my hand. I feel fairly equipped in playing power games. Which is what business is, it is what social interaction is with people you don't know. It is this feeling each other out. I attribute that a lot to how you prepared us, gave us the dialogue and gave us understanding of why. I think another positive side effect of you calling me out on my abuse of power was that *I felt powerful*. I was like, "Oh, I do have power." Which was good. Then you realize you have it and you know it. It is something you don't have to flaunt once you believe you have it. It's in your tool kit.

TINA: Can you think of any stories when you might have expected a more closed or authoritarian response from me; when I might have used my power more or differently? Maybe when you were older, a teenager, perhaps?

CHRISTIAN: I am thinking of that time I came home stoned (ninth grade) and you decided to confront me and talk about it. It was done in a respectful way. There were many more questions that were about, "I want to know what is going on in your head"; "I want *you* to know what is going on in my head"; "I want you to know what was going on in *your* head." I think I would have preferred for you to yell at me at the time. I was expecting something more severe instead of the counseling that I now know I should have expected [we all laugh].

TINA: Tell me more about that. In retrospect … What about being yelled at would have been preferable?

CHRISTIAN: At that age I was *really* trying to figure out some independence. I think every ounce of my energy went into independence. So, I think stopping and explaining where I was felt like a step back into childhood instead of a step forward into adulthood. I mean, it wasn't that. But I think at the time, I think it felt like that. It was like "Why am I talking to my mom about what I am doing outside of home? That is me figuring out me." I really wanted to make my own mistakes. At the time, that was really more of an issue with Pop, but I really wanted to make my own decisions and figure out and solve my own dilemmas. Knowing myself quite a bit better now, I think I just really enjoyed being able to understand my conclusions. And have conviction for how I was understanding the conclusion to whatever the problem was. For example, "This is a problem, and this is why, and I figured this out, and it failed, and I know why, and I own it 100 percent. Whereas if it was someone else telling me, then I would think, "Now I have to go find my own experience to prove it to myself. That one was figured out for me."

TINA: Oh, well. I'm not a yeller, so that doesn't really work very well for me [laugh].

CHRISTIAN: Yeah, and honestly, it wouldn't have worked as well if you had reprimanded me. You know, I figured out dialogue in that conversation. I could see how I was blaming Chase. I could see myself younger than I wanted to see myself in my head. Which was an important lesson.

A respect or openness thing, or all of the above, was when you let us have that party at the house [Christian was 15 and had a closed party with eight friends at the house with me present. Chloe was 15 and had a closed party with one friend at the house with me present]. You gave us rules and you gave us the environment. We didn't follow the rules, but I was aware of them and I was aware of what was going on. It was safe, and I learned some important stuff. That was a situation that was very open, respectful and gave me lots of room to work within my own power.

TINA: Yeah, from my perspective, I realize I only know a fraction of your experience, but when I look back on that experience for you and the one that we staged for Chloe, I think if I had to do it again, I would do it just the same because I think you both emerged on the other side of those events so much wiser and able to manage parties on your own better.

CHLOE: And we felt like we could be more open with you because you had opened the door for us to experience something like that, then if we were to experience something like that at a party. I felt way more open and able to share that with you and ask for your help. I think that was a big part of that.

CHRISTIAN: I would totally agree with that.

TINA: That was part of what I wanted too. That you would feel safe to come talk to me – to see me as a resource to you. Christian, you kept much more to yourself, than you did, Chloe. But I think that was part of being male and part of who you are. And that was fine. You guys did what you felt was best for you at the time – and ultimately I think you knew I was there.

CHLOE AND CHRISTIAN: Yeah, totally.

TINA: How did I manage power in our relationship? When did I use it, when did I hold it back? How was that for you? Was that confusing? Why or why not? How free did you feel to tell me things that would disappoint me? Can you think of any stories?

CHRISTIAN: Me, personally, I generally did not like disappointing you.

TINA: Yeah, I think there was a lot you didn't tell me.

CHRISTIAN: Not anything that is all that surprising now. But then, it was so much easier not to. I think it had more to do with consequence and you trying to teach us it's respectful to learn about the consequences of our actions. You wanted to help us learn about them. It was not so much you showing that you could punish. You didn't really punish us. I don't really remember that. I just remember you teaching us this was a consequence to our actions. And I associated that to there being consequences *to being caught*. So, like, you can avoid most consequences if you just don't get caught. That may not be ethical, but as you are learning things as a kid you think, "Don't get caught if you are going to have the best experience." Maybe because you taught me consequences. Maybe you taught me how to play the game so well that I could get away with a lot, because we did. I cannot believe my group of friends all came out of high school with clean records. That is insane. It really is. And a lot of that was everyone's problem-solving skills, and not wanting to get caught, and being lucid when we needed to be.

TINA: When you say I taught you to play the game well, what do you mean? What do you think I did? How do you think I did that? Say more about that.

CHRISTIAN: I think if you understand the consequences of your actions well enough, then you can avoid them. I got in very few fights in high school because I knew how to manage situations – manage people. Understanding this allowed me to get the most out of the experience without pushing it to the point where consequences became exponential or doubling, or more than I wanted to manage. It's kind of this razor's edge and we kind of knew how to play that edge most of the time.

CHLOE: You were smart about your stupid decisions.

CHRISTIAN: Yeah, I also understood we were all after a thrill. We all knew that. We all knew we were going to do that, we were going to lean into it, so we got good at it. How do you get thrill and still be able to do it again the next week without the consequence so that you can't.

TINA: Boys! Ugh! And not having a pre-frontal lobe – it's so scary!

CHRISTIAN: I had a conversation with a boss of mine years ago whose son was 12 at the time. He was trying to figure out how to get him to make smart decisions. I liked my response to him. I said, "There has to be something more important than maxing out your night. Something *that's really fun* you look forward to the next day." Like passions have always won for me. Like snowboarding. If I'm going snowboarding the next day, I am thinking about that the whole time. So, we can push it as far as we want, but I am doing *that* [snowboarding] tomorrow. Having those things that took priority would temper me. As long as you don't lose one of your passions because another thrill is taking its place – work hard, play hard.

TINA: On the day you came home stoned, I remember saying to you at one point "At what point would you be so worried about Chase's pot use that you would actually want to say something to him?" And you said, "When he was using so much that he stopped skateboarding." To me that said, "He would have traded in his passion for pot." Is that what you are getting at here?

CHRISTIAN: Yeah. It's that play hard, work hard, party hard. As long as you don't lose one of them because others are consuming that space. Any of them. Work hard, you can't play hard. Play hard, you can't work hard. Play hard meant something very personal. These were the things I was developing in myself. Party hard was the social side. But if I partied too hard to play, then I was really doing myself a disservice. I still believe that. But now I work. [Laugh]

TINA: [Laugh] Yes, yes, you do. What about you Chloe, around disappointment and power?

CHLOE: It doesn't bring up the concept of power either. It touches something else in me other than consequences or power. It's that I respect your opinion so much, and want your approval so much, that if I already know that what I want is not going to meet that, is not going to be what you think and want, I have a hard time telling you. So maybe it does have something to do with power – but it is power that I have given you – because I have given so much power to your approval over the years that I still have trouble standing on my own two feet and saying that I am making this decision for me, regardless. And I feel 100 percent OK about that. And I am almost 25 years old. A part of that is the power I give you and a tiny part of that is that you know you have that power. But I think I've given a lot of it to you. Of course, I want to make you happy and of course, I know you want what is best for me. That has never been a question in my mind. But there are going to be times when what you think is best for me and what I think is best for me are going to be different. This stage of my life has to be about me being OK with making a decision and standing in that decision on my own. It just has to be. I think the only time I have been afraid to tell you something is because I crave that approval so much, above all else. Really, I think it's made me question my own decisions. Which is frustrating because although I have so much strength in my decision-making, when it comes to your approval, I start to waver.

CHRISTIAN: It sounds to me like it is momentary decisions – not who you are fundamentally. For example, at my core I don't think I could ever truly disappoint mom. However I decide to paddle down this river, I have good faith in myself and in my better judgement that I won't disappoint mom. So that feels very freeing.

TINA: I think that is so true – for both of you.

CHLOE: But you can say mean things – especially around tattoos and piercings. I think you will absolutely accept me for exactly who I am for the rest of my life. You always do. And every time I make a decision that you may not be happy with, it will take maybe about a month before things will settle out again and we'll be fine. And you'll be proud of my decisions again. That's what it feels like. But you do, at times, say things that are mean when you are bummed about a decision I am making. You hold a lot of weight and you know I am very sensitive. And there are times that I wish you could be disapproving and also respect how much I care about how much you think and be more careful about what you say.

CHRISTIAN: I don't know what to tell you. I just don't open up that door. I would be hurt too.

CHLOE: But for me opening that door *is* walking through the door.

TINA: Because they are all about tattoos and piercings. They are all about that. They are not about anything else.

CHLOE: But I don't think we can single out this one thing. I don't think we can talk about having openness to my perspective and respect, but there is this one thing you have the right to cut me to the core.

TINA: I hear you.

CHLOE: That to me feels very jarring. It feels like I have one experience of being very respected and given power to make my decisions and to own the consequences if there are consequences. And then there is this one part that is about the physical appearance that I don't feel respected. I don't feel there is curiosity about what these things mean to me. I just feel like you're hurtful.

TINA: Yeah, I hear you. It is really hard for me. I have to work really hard on it because it is really hard for me.

CHRISTIAN: It sounds like you handle it pretty well for it being as hard as it is on you. I think you guys have a very unique relationship.

TINA: I do need to work on it and I do hear what Chloe is saying. And it may just be that I keep my mouth shut and I just give myself distance for that month. Because it is hard for me and I don't like it. But to what you are saying Christian, to the broader picture with both of you, I respect who you are so much as people and I appreciate who you are so much, I don't imagine anything you will do in your lives that I won't be 100 percent behind. I admire you both so much.

CHRISTIAN: Chloe, are you hoping that someday you will come home with some body modification and mom will be approving?

CHLOE: No, just not condemning. I completely understand our differences of opinion. I completely understand why mom feels the way she does about body modification. I do. And if I was a parent, I would probably feel the same. It's more that I don't want to walk in the door and know I am walking into a fire when there are so many other things that feel important and relevant to me.

CHRISTIAN: Closing statements?

CHLOE: Don't say mean things.

TINA: Okay.

CHRISTIAN: Chloe, I think you could probably count on one hand the number of mean things mom has said to you in your life – maybe two? That's pretty f-ing awesome.

CHLOE: That is! It truly is.

CHRISTIAN: So, let's just keep things in perspective the standard that we have for mom and daughter.

CHLOE: Yes, it was just part of the answer to the question [laughter].

TINA: What do you take from our life together, from my parenting, that you imagine you will want to do when or if you decide to be a parent? Why? And what will you want to do differently and why?

CHRISTIAN: Something I want to focus on is being respectful of the child at each stage. I think that is humongous, because you hold them to the standard of their age. That level of empathy is difficult and takes a lot of intention.

Additionally, there is something that I don't necessarily want to do differently, but I think I will because I am a different person – a mixture of Grandpoop and you on that level. I think I'll have more expectations of, say, a seven-year-old – a little more "this is what makes a man a man." I kind of see it in myself and I like it. And when I see it in others, I kind of like it, if it is done in a way that is not condemning. Because it was stuff I loved – being held to a standard of adults and then being praised when I understood the concepts that adults understood, at a younger age. It was not being condemned, it was being taught the concepts and then being able to perceive them and then when I unintentionally showed I understood those concepts and was praised for them, that was pretty cool. And I think maybe that is a man thing. It's a mixture.

CHLOE: I think openness is a big one for me. I know sociology is so ingrained in me now. And I look around and see so much disparity and see race, SES and gender. So, I want to really raise children to be empathetic when it comes to other people's situations and be open to different lifestyles and different religions and different situations people find themselves in. I think that is really important, because as humans we like to categorize people when someone is different and then make a hierarchy. And I felt as children, we saw a lot of diversity in terms of life situations. I feel like I categorized, because I think that is natural. But as far as hierarchy, I feel that wasn't as much ingrained in me in terms of race. I mean, of course I have racism in me, of course I have sexism in me, it's part of culture. But I feel like I have less of it because I was shown so many ways of being and urged to be open to it. I was asked questions like, "How do you think that person feels?" Or a homeless person? I was nannying a couple of years ago and the little boy I was taking care of said, "That man has no home." And I asked, "I wonder why?" And he said, "My mommy said, maybe because he is sick, or maybe because he doesn't have a job or a family." They felt so much empathy for this person. Instead of this difference – like *you* are less than me – it was, this person *has* less than me. That is so, so important. Along with what you said, Christian. Respecting where children are in their life developmentally and then showing children how to be open and respect where other people are in their life. It's all OK – and how do we understand those things better.

CHRISTIAN: So, what would you do differently?

CHLOE: Not much, honestly. So, even the shitty, shitty parts. Like them getting divorced and us living in so many different places with Pop and whatever, I think all of those things were dealt with in a really good way and a really open way. If anything, and mom and I have talked about this so many times, I think the one misstep (and to just have one in all of this is pretty insane) was we got a little too close during a couple of those years right after Christian left for college. I think it affected both of us and it is something we have processed a lot to know how we would do things differently if we were in that situation again. If I found myself in a situation like mom found herself, I can understand the difficulty in not opening up to your child who is of an understanding age, who is very sensitive and very compassionate. I can understand how hard that would be – and a challenge, but I would really want to try and separate it more. Really though, if that is the only thing I would do differently that is pretty phenomenal.

TINA: Thank you both so much.

CHLOE: I love you.

CHRISTIAN: Yeah, I love you guys too.

TINA: I love you more!

23

UNPACKING A STORY OF RACE

Kenneth Jaimes and Kathleen Blair Jaimes

As we sat down to brainstorm for this book chapter, we were both struck by how difficult it was to begin the process. We agree that our racial differences, history, and experiences constantly shape and influence our relationship. And, as systems therapists, we actively discuss other power dynamics in our relationship. For instance, Kenneth holds power as a hetero, cisgender male with a graduate degree. And yet, as a Latinx son of an immigrant, racially ambiguous looking person, the power he holds often varies. On the other hand, Kathleen is a hetero, white, cisgender female, who also has a non-visible disability. In some spaces toxic men give Kathleen the runaround, while in others Kenneth anxiously code-switches between cultures in order to appease the dominant culture around him.

As narrative-leaning therapists, we prefer to metaphorically think of our relationship as a bookshelf holding lots of unfinished books. Each book represents an aspect of our relationship including experiences, thoughts, and conversations that add to our story. Books on the shelf range from titles such as *"Places We've Travelled Together," "Awkward Family Dynamics," "Cats Rule, Dogs Drool,"* and *"Coping with Stressful Situations." "Race"* is another, big, meaty, weathered book sitting on our shelf, and, like good nerds, we have curated our bookshelf so that *"Race"* sits near other books that give it a more meaningful context such as *"Differences in Ability"* and *"Smashing the Patriarchy."*

Race, gender, family dynamics, sexuality, etc., are all different layers of one's life, and as systems therapists, it should be instinctual to consider how these various layers intersect. Additionally, sometimes the work of systems therapy is to pull systems apart and give each part particular attention. This chapter is such a moment, when we analyze the parts of our relationship that intersect with race specifically. This is an example of how we use the *ORCA-Stance* to examine the particulars of our lives.

On a recent international trip, our involvement in a friend's wedding brought us into frequent contact with an older, cis, white, American wedding guest. He consistently vocalized his anti-immigrant and Islamophobic viewpoints, and aggressively doubled-down when others challenged him or raised concerns. As guests, neither of us felt much agency to set appropriate boundaries with this man. We both had negative, taxing experiences with this person. However, our negative experiences were vastly different, informed by poignant differences in our personal histories of race. We both felt icky, flustered, and angry with said person, and limited in our ability to effect change. Beyond that, Kenneth's sense of security plummeted for the remainder of our time in the predominantly white, elderly, European city.

This encounter also impacted our relationship. We might be able to guess some of each other's feelings, but we are not mind readers, and had a conversation checking in the next day. Our conversation proceeded as follows:

KATHLEEN: [noticing something was clearly wrong with Kenneth]: What's going on?

KENNETH: I just feel tired.

KATHLEEN: It seems like there's something else. Are you bothered by the negative comments from last night?

KENNETH: Yeah, that was pretty upsetting. I think more than feeling upset or flustered with him, I feel unsafe. And beyond that, I don't feel safe being in this city in general.

KATHLEEN: Is there something you need me to do to avoid being around them? I know we're sort of dependent on them for rides.

KENNETH: Not necessarily, I know you need to be here for your friend, but I needed you to hear that that's how I'm feeling.

KATHLEEN: Thanks for telling me. I'm sorry we have to be around them.

Kenneth's Reflections

While Kathleen could safely assume that I also had a negative experience of said person, she was unaware as to how unsafe I felt with both said person and as a foreigner in a predominately white nation. Kathleen's whiteness allowed her to both blend into the dominant culture and not feel directly threatened by this man's xenophobia; I could do neither. Holding less power in such situations, it felt tenuous for me to name how unsafe I felt, yet I needed an ally in my partner. It was important for me to present my experience in such a way that activated Kathleen's ally-ship and remained open to her negative experiences (she was, after all, a target of his sexism). My history and experiences with Kathleen facilitated my openness to exercise my voice and explain my concerns. Kathleen practiced respect to my experience by listening to my fears and not discounting or diminishing them.

Kathleen's Reflections

When Kenneth shares with me his feeling unsafe, I have a few options, ranging from denying how he's feeling, telling him he doesn't need to feel that way, or listening and believing him. Leaning into an ORCA-Stance and holding myself accountable to my power as a white person, I need to recognize when my experience does not align with Kenneth's. Both as a therapist and as a partner, it is my aim to validate the feelings of those around me. It is a continual process for me to take things regarding race at face value when they are presented to me, and part of my personal work of dismantling white supremacy.

I also know I tend to want to come up with a solution to "the problem." Part of our relationship has been my own learning process of sitting in the discomfort with someone else; there is not always a fix. I had to practice openness to holding the discomfort with Kenneth, while recognizing that I would not feel the same level of danger that he did.

Conclusion: History on Repeat

As we discussed the content of this chapter, we found ourselves in a familiar tension. Previously, in our graduate student days, we collaborated along with other peers to advocate for more equitable and inclusive changes within the clinical institutions to which we belonged. While our voices made an impact, Kenneth could not help but wonder if his concerns regarding the racial dynamics of said institution would be heard or taken seriously without the support of more powerful white voices.

Here we were, an interracial couple made up of a Latinx man and a white woman collaborating once again, asked to write on ORCA and race. We contemplated how it seemed that the voice of an ethnic minority needed a white voice in order to be palatable to more audiences, or that adding a white voice somehow added value that the editors might be looking for. As we got into this discussion, we felt it appropriate to end this chapter on "race" on this uneasy note. There are no "conclusions" on how to handle race dynamics interpersonally – as clinicians or at a societal level – without taking a moment to ask: "Who is at the table?" and "What power do they hold?" The tension of racism and other -isms are not resolved through ORCA, but ORCA does provide a lens through which we can examine and sit with these tensions. Perhaps accountability to power is the most challenging tenet of ORCA to exercise in a world shaped by societal and social hierarchies. And so, we end with that tension.

We hope you will take these concepts and continue to apply them to your own lives or clinical work. We hope that you continue to add books to your shelves. Might we suggest starting with a quick read of "*Cats Rule, Dogs Drool*" followed by a deep introspection on "*Race: Where Is My Place?*"

24

FAMILY THERAPY TRAINING

*Scott Edwards, Hee-Sun Cheon, Claudia Grauf-Grounds
and Peter M. Rivera*

My wife and I are in Berlin right now working with a church leadership structure that has sought "coaching." Whatever it is we are doing for and with them, it doesn't feel like coaching to me; it feels collaborative, and I have to say that Bowen, Narrative, and overall systemic ideas are making a great difference here. Folks are loosening their grip on a modernistic critique and becoming more open to appreciating the differences. The church here loves ORCA. Me too. ... Thank you for relationship. Your spirits have invited us into a safe and supportive community. I have the feeling that any of you would respond to our needs – we would just need to say the word and you would be there. I came into this program feeling like a stranger. I leave it with an internalized certainty that no one is alone. I am a witness, and I carry at least a small part of your wisdom and love into the future with those I'm blessed to attend.

(Scott Green, 2010 alumnus, excerpt from an email to faculty dated June 29, 2010)

The *ORCA-Stance* was developed by our clinical faculty to identify core relational values that we hoped we could embody within clinical and personal relationships. Teaching students to attend to these core values is empowering for their lives and the lives they encounter. We are aware of the level of expertise and authority others bestow on us as educators and clinicians. However, simply teaching a way of being, in and of itself, would be a thin endeavor. The ORCA-Stance is not simply a group of values that we teach or hold; rather it represents the interpersonal dimensions which we practice and strive to uphold in daily interactions with students, clients, and colleagues.

How do we, as a clinical faculty, integrate and thicken the experiences within our family therapy program while simultaneously embodying those same values we have identified? Through the practice of humility, specifically cultural humility when differences exist, we acknowledge we are not all-knowing and attempt to remain mindful of our limits. We thicken the relational experiences within our training context by intentionally attending to "how we are in relationship," and striving to embody the ORCA-Stance ourselves in our personal encounters within our cultural contexts as well as integrating intentional structures and processes within our training program.

A central concept within our systemic perspective is that of isomorphism, which attends to parallel structures and processes at different but related contextual levels. We are aware that each student in our program is part of various layered contexts, such as being part of a supervision group, which is part of a classroom cohort, which is part of a graduating cohort, which is part of the program, and so on. Additionally, our training program itself exists within the layered contexts of faculty, department, school, university, profession, and cultures. By intentionally attending to the congruency between program structures and processes and how we embody the ORCA-Stance, we practice what we call "isomorphic accountability" (Edwards, Grauf-Grounds, & Cheon, 2011; Grauf-Grounds, Edwards, MacDonald, Quek, & Schermer-Sellers, 2009). Intentional programmatic structures and processes infused with the ORCA-Stance allow us, as educators, to come alongside our students in ways that support their development on their journey to becoming a clinician. As we support each student in finding their own direction, our training program intentionally attends to our structures and processes within our training program. We have developed numerous program structures and processes, which lay the foundation for, foster, and facilitate the embodiment of the ORCA-Stance.

Each week, we gather as clinical faculty for a 90-minute marriage and family therapy (MFT) department meeting. It is an honor to intentionally spend the first 30 minutes creating community time, checking in with each other prior to dealing with departmental business. Specifically, we attempt to embody and practice an ORCA-Stance with each other. Our "check-ins" allow time for us to connect in relationship, share our professional and personal lives, re-connect, and ground us in a relational stance with each other. This is an example of an isomorphic structure in which we intentionally attempt to embody the ORCA-Stance as in essence we practice what we preach within a culturally humble stance. We also attempt, as teachers in the classroom and supervisors in clinical practicum supervision, to check in with students and pay close attention to the multiple layers of relationship. This promotes intentional ways of educating congruent with the values embodied within the ORCA-Stance.

Structurally, our training program intentionally begins with the ORCA-Stance as a foundational experience. We do this first with a two-day overnight retreat for incoming students providing relational experiences as we embody the ORCA-Stance, and second with an all-day experiential ORCA training session. During this new student retreat that takes place one week prior to the beginning of term, we start with building relationships among the faculty and incoming cohort of approximately 30 students. An intentional example of engaging in our

ORCA-Stance is facilitating an activity during the first evening where small student groups are formed and prompted to be curious with and about their faculty. Each group has the opportunity to ask an individual and/or all faculty any question resulting from their group's curiosities. The faculty attempts to model openness, respect, and accountability to power by responding to the questions; we also draw boundaries within our answers. Questions range from "What are your pet peeves in the classroom?", "How are you able to teach marriage and family therapy as someone who has been divorced?" to "Describe an awkward moment you had in session with a client." This activity offers students permission to be open and curious with each other while the faculty tries to embody the ORCA-Stance. This experience provides a foundational interchange of relationship formation for individual students with their cohort and faculty, regardless of the content of the student questions and responses.

At the end of the first week of classes, incoming students participate, along with several returning students/second-year students who are willing to participate, in our all-day ORCA training session. This day-long encounter provides both the language and another experiential example of our ORCA-Stance embodied in relationship, facilitating foundational relationship experiences. Isomorphic accountability of integrating the ORCA-Stance within our program shows up during the first foundational encounters that students have with our program, within program structures and relationship processes.

We empower students to self-select the option of completing our program on a full-time two-year track, a part-time three-year track, and even constructing a part-time four-year track. Courses and supervision groups are structured so that various tracks are combined at different times over a student's journey, resulting in the broadening of diversity. The blending of these full-time and part-time cohorts within each student's program experience expands the breadth and depth of exposure to different students, worldviews, and clinical applications. In other words, we structure the program to maximize "how to be in relationship with difference," allowing for numerous opportunities to engage in/be in relationship with difference while embodying the ORCA-Stance.

Although structure alone provides opportunity, albeit thin, to practice the ORCA-Stance, we intentionally infuse ORCA throughout all courses and supervision experiences. Our primary role is to develop the clinical competencies of our students. As teachers, it can be challenging to build a relationship with the class as a whole, with students individually, and to help to facilitate the development of relationships between students. In our program, not only do we aim to model our relational stance to our students while in the classroom, we also hope to develop their capacity to congruently live out the ORCA-Stance in meaningful ways in their everyday interactions with each other, clients, family, and friends. For instance, it is not uncommon for graduate students to challenge their teacher's point of view or views being communicated through course content. It is possible that such challenges may be received with antagonism, especially if the teacher lacks humility or senses that their authority is being challenged. However, the ORCA-Stance provides an alternative response to this scenario, as the teacher in front of the class has opportunities to live out the ORCA-Stance in the moment in meaningful ways.

When living out the ORCA-Stance, even in the context of being challenged by a student, we would recognize the need to be open to receiving what students are offering, but also the need to expand ourselves so that we can begin to understand where our students are coming from. Respect allows us to recognize the inherent worth of our students, and even when feeling challenged or disrespected, calls us to model respectful behaviors. At the same time, we would remain curious by asking questions about our student's views, promoting the development of a deeper understanding. Finally, accountability would challenge us to take ownership of our reactions to being challenged by students and the effect of those reactions on our interactions with our students in the context of the power differential.

Teachers also play a pivotal role in orchestrating relational processes between students that allows them to develop awareness and intentionality with how the ORCA-Stance shows up in their interpersonal interactions. For instance, teachers are often tasked with the responsibility of facilitating classroom conversations, which can be challenging when welcomed differences of opinions are expressed. However, such conversations are prime opportunities for teachers to help students to increase their awareness of how they connect and rely on the ORCA-Stance when differences exist. This process first requires that teachers become aware of the opportunity to engage students in conversation around their current dialogue, and also requires a degree of confidence to be able to slow the process in order to allow students to better track their interpersonal and internal processes. Teachers may ask students if their contributions to the conversation reflect an ORCA-Stance, and, if so, how. Teachers may pose their curiosities in conversation about how the ORCA-Stance may be showing up (e.g., "I wonder if and how curiosity is at play in our current interactions?" "If curiosity is not present, I wonder how we could benefit from it being present?"). Teachers may even consider asking students to explain how they are exhibiting ORCA principles in their current interactions. However we choose to bring ORCA into the classroom, our approaches must share the common objective of developing our students' capacity to practice ORCA in their everyday interactions with each other.

In addition to classroom interactions, we intentionally integrate the ORCA-Stance within the structure of practicum where we provide group clinical supervision. Practicum is a powerful space where the ORCA-Stance comes alive in the most intimate and active way. Influenced by the systemic framework of isomorphism and our attending to isomorphic accountability, we believe that if the ORCA-Stance is something we wish to see embodied in our students' clinical work, then it must be seen, experienced, and challenged in our supervisory relationships. With this in mind, we structure our practicum in a way that infuses the ORCA-Stance throughout the entire program and within each practicum meeting.

An example of an intentional structure and process within clinical practicum that fosters the ORCA-Stance occurs during the first of seven quarters of our practicum sequence. Groups are formed and divided into full-time and part-time cohorts, as part-time students have already begun to meet with clients during the second year of the three-year track. At the beginning of the second quarter of practicum, our Director of Clinical Training forms new small groups of no more than six students with differences in mind accounting for full- and/or part-time tracks, age, gender, internship site, life experience, and theoretical preference. These groups remain together for the remainder of the practicum sequence over the next six quarters. The formation of these small, stable practicum groups provides our students with an opportunity to develop a safe, supportive learning context for developing clinical competencies and exploring their self-awareness. In addition, we intentionally rotate a different supervisor through each group every six months, exposing students to a variety of supervision styles and providing more relationships in which to experience difference and the ORCA-Stance.

Parallel to the structure of our faculty meeting, each practicum meeting starts with a "check-in" where students can experience the grounding in "relationship with other" through the sharing of aspects of their professional and personal lives. This structural open space invites students to connect with themselves and with the group members, building relationships that foster the ORCA-Stance. During these check-ins students and supervisors learn to stay open and curious about themselves and each other, which often leads to deeper insights, understanding, compassion, and connection. When students feel seen and heard by a group of colleagues and supervisors, we often witness an increase in our students' sense of safety as well as in their capacity to gain additional competencies.

Although we strive to embody the ORCA-Stance ourselves, we humbly admit that there are many unfortunate and painful moments when we miss, overlook, and/or run away from opportunities to use the ORCA-Stance with our students and ourselves. For example, during the check-in one student shared her personal low, which involved being disrespected by the opposite gender in public. Students in practicum showed empathy and provided support as needed. One particular student, however, appeared quite upset and frustrated, making generalized comments about gender with no sense of curiosity. The supervisor missed the opportunity to be curious about this particular student's experience and was rather quick to judge this student, which ironically and isomorphically was the very reaction noted in the student. After the supervisor wrestled with her own ORCA reflection, she reached out to the student, humbly shared her observation and wondered about the student's experiences. After the superior and student revisited their own respective stories through a series of meaningful conversations exploring gender, they began to come to a more capable position of using the ORCA-Stance in a reflective and compassionate stance for themselves and others.

During each quarter of practicum we also are intentional to facilitate student reflections on their own ORCA-Stance ideas as it pertains to the case they presented as well as how the ORCA-Stance was honored in their practicum by themselves and supervisors during the group process. This process-related reflection is facilitated in various formats, both formal and informal. Formally, students are prompted to provide online feedback on practicum overall and the ORCA-Stance more specifically in an anonymous way. Informally, we strive to regularly invite the students to share their experiences of the supervision process. Due to the unequal nature of the supervisory relationship, we are mindful that our students are unlikely to initiate challenging discussions until they perceive our openness, curiosity, and genuine willingness to do so. Thus, inviting our students' experiences of the ORCA-Stance in supervision and remaining open to feedback from them has been a major way to hold ourselves accountable to the ORCA-Stance and to help our students to be better equipped with ORCA. We strive for students to experience our accountability to our power in our relationships with them.

At the conclusion of our program during the seventh clinical practicum, our students present a Final Clinical Portfolio informed by their relational experiences of our ORCA-Stance and reflective of their clinical work across the program. Their training is bookended with the ORCA-Stance, as it becomes a reflective tool for training. After the day-long training session during their first week of school, students write a reflection paper describing the ideas that they were introduced to and their own connection to the concepts. This reflection paper becomes the first chapter in their capstone project – their Clinical Portfolio.

Each quarter, we require students to add an additional chapter to their written Clinical Portfolio which ultimately includes a reflection paper on the ORCA day encounter; a description of their beliefs about human functioning and change; an in-depth description and critique of a specific theory applied in their clinical work; a comprehensive review of a family therapy case including a three-generation genogram; and a personal reflection of their own embodiment of the ORCA-Stance. Within both the theory and case sections, the student reflects again about the ORCA-Stance as they describe how each of the four characteristics of the ORCA-Stance is demonstrated within the particular theory they use. For example, if the student selects Narrative Therapy as their theory of choice, they might tie the idea of curiosity in the ORCA-Stance to Michael White's notion of taking a "not-knowing" position within the therapeutic relationship.

We integrate our training and experience of the ORCA-Stance further within the case section. The student reflects upon how the ORCA-Stance could be noted and become useful in their relationship with their clients. For example, in one student's case chapter, they reflected on the challenge of becoming respectful and curious when working with a young man who was involved in a gang. The student internally reacted to this client's value choices and reported difficulty in establishing a therapeutic relationship. However, in consultation with his supervision group, he was asked to think about and depend upon the ORCA-Stance as a practice of cultural humility. The student began by asking about the history of this young person's involvement in the gang and discovered that it had been influenced by his older brother's gang participation, which fulfilled the need to be part of a group in response to feelings of isolation and depression. The student had also struggled with isolation and depression, and had joined a church youth group that became a useful context for his own growth. By using the ORCA-Stance positions, the young therapist began developing cultural humility as he connected with, increased compassion for, and gained more understanding of his client's world more deeply through this reflective exercise.

Furthermore, in each quarter of their clinical practicum supervision, a student must provide a formal case presentation that includes a completed mental health assessment at individual and family level, a treatment plan, and an evaluation of the effectiveness of the therapy. In each presentation, the student is required to revisit the ORCA-Stance ideas as they pertain to the respective case. For example, if a student depended upon feminist perspective in their clinical encounter they might reference their accountability to social power in their work with a young child. The Clinical Portfolio along with a two-hour oral presentation that demonstrates their therapeutic orientation and development as a therapist is included in the last quarter of their training. It is given to a group of peers and is formally evaluated by their site and school supervisors.

Throughout our family therapy training program, we bring in the ORCA-Stance as a means for our students to reflect upon their clinical work with their client as well as self-of-the-therapist awareness. As students graduate from the program, we hope that it becomes a means to do self-supervision on their clinical work as they humbly interact with various cultural contexts.

It is a unique privilege to experience the ORCA-Stance with the students who participate in our MFT program. Whether during lectures or practicum supervision, the opportunities to embody being open, respectful, curious, and accountable to power are plentiful. As educators and role models, we take our isomorphic accountability and embodiment of the ORCA-Stance seriously. We hope that our students, the next generation of relational therapists, will do the same as we grow from them and they from us through our ORCA-Stance encounters embodied with cultural humility.

References

Edwards, S.A., Grauf-Grounds, C., & Cheon, H. (2011). Competencies with an ORCA stance: Developing the self of the therapist. *Family Therapy Magazine*, 10(5), 46–47.

Grauf-Grounds, C., Edwards, S.A., MacDonald, D., Quek, K., & Schermer Sellers, T. (2009). Developing graduate curricula faithful to professional training and a Christian worldview. *Christian Higher Education*, 8, 1–17. Retrieved from www.tandfonline.com/doi/pdf/10.10 80/15363750802134931?casa_token=Pbd4pYB0OvYAAAAA:6M5oDiQ6mmEd3iKsY-xms4X32Tj96hic_-5AmB753tSTgrAJ7VYVIwy5fu8AclUsCZcqpOD73w.

25

FAMILY THERAPY ALUMNI REFLECTIONS

Robin Moore, Marcus Comer, Rose Joiner,
Blake Griffin Edwards, Christina L.P. Steere,
Lauren Rimkus Pallay and Delene Jewett Galvin

Dozens of our alumni are currently out in the real-world therapy trenches, using the *ORCA-Stance* with clients, colleagues, and in other relationships. Seven of our former students, representing a wide range of therapeutic settings, were generous enough to share their observations and experiences with the ORCA-Stance and how it's impacted their lives.

Robin Moore

On the day that I was first introduced to the *ORCA-Stance*, the class did an exercise where we faced a partner, closed our eyes and spread our arms in relation to how open/closed we felt. When we opened our eyes, I remember thinking that I was the only person in the room with their arms almost as wide as they would go. This was very powerful but also searching – to be so open meant that I needed to pay attention to my power as a therapist and be accountable to that, i.e., develop boundaries.

About a year into full-time practice, I started teaching the ORCA-Stance to couples (I always credit my program when I share this information). This was so helpful that I started sharing it with all of my clients. I tell them that it is a stance, a way of being toward all fellow human beings. I usually bring up ORCA when my clients are feeling very closed, and it becomes a teachable moment. We talk about how it's easier to respect similarities, but much harder to respect differences. I spend most of the time on curiosity – how our brains are wired to make shortcuts and tend to leave out rich information about a person if we can't stay in a place of wonder. We talk about assumptions being the opposite of curiosity, and how asking "why" can be done non-judgmentally. When I share accountability to power with couples, I link it with attachment theory to help them to understand how much power they have in the relationship.

Because of my own experience as a white, heterosexual, middle-class, middle-aged, college-educated therapist, accountability to my power has been the most life changing. I am so much more at peace, perhaps even excited, when I am working with fellow human beings who have been marginalized, because I have become aware of the power that I have, and because I have been given tools to help me not to abuse this. I feel competent in passing on the good news – that we can own and use our power well! Taken together, the ORCA-Stance puts me in a grounded, compassionate head-and-heart space in all my relationships, at home and at work.

Marcus Comer

In my constant pondering, specifically while driving, the following summary of the ORCA-Stance came to mind. I felt I must share it as I continue to observe excitedly how pieces continue to fall together, evolve, and expand.

Openness: A state of being open to the idea that there are realities beyond our own; ours is *a* reality but not necessarily *the* reality. Openness – as a position or stance – is the readiness we are in, shown through the outward expression of respect.

Respect: Action/interaction with others; allowing for and creating space for others to experience or express their realities, ideas, and opinions free of judgment and persecution. Respect – as a position or stance – invites others to feel safe to share their experience with us.

Curiosity: An expression and method of receiving information from others and our experiences. Curiosity is our furthered exploration of experiences when we are open and respecting of realities/experiences of others and of our own. This may also be a further expression of respect and openness, a continuation of our invitation to others to share safely with us.

Accountability to power: Awareness mobilized in our actions and/or responses as a continuation of openness, respect, and curiosity. Accountability, particularly to social power is how we share information or respond to information, when others have felt secure to share their experience, such that we are careful of what influence may or may not come from our response and presence.

ORCA may also be understood in the following way:

- Openness: Open to receive information.
- Respect: Care in how we hold/manage/maintain information.
- Curiosity: Exploration/understanding/interpretation of information.
- Accountability: Care in how we reflect and share information.

The first three concepts/ideas relate to the reception and holding of information. Only the final one describes how we outwardly express information or not.

We may interpret this as a clue that listening is of great importance, our response being necessary or not. Albeit that others have expressed that we have two ears and one mouth, let us listen more than we speak.

Rose Joiner

I am an alumna of the class that graduated from the MFT department in June 2012. I was energized and excited to hear that the ORCA-Stance has been something that Seattle Pacific University would like to highlight. This stance has been incorporated into my everyday work as a therapist; it is the perfect lens through which to see clients, friends, or family. I am currently working as a full-time therapist, and will soon be licensed to practice in the state of Minnesota. I am working at the American Indian Family Center, immersed in a culture that is unknown and different to the one that I am used to.

As a Licensed Marriage and Family Therapist Associate, I am using openness towards a culture that is different. I find that this allows me to create a friendly closeness and opportunity to join with my new clients. I find that being respectful allows me to participate in "smudging" and in traditional Native American prayers, such as the passing of ceremonial tobacco; this brings me closer to my clients and allows me to partake in something that is greater than myself. I find that being curious with my clients takes judgment out of the equation, allowing a dynamic untainted therapeutic relationship to unravel in a unique and significant way. Finally, when I encourage my clients to be accountable to their own goals, and their own obligations, this honors them in a way that they may have never felt honored before. Being a therapist to someone and holding them accountable to their own truths and their own desire for change can be an extraordinary honor. Being a therapist with the ORCA-Stance has been eye opening, and it is woven into the person I am proud to be. It should be incorporated not only by therapists, but also by everyone in leadership, in homes, schools, etc.

Blake Griffin Edwards

In my current role, I serve active duty military service members at a base Fleet and Family Support Center. I often think back to the ways in which I was challenged as a student at SPU to remain aware of isomorphism, parallel emotional processes that help to inform and guide us during the course of therapy.

At every turn, I believe that it is my responsibility to circle back around to mindful reflections of my therapeutic interaction with clients. I tell them about my experience of them – what I have felt, wondered, observed, and thought, including my evolving hypotheses. I sometimes go to great lengths to reflectively communicate with my clients about some of the basic relational dynamics taking place between us in therapy in order to stir perspective and creativity *outside* the therapy room. An immersion in ORCA principles provided early and formative shape to my values and posture as a therapist. I have found that engaging at this level infuses transformative power into the therapeutic process.

Christina Steere

As an MFT alumna, I have incorporated ORCA into many aspects of my life. The main way I have incorporated into my professional life is by using it as a framework for teaching introductory lessons to groups of people. For example, I have used ORCA to teach a group of high school students and adult volunteers from our church who were preparing for a short-term mission trip in low income areas of the United States. I also find it to be particularly influential when speaking with individuals and groups who identify themselves as being of the millennial generation. It seems to appeal to their sense of wanting to know themselves better and make their relationships more meaningful. I appreciate learning the simple structure that has proven to be a firm foundation for my private practice and public speaking engagements.

Lauren Rimkus

I must admit that when I first heard reference to ORCA, I passed it off as a distinctive marketing phrase for an MFT program situated in the beautiful Pacific Northwest. However, as I began meeting with clients in the second quarter of the program I quickly realized that the acronym was a powerful foundation for the overwhelming task of attempting to gain competence as a therapist. I pictured it as a chair – literally as one professor had demonstrated – that allowed me to physically calm my anxiety in session and create space to connect with the individual across from me.

- Am I open: who is this person? Have I already made assumptions about them that may narrow the possibilities of our time together? Am I fully present right now? Can I attempt to set aside my own bias to be aware of the many layers of information they are offering within their story?
- Do I have respect for them: have I grown cynical? Do I believe that this person has resources and is capable of healing? Do I trust that they know themselves better than I do? Do I believe that as a human being, they are just as much deserving of grace and presence as anyone else? Do I take their issues as seriously as they do?
- Am I curious: have I allowed myself to jump to any conclusions prematurely? Have I consciously made an attempt to ask one more question before making a statement? Do I trust my intuition and slow down accordingly when caught by a phrase or emotion? Am I relaxed and connected enough to be playful when appropriate? Am I beginning to understand their story from their perspective wholly?

- Am I accountable to power: have I paused to consider the other dynamics that are present within and outside of the room? Gender? SES? Age? Race? Culture? What might get in the way of me reflecting and assisting this person and/or acting on their behalf? In the case of a couple, how are these unspoken dynamics of power playing out between them as well?

The usefulness of this foundation has extended beyond my graduate studies and into my growth as a professional. When I feel confused, stuck, or confounded, I often find myself taking a deep breath and reflectively moving through the checklist again. It somehow cuts through theoretical concepts, interventions, and diagnoses that are completely necessary but can also serve to muddy the waters of relationship. ORCA grounds me – a concrete way of finding center as a therapist.

Being in a program that focuses on openness, respect, curiosity, and accountability has been an integral part to my personal and professional development. I spent a year in a graduate program that seemed to breed arrogance, narrow-mindedness, and the idea that the therapist knows all. It's been liberating and healing to go from that atmosphere to a program that centers itself in quite the opposite way. The intentionality, reverence for clients, and humility that the ORCA-Stance teaches is profound and fundamental to truly compassionate therapeutic care.

Training therapists with the ORCA-Stance not only empowers clients, but therapists as well. It take the weight off the therapists to be "experts" in others' lives and authoritive in the relationship. ORCA teaches therapists to be authentic and gracious with anyone they come into contact with. It empowers clients by truly honoring their stories, their experiences, and the courage it takes to bring what they can into therapy. There is no other foundation from which I would want to practice from. ORCA informs every area of my work, both professionally and personally. I am confident that its foundation helps me to be the best therapist I can be.

Delene Jewett

When I was a supervisor at Catholic Community Services in Tacoma, I introduced the ORCA-Stance to therapists and caseworkers. I have found it a truly valuable tool to remind myself of how to be present with clients and to be mindful of how I am conceptualizing a situation and presenting myself. I still think about the ORCA-Stance, and I graduated nine years ago. There are so many therapy theories, articles to read, new research, techniques … and for me to remember and use something I first learned about at the beginning of graduate school, during a one-day training session (on my 24th birthday, when I would have rather been doing something else!) shows that the ORCA-Stance made an impact on me. I find it useful and it has stuck with me.

26

ETHICAL DILEMMAS

Don MacDonald and Peter M. Rivera

Ethics is knowing the difference between what you have a right to do and what is right to do.

(Judge Potter Stewart)

Therapists can hurt as well as help. In addition, therapist neutrality is a myth; therapists highly influence what does or does not occur in therapy. Furthermore, the privacy inherent within psychotherapy necessitates that clinicians be self-monitoring, self-aware, and self-managing in order to provide responsible and effective services (Hubble, Duncan, Miller & Wampold, 2010; Wilcoxon, Remley & Gladding, 2013). Taking all these factors into consideration, it is vital that therapists have guidelines for providing services. Ethical codes seek to provide such structure.

Ethical codes afford broad guidelines for appropriate therapist conduct (Wilcoxon et al., 2013). As such, their relationship with openness, respect, curiosity, and accountability to power is primarily in terms of accountability. That is, the therapist is accountable to clients, colleagues, professional organization(s), and society as a whole.

Guidelines, however, cannot address the idiosyncrasies of each ethical issue that arises. Therapists must exercise their professional judgment and, in consultation with others, decide upon appropriate courses of action vis-à-vis particular clients dealing with particular issues in particular contexts (Cohen & Cohen, 1999). This is where ORCA comes to bear. The four constructs, as discussed in other chapters, help clients to share their stories. Among other issues, these stories contain matters with ethical and/or legal ramifications that might call for intervention to address those issues.

One way that society, via the legal system, reminds therapists about accountability to power is through disciplinary measures, including malpractice suits.

Charges of malpractice apply when therapists (a) fail to provide appropriate services for clients and/or (b) provide faulty services (Wilcoxon et al., 2013). If clients experience demonstrable harm through therapists' inaction or faulty action, then malpractice pertains and the therapists have belied accountability.

Case Study

I conducted therapy with a 20-year old Euro-American man. His stated interest in therapy at this point in life was to "sort through some family issues." Developmentally, the issue was a common one for young men and women who are launching or preparing to launch from their families, particularly families that have resided in the United States for several generations (Berger, 2014). He said that he was the elder of two children, with a 17-year old sister still at home. His parents were in a first marriage of nearly 25 years. The parents had married at nearly 30 years of age, having focused a lot on their careers during their twenties. His father had risen to a prominent county government position and was likely to retire in a few years' time in order to begin a second occupation. After the children were born, his mother became a full-time homemaker. When his sister was aged about 12, the mother returned part-time to the workforce as an accountant.

During our second meeting the young man described the relationships between the four members of his immediate family and members of the extended family as very close, "sometimes too close." When he said "too close," I noticed that his voice inflection dropped and he broke the eye contact that he usually held with me. I became curious about these differences from his baseline behaviors and asked him what he meant by the phrase. He hesitated, avoiding eye contact, and said that he did not want to talk about it, at least not now. I respected his wishes, even though I was sure that he was feeling quite anxious and perhaps conflicted about how much detail to share; besides, this was only our second session and he was still deciding how trustworthy and/or safe I was around difficult issues. Wanting to convey respect, I asked him what he wanted to do next and he chose to talk about other family-related matters such as cousins who were about his age being some of his best friends.

At the start of the third meeting, it was apparent that the young man was anxious. He walked into my office lightly wringing his hands, avoiding eye contact, and walking directly to a chair, sitting on the front edge of it and leaning slightly forward. Out of respect and continued openness, I sat a little further away from him than usual, inferring that my physical closeness might provoke even more anxiety. Following an initial silence, he blurted out that for as long as he could remember his father almost always bathed him and his sister. He bathed each child separately. He said that when he was seven or eight years old, he began to feel uncomfortable with part of the bathing process that involved washing his genitals. He stated that he had said nothing to his father about his discomfort until he was around 11 years old. He said that when he voiced his discomfort, his father stopped bathing him altogether and never explained why. The client did not know about his sister's bathing experiences, as the siblings never discussed it.

After discussing the bathing experiences further, I reminded him of the informed consent form and process, wherein I was accountable as a mandated reporter of potential sexual abuse. He acknowledged reading that part of the consent. I also stated that since his sister, a minor, still resided in the home of his father, I was legally required to notify Child Protective Services. He was vexed that I had to make a report. I said that I realized he was naturally upset, as he had stated that he loved his father, despite his misgivings over the bathing actions. He was also aware that disclosure of sexual abuse allegations might jeopardize his father's career and retirement, which helped to fuel his distress. I acknowledged that this was indeed a dilemma and we talked about possible ramifications for his father and family.

Given that I was a mandated reporter, I gave the young man a number of options for reporting (Stadler, 1989). He chose to call his father himself and tell what he had shared with me, while I was present in the room. I was glad that a conversation about this suppressed issue had begun between father and son. I was also glad that the young man and I were able to immediately debrief the conversation. We also talked about how he might continue conversations with other family members. Finally, I gave him information about family therapy services in the vicinity of his family's residence, in case other family members sought assistance.

Hearing about this young man's concerns was difficult. I have heard versions of this sad story many times over the past 40-plus years, and the experience gets no easier to hear. Being the father of sons, this instance felt somewhat personal as well, as the notion of sexually fondling any of my sons was revolting to me. Nevertheless, I sought to remain open to hearing the young client's entire story, recognizing that helping him to get it out was the start of his healing and hopefully of family healing as well.

Ideas for Best Practice

- An obvious yet perhaps overlooked idea is to be familiar with current ethical and legal codes. When a potential concern with ethical overtones arises in therapy, a therapist who knows the codes can quickly and intentionally decide how to draw upon ORCA and other resources to help the client(s).
- A second idea is for the therapist to understand him or herself well enough to recognize how the therapist is responding to the client(s) as the session progresses. Ethical decisions are easier to sort out when the therapist sees how client issues affect issues in the therapist's life and vice versa. For instance, a therapist's blind spot about his or her own self could compromise openness, curiosity, and perhaps respect when the therapist unconsciously feels threatened by what the client(s) shares.

- Related to the second idea is a third one of honestly assessing therapeutic competencies. Therapists are ethically obligated to work within their competencies so as to avoid possible harm to the client(s). Openness to this aspect of self will enable the therapist to realize when it is important to refer, confer, and/or seek supervision.
- Curiosity is a fourth aid for ethical therapists. Clients often raise issues that are either new to therapists or nuanced in ways that are unfamiliar to therapists. Issues such as race, culture, ethnicity, language, and national origin frequently bring into sessions matters and experiences not encountered in the therapists' own history. Therapists seeking to operate in the spirit of ORCA will become curious and engage in professional growth activities (e.g., supervision, continuing education) so as to increase the quality of services that they provide.

References

Berger, K. (2014). *The developing person through the lifespan* (7th edn.). New York: Worth.

Cohen, E.D., & Cohen, G.S. (1999). *The Virtuous Therapist: Ethical Practice of Counseling and Psychotherapy*. Belmont, CA: Wadsworth.

Hubble, M.A., Duncan, B.L., Miller, S.D., & Wampold, B.E. (2010). Introduction, in B.L. Duncan, S.D. Miller, B.E. Wampold, & M.A. Hubble, *The Heart and Soul of Change: Delivering what Works in Therapy* (2nd edn., pp. 23–46). Washington, DC: American Psychological Association.

Stadler, H.A. (1989). Balancing ethical responsibilities: Reporting child abuse and neglect. *The Counseling Psychologist*, 17, 102–110. Retrieved from https://journals.sagepub.com/doi/abs/10.1177/0011000089171006.

Wilcoxon, S.A., Remley, T.P., Jr., & Gladding, S.T. (2013). *Ethical, Legal, and Professional Issues in the Practice of Marriage and Family Therapy* (5th edn.). Boston, MA: Pearson.

27

CLINICAL SUPERVISION

Lori Kimmerly

I began with ORCA supervision quite by accident. I was a student in a practicum group with younger students and our leader was not always ORCA oriented. I would often step in and attempt to embody ORCA, to build up my fellow students. It became great practice for my supervision style, unknown at the time. Because I come from an ORCA-based program, ORCA is the subconscious way I tend to think and supervise. This chapter will unravel and examine the similarities and differences of ORCA principles when applied during or outside supervision.

Openness

I tend to be open about my process and history of growth, coming as I do from a program where self-of-the-therapist issues are explored. When giving supervision to student interns, I will often wonder aloud about what is happening for them with clients and ask why. The supervision process tends to be influenced by both the supervisor's and the supervisee's own awareness, often referred to as isomorphism. Isomorphism, by definition, is when things take on a similar form. In therapeutic terms, it is when the client/family, therapist/trainee and supervisor take on a similar form either consciously or unconsciously (Weir, 2009). This interaction and sameness can often bring up multiple layers of self-of-the-therapist issues that the therapist/trainee and supervisor discuss and work through.

For one of my supervisees, there was nothing more activating than a suicidal client, who also happened to be her first client. She called to have live supervision because she suspected that a new client was suicidal. We were suddenly knee-deep in the client/trainee/supervisor isomorphism process, in which openness was required yet felt personal and blurry for both of us. Aponte (1994) looks at the person/practice process of supervision and the differences between personal therapy and supervision. Does it become a dual relationship with both trainee and supervisor swimming in their own stuff? As defined in Aponte's 1994 article, there is a "relationship with dual qualities in contrast to a dual relationship in which the trainer being paid to train a therapist simultaneously accepts payment from the trainee as a patient" (p. 4). In this case, I encouraged the supervisee to examine her own self-of-the-therapist issues in order to remain open to the therapeutic and supervision experience.

It's hard to know in the moment, as a supervisor, about what to disclose. If I've been suicidal myself, do I tell a trainee that information, taking on an open stance? A disclosing, open supervisor (Storm & Todd, 1997) would talk about their own experience with clients in the past, about feeling nervous, about their own family of origin issues and how they use self with clients. In contrast, a non-disclosing supervisor would not talk about what they would do in the situation or the issues it could bring up for them. One thought could be that a non-disclosing supervisor might actually be more likely to allow the supervisee to have their own experience.

What are the boundaries, I asked myself, as I watched a trainee become tearful about how the process of having a suicidal client has shaken her into wondering whether she should even be a therapist? How do you decide whether or not to disclose when issues come up for trainees and/or supervisors? We are contracting to have only a professional relationship during supervision. Roles are clear and defined. Does this slow down openness?

There was an occasion when I was fully open to one of my interns in a way that I never had been before or since. There was a school shooting on the Seattle Pacific University campus and I got a text from one of my interns; she was near campus and didn't know what was going on, but requested prayer. In our back and forth dialogue via text, when things felt unsure, I blurted out in text, "I love you." I felt that this was too open, even in this difficult moment, so I followed it up with, "In a supervisorly way." When the air had cleared, this moment became a touchstone of both care and humor. Did this cross the line of boundaries between supervisor and supervisee? In both of our collective opinions and discussions, it did not, and with openness in the *ORCA-Stance*, we were able to have this conversation, in depth.

Respect

I once was supervised by a person who took his role as an authority figure *literally*. I understood that I was to follow the policies and procedures of the office in his way. This type of supervisor would bring to the training process a modernistic worldview, looking at supervision with a more expert stance. There is a clear path to being supervised and the supervisor provides the answers. This type of supervisor would possibly bring to the table a desire to know and share the answers with supervisees, perhaps limiting openness. As Aponte describes though, therapists are regarded as less like the authority figures than they once were and this seems to be the case with supervisors as well. Over time, our therapies have become more personal and interactive and thus more collaborative, leading to a lessening of the modern stance in a supervisor role (Aponte & Carlsen, 2009). It could also be described as holding cultural humility as a supervisor and understanding how being less authoritative would lead to more respect, not less.

In contrast, I have supervised millennials almost exclusively (the generation of individuals born between 1980 and 2000) and I try to embody a postmodern worldview. According to Riggio (2010), millennials are known to "play well with others" so I have focused on following a "team" approach with all trainees doing co-therapy with at least one other team member. Millennials also want recognition and to be taken seriously, so I provide lots of praise and feedback along with giving them the ability to make decisions that impact the practice and procedures that we follow. Additionally, Anderson et al. (2017) discuss how important timely feedback is to trainees and how difficult it is to provide it in supervision. Millenials want their workspace to be employee-centered and fun, so we have regular team meetings in which we talk collaboratively about how to make the office better. I am not in a clear leadership role, but rather I tailor my role to be equal with theirs in order to fit their needs and desires – which has led to mutual respect and teamwork. On several occasions, I have had millennial students tell me how respectful this is and how it fits their communication style. I take in the experience of the student and tailor the supervision in a non-rigid way, knowing that I may not have the ultimate answer or directive in my own, more postmodern approach to supervision.

There are many styles of supervision and Storm (1997) examines these. Both the authoritative and directive supervisor would fall under the "modernistic supervisor" lens. An authoritative supervisor directs the supervision and is closed, rather than open, with trainees. A directive supervisor would tell a supervisee what to do. An example might be a supervisor who takes on a solution-focused stance, which is about the here and now – what did the supervisee experience in the session that is reportable? This would possibly be seen as disrespectful to the trainee's experience, inviting very little, if any, discussion about self-of-the-therapist issues.

In contrast, a postmodern style of supervision would be a supervisor who is affiliative, who asks what the supervisee is hoping to get out of supervision, or who takes a non-directive stance. A less directive approach might be psychodynamic in nature, or might look more at countertransference and the like (Storm, 1997). Both of these styles of supervision could be considered postmodern and possibly more suitable to millennial trainees who are open to collaboration, feedback, and team building (Riggio, 2010).

Curiosity

Therapists tend to wonder out loud about things and certainly supervision is influenced by this natural state of being. I wonder about what clients and sessions feel like, what trainees are learning, their successes and perceived failures. The isomorphic process very much comes into play in my curiosity in how and why it influences all the systems involved. This isomorphic process is influenced by either opening or closing down their inherent curiosity.

Supervision is heavily influenced by isomorphism, whether conscious or not. There are three types of isomorphism: mimetic, coercive, and normative. A mimetic style of isomorphism is when a supervisor models an approach to therapy and expects trainees to mimic them in their work. It gives structure and something to hold on to for both parties in the training process. Coercive isomorphism involves the reality that therapy is a business and is beholden to systems that provide funding and payments, such as insurance companies and state-funded plans. Normative isomorphism is led by the critical areas of development, accreditation standards, and ethics (Weir, 2009).

The various levels of isomorphism become more obvious according to the training setting. In a university or academic setting, the structure of supervision is usually well defined with a set framework. The institution would also have expectations for supervisor responsibility (Storm & Todd, 1997). The supervision contract is primarily between the supervisor and the institution and thus influences my normative isomorphism related to accredited program ethics, standards and faculty feedback. This setting with normative isomorphism might lead to less freedom to implement curiosity (Weir, 2009).

I was trained in a community mental health organization and saw at first hand the complexity of coercive isomorphism. Clients must meet certain criteria to become clients in the first place, which can lead to organizational politics and policies that influence treatment. A trainee might be trained somewhat isomorphically (or directly) by more evidence-based practices or designated criteria based on the politics of the setting. The presence of politics and procedures are not curiosity friendly. The system likely may be very structured with defined tasks that must be completed, and curiosity could be limited by the number of cases and time allotted to supervision. Added responsibilities of paperwork, recordkeeping, case notes, etc., only add to the complexity (Storm, 1997).

I train students in a private practice setting. While my practice is certainly influenced by normative isomorphism, along with the need for ethical standards and a fit with the university program with which I am associated, it is not heavily influenced by either. I am openly curious about process most of the time. I am careful not to let my particular passions about therapeutic approach influence any trainee to choose the way they practice themselves. As each of the clients pay according to a sliding scale (private pay), it doesn't fall under coercive isomorphism, as we are not trying to keep anyone happy except the clients. I only do one-to-one supervision as well, leaving time to discuss as many or as few cases as needed for each trainee. It's not a perfect system, but has been key to open curiosity on both sides.

Accountability

As hard as I try to be postmodern and ORCA-influenced in my approach to supervision, nowhere is the unequal nature of the supervisor/supervisee relationship more unequal than when dealing with ethical and legal issues. A key job of the supervisor is to assesses what the student needs developmently (such as their level of clinical skills) and to match their style of supervision to meet the training standards and goals (Morgan & Sprenkle, 2007). Regardless of the blurriness of the dual relationship, indistinct boundaries, legal and ethical issues, and awareness of all parties, the supervisor is the ultimate authority. When legal and ethical issues come up, the intern-supervisor relationship becomes unbalanced and unequal, making it hard for both.

For example, one of my trainees reflected,

> After practicing for about two months, I had a person on my caseload where I thought I would need to call CPS [Child Protective Services], but the situation was complex and confusing. I called Lori, who utilized openness and curiosity to ask questions about the case. I felt entirely respected and that my experience and opinion mattered. At the same time, she was accountable to her position of power as my supervisor, a stance that I greatly valued as a new therapist trying to understand my professional responsibility in a complex situation. I felt held and reassured, while at the same time empowered to own my position as the therapist on the case. Having a supervisor who embodies the ORCA-Stance is invaluable, both for role modeling and for teaching. I have felt supported, understood, and valued in my supervision, and this story in particular highlights the importance of ORCA in providing meaningful supervision for the supervisee.

The challenge of making the abuse call is the possibility of ruining the therapeutic relationship of all the parties involved. At times a supervisee is hoping for a loophole to not have to call CPS and ultimately it is something that has to be done. The supervisee is the one who has the relationship with the individual or family, and risks losing it, along with the possibility of hours needed for licensure.

Liability comes into the accountability to power equation, no matter the setting. A male supervisee at my practice wanted to take on a couple where there was a potential domestic violence issue in which neither I, the supervisor, nor the supervisee had little to no expertise. The supervisee thought that he could handle the case and the supervisor has to make the ultimate decision as to whether or not such a case could lead to liability or safety issues for the client(s) or supervisee. I needed to set a limit which protected my practice; this decision fit with an

ORCA-Stance focus on accountability. The supervisee experienced the limit as making a decision without him; it also reduced the number of his clinical hours toward licensure. I could understand his concerns, but also needed to attend to my own. The tension that exists in the supervisor/trainee experience can and does feel difficult to manage within the relationship. It is imperative, especially in the area of accountability to power, to hold a stance of cultural humility: the supervisor holds and acknowledges the inherent lack of ability to hold a postmodern stance and how this could impact supervisees and their sense of their own internal power or lack thereof. In such circumstances, it's vitally important to bring in the other portions of the ORCA-Stance as a supervisor – of being open, respectful, and curious in those conversations in order to balance this sector with supervisees.

References

Anderson, T., Crowley, M.J., Binder, J.L., Heckman, B.D., & Patterson, C.L. (2017). Does the supervisor's teaching style influence the supervisee's learning prescribed techniques? *Psychotherapy Research*, 27(5), 549–557. Retrieved from http://dx.doi.org/10. 1080/10503307.2015.1136442.

Aponte, H. (1994). How personal can training get? *Journal of Marital and Family Therapy*, 20 (1), 3–15. Retrieved from https://onlinelibrary.wiley.com/doi/abs/10.1111/j.1752-060 6.1994.tb01007.x.

Aponte, H., & Carlsen, J. (2009). An instrument for person-of-the-therapist supervision. *Journal of Marital and Family Therapy*, 35(4), 395–405. Retrieved from www.sfvcamft. org/resources/Documents/Aponte%20Article.pdf.

Morgan, M., & Sprenkle, D. (2007). Toward a common-factors approach to supervision. *Journal of Marital and Family Therapy*, 33(1), 1–17. Retrieved from www.wyomingcouns elingassociation.com/wp-content/uploads/Morgan-Sprenkle-2007-Common-Factors-S upervision.pdf.

Riggio, R. (2010). How to lead the Millennial generation. *Psychology Today*. Retrieved from www.psychologytoday.com/us/blog/cutting-edge-leadership/201005/how-lead-t he-millennial-generation.

Russell, C.S., DuPree, J.W., Beggs, M.A., Peterson, C.M., & Anderson, M.P. (2007). Responding to remediation and gatekeeping challenges in supervision, *Journal of Marital and Family Therapy*, 33(2), 227–244. Retrieved from http://dx.doi.org.ezproxy.spu.edu/ 10.1111/j.1752-0606.2007.00018.x.

Storm C., & Todd, T. (1997). *The Reasonably Complete Systemic Supervisor Resource Guide*. New York, Lincoln, and Shanghai: Authors Choice Press. Retrieved from https://book s.google.com/books?id=QEwwmlUc6UIC&printsec=frontcover&dq=The+Reasonably +Complete+Systemic+Supervisor+Resource+Guide&hl=en&sa=X&ved=0ahUKEwjc 9Kn6z6bhAhXT-lQKHWfAB4gQ6AEIMTAB#v=onepage&q=The%20Reasonably% 20Complete%20Systemic%20Supervisor%20Resource%20Guide&f=false.

Weir, K. (2009). Countering the isomorphic study of isomorphism: Coercive, mimetic and normative isomorphic trends in the training, supervision, and industry of marriage and family therapy. *Journal of Family Psychotherapy*, 20, 60–71. Retrieved from www.tandfon line.com/doi/full/10.1080/08975350802716517?casa_token=81rBR4SF_IUAAAAA:pS HDxhqEAh6ZJbgmpOjlZ51RowXls859nwLmzbqBCXlSSmuMKrJbBvZIpN6TzrJTU vOLFU5iVA.

28

COLLABORATING WITH CHURCHES

Strengthening our Communities of Meaning

Tina Schermer Sellers and Shawn Whitney

> When we learn to think with the mind descended into the heart integrating cognition and emotion with other faculties like sensation, intuition and bodily knowledge, the result can be insight, wisdom and the courage to act on what we know.
>
> *(Parker Palmer,* Healing the Heart of Democracy*)*

Speaking the Unspoken: Sexuality and the Church (Tina Schermer Sellers)

I recall one of the first times I was asked to walk with a congregation into the wild wilderness of how to begin to talk safely about sexuality. It came after a colleague and her pastor returned from a women's retreat where participants told stories about transformative moments in their lives. Isabelle (fictitious name), a colleague of mine, had opted that night to share how her life had been transformed after writing her sexual autobiography in a graduate human sexuality course, and how she had come to embrace her body and sexuality as gifts rather than burdens as a result. Her slow journey of healing had begun to transform her as a woman, a wife, a daughter, a friend, a therapist, and a believer in Jesus. Her story struck a chord, and you could have heard a pin drop as she spoke in the conference hall. As soon as the story period ended, women came up to her one by one to tell their stories of sexual pain. Jane, the pastor, decided with Isabelle that night that they must find a way to address the issue of sexuality in the church and to open this library of untold pain that so desperately needed a compassionate and loving witness. But how?

Jane called me the next week. Together, we strategized on how to begin this tender conversation. We all recognized the amount of fear, pain, and shame that shrouded most of the sexual stories they had heard at the conference. Yet we also saw a paradox in how little most of them understood about that shame or that story. The combination of great shame and great ignorance was the recipe for high anxiety and even higher reactivity – an emotional landmine. We designed a two-day workshop for Jane's church, in order to ease us into this conversation. Friday night's session introduced the principle of ORCA, describing the importance of creating a safe place for everyone who was there. I reiterated the pain and suffering in the majority story, and how we needed to bring enormous grace, compassion, and love to ourselves and to each other as we gently moved through the conversation. I let them know that if I got a sense that we were straying away from our ORCA-Stance, I would stop us and gently move us back.

That set the stage for our first exploration into the landscape of the sexual developmental lifecycle. I began there because I wanted everyone to start on the same page with basic education about what normal developmental curiosity looks like. I wanted them to normalize their own stories and to start to extend grace to themselves. Before beginning another section, we would return to ORCA and to a question-and-answer period. The next day we covered some anatomy, along with some male and female neurobiological differences that show up frequently in heterosexual relationship dynamics. I also introduced some ideas from ancient Hebrew mysticism for heightening intention, connection, and pleasure that can allow for ecstatic and transformative spiritual experiences to occur during sexual sharing with one's partner. We then spent over an hour discussing any question that came up over lunch and in the small groups, which allowed us to cover a lot of ground that we hadn't covered in the formal prepared talk. Our organic discussions, in the context of our ORCA-Stance, were as fertile and integral to the learning as our planned topic discussions. We also recorded the audio of the entire two-day experience so that anyone in the congregation could go back to the discussion at any time and listen again.

The two-day event, titled "Beginning the Conversation: The Sacred Gift of Sexuality," ended up being the first of several talks held by that congregation. They later put together an event for parents known as "Raising Sexually, Spiritually, and Emotionally Healthy Kids," and another one for parents and leaders of youth, known as the "Youth and Adult Sexuality Forum." They ran yet another seminar on gender challenges for men and women co-leading in the church, and one for pastors and their wives, called "Nourishing Private Spaces to be Your Favorite Places." If you haven't been part of the conservative Christian church, it's hard to appreciate the delicate nature of this subject, the amount of reactivity that pervades any mention of sex, and the depth of anguish involved for many people in speaking about such things – and hence the magnitude of the accomplishment by this church! The pastor is a courageous woman who saw a felt need in her congregation and she was willing to figure out how to try and meet it, even if it meant risk and mess. Interestingly, it wasn't as messy as she had feared, and people were grateful for the chance to be seen, known, loved, and accepted in their truth. In many ways, the church's conversations were a testament to the container that is created when ORCA is used well: how it can hold tension and difference, allowing people to wade their way through a tough issue together as a community of radically valuable and radically imperfect humans.

Using ORCA as a Model for Dating and Marriage (Shawn Whitney)

The ORCA-Stance can also be applied well to issues of marriage. In religious circles, there is often a very strong focus on marriage preparation and on premarital counseling for couples who are engaged. From counseling to videos, to books to retreats, a multitude of resources exist for couples once they become engaged, but in my experience, the same isn't true for dating couples. This is quite unfortunate, given the major decisions couples make about their relationship while they are dating.

When my wife Melissa and I discovered the lack of resources in our faith community and city, our church supported us in starting a class for dating couples. For several years, we had 15–25 couples each quarter agree to explore their lives, their faith, their sexuality, and the future of their relationship with us. We began each eight-week session by introducing the ORCA-Stance as the posture we encouraged each participant to take while they explored topics in and out of class with their partner. Each time we introduced ORCA, a collective exhale could be heard around the room, as if to say, "I can feel safer being vulnerable if we seek to embody this stance with each other." This kind of safety was essential to exploring the challenging weekly discussion questions we provided as homework. As it happened, each quarter at least one couple would decide to end their relationship, but in our opinion, these couples didn't fail to embody ORCA or to apply the information learned. Rather, the opposite occurred: they took risks to be transparent with their partners, discovered a new level of clarity, and decided to end the relationship as a result of the work they had done. Their decisions to humbly examine their relationships proved to be challenging and meaningful.

In general, the dating couples we encountered were earnestly seeking direction and mentorship for their relationships. We commonly continued our conversations after class at the community dinner that our church provided on Sunday evenings, and the couples wanted to hear more about the relationship between Melissa and I, solicit advice for their relationships, and gain wisdom about how to embody ORCA with others. Melissa and I would often look at each other and laugh when we were asked for guidance, because we knew that we were no different from them. We could certainly relate to their desires for answers since we were looking for them in our own relationship together.

One dinner conversation stands out to me as particularly significant. Three dating couples joined us with the purpose of understanding how to embody

ORCA when the other partner does not. We collectively provided examples of conversations over the years that had gone well, and examples where things had not gone so well. As we spoke, a common theme emerged: a desire to engage with the other. Regardless of the topic, that desire for engagement was what caused all of us to initiate conversations in the first place. The trajectory of each interaction was largely influenced by the amount of openness present. When we were open, the conversation often resulted in increased connection. On the other hand, a lack of openness would typically stall our ability to embody ORCA. "What do I do when he's not open?" one woman asked me. "Excellent question," I said. "It's important to remember that the elements of ORCA perpetuate each other. For example, if you are curious instead of defensive about his lack of openness, he might open up." With a smile forming on her face, she turned to her partner and said, "I'll try to be curious." I won't soon forget his blushing face, nor his reply: "I know you're for me." Simple, yet significant.

Ideas for Best Practice: The Power of ORCA

In the ORCA dating class, we talked about how this stance was helpful in four different ways when it came to building a strong intimate relationship that could stand the test of time. We broke it down in the following ways and discussed how these features could be understood and strengthened when navigating all the times of growth and challenge that couples inevitably face.

- *All four aspects of ORCA beget the others.* Partners often know each other's vulnerabilities. Being accountable to power and choosing to affirm instead of hurt can often result in greater mutual respect.
- *Modeling has the power to transform.* When partners model openness, they have a difficult time remaining closed. While they may not respond immediately, persistence and time are often what it takes to help them to open up.
- *Trust is essential.* Often a partner's resistance to connection is related to a lack of trust. Without trust, partners will struggle to embody ORCA. Although it can be challenging, particularly after a betrayal, rebuilding trust can enliven ORCA between partners.
- *Emotional safety is worth the effort.* Related to trust, emotional safety is key to building and maintaining a culture of connection for partners. When a partner is resistant, it is important to validate it and be curious about it. If a resistant partner receives curiosity instead of criticism, they will likely feel an increased sense of safety.

In general, people want to know their partner is "for them," that they are safe. Embodying the ORCA-Stance is a powerful way to reinforce this experience of being seen, known, loved, and accepted. We appreciate that vulnerability and transparency are risky postures, and yet taking these risks can elucidate the truth of our relationships. That clarity is an imperative aspect of a healthy foundation for intimate relationships.

ORCA as a Way of Life

People, and all of their diversity, strengths, and flaws, are central to the existence of churches. Without people, a church is just another building with a signboard out front. Similarly, people embody the ORCA-Stance. Without people, ORCA is merely a concept. Both churches and ORCA are meaningful because of people and their capacity to engage relationally with one another. Yet the quality of the church experience and the quality of a relationship is to be found in interpersonal intersectionality – what happens between the people, how they engage each other – how they embody cultural humility. ORCA provides the scaffolding, the "how," for doing connection in meaningful, grace-filled ways.

We feel strongly that embodying the ORCA-Stance is necessary in order to dig more deeply with people, both inside and beyond the walls of faith communities. Bringing each other openness, respect, curiosity, and accountability to our power offers an opportunity for us to learn about our similarities and our differences in a deep and consequential way. It enriches each of us, allowing us to be for each other, rather than against each other. As we said above, people yearn to be seen, known, loved, and accepted. Shame, fear, and isolation hurt our ability to experience these truths. Our hope in bringing the ORCA-Stance to churches is to invite them to extend this grace-filled way of being to every person they meet. ORCA can reduce shame and increase curiosity about soulful matters, bringing diverse individuals together in community and emulating a loving presence – one that is at the heart of the faith experience.

References

Palmer, P.J. (2014). *Healing the Heart of Democracy: The Courage to Create a Politics Worthy of the Human Spirit.* Hoboken, NJ: John Wiley & Sons. Retrieved from www.courager enewal.org/wpccr/wp-content/uploads/HealingHeartDemocracy-Prelude-ParkerJPalm er.pdf.

Schermer Sellers, T. (2017). *Sex, God, and the Conservative Church: Erasing Shame from Sexual Intimacy.* New York: Routledge. Retrieved from https://books.google.com/ books?id=K5y8DgAAQBAJ&printsec=frontcover&dq=S ex,+God,+and+the+conserva tive+church%E2%80%94Erasing+shame+from+sex ual+intimacy.&hl=en&sa=X&ved= 0ahUKEwjG4Yqk0KbhAhXxwMQHHRfQApcQ6AEIKjAA#v=onepage&q=Sex%2C %20God%2C%20and%20the%20conservative%20church%E2%80%94Erasing%20shame %20from%20sexual%20intimacy.&f= false.

29

COLLABORATING WITH PHYSICIANS

Jackie Williams-Reade

> It is unsettling to find how little it takes to defeat success in medicine. You come as a professional equipped with expertise and technology. You do not imagine that a mere matter of etiquette could foil you. But the social dimension turns out to be as essential as the scientific – matters of how casual you should be, how formal, how reticent, how forthright. Also: how apologetic, how self-confident, how money-minded. In this work against sickness, we begin not with genetic or cellular inter-actions, but with human ones. They are what make medicine so complex and fascinating. How each interaction is negotiated can determine whether a doctor is trusted, whether a patient is heard, whether the right diagnosis is made, the right treatment given. But in this realm there are no perfect formulas.
>
> *(Gawande, 2008, pp. 81–82)*

Often when therapists collaborate with physicians and other medical professionals, we experience a variety of emotions, ranging from excitement at being able to take our place as colleagues with those in the medical field, to a sense of calm confidence that we are providing holistic care to our patients, or to disillusion-ment that the medical professionals we are working with do not appear to value our expertise nor share our same vision for patients' overall health and quality of life. We often come into contact with physicians whose sole focus seems to be only on "the sickness" (as mentioned in the quote above) and not on the person experiencing that condition. While it can be challenging at times, I believe that we can more easily grapple with these issues and experience a positive, colla-borative relationship with physicians if we consider the ORCA principles in our collaborations.

First, let's consider the training and frame of mind of a typical family therapist. For therapists, witnessing the sufferings, grief, and losses of others can come at a significant and personal emotional cost that can, at times, feel unbearable.

Therapists struggle with this reality of their work constantly and are typically trained and acculturated to know that they can bring these issues up with their trusted supervisors and colleagues. In addition, there are schools of thought that emphasize that they *must* attend to these "self-of-therapist" issues in order to ensure that their clinical practice is ethical and unencumbered by personal issues that can cloud the therapeutic relationship. Thus, ORCA principles often resonate with therapists at any stage of training and open up life-giving and renewing conversations.

Now let's imagine the world of the typical physician. Imagine if in training you could participate only in the technical aspects of your work. Assessments, interventions, and outcomes are the sole currency of your clinical relationships. You are applauded for your ability to provide quick and effective interventions and make instant decisions with certainty. Your workload consists of back-to-back patients and your schedule has no margins for error. You are regarded as the leader of the team and your time spent with patients helps to pay the salaries of your colleagues. Attempts to discuss your feelings about your challenging patients, of being overwhelmed, or your uncertainty about your effectiveness are dismissed by your supervisors. An omission or perception of lack of confidence is responded to in a way that suggests that you actually *are* incompetent. Imagine making a mistake with a patient that you knew could have significant negative effects and being advised to stay quiet and move on to the next one.

As you think about the differences between these two ways of working, what ideas or feelings come up for you? What do you think the effects of working in the second scenario would have on your clinical work, on your professional role, and coping with the emotional aspects of your job? How do you think working in the second scenario would impact your personal life, including your mental health and relationships with loved ones? How do you think you would conceptualize the importance of ORCA principles and how would you apply them in your work?

Now that you have begun to think about the differences between the mindsets of physicians and therapists, it is important to note that we are not just interacting with individual personalities and ways of being when we talk about collaboration with physicians, rather we are engaging in the intersection of two very different cultures of thought, training, meaning, and expectations as illustrated by the exercise above.

In my work as a professor and supervisor of medical family therapists, this tension between our two *cultures* – medicine and family therapy – is the main issue my students grapple with as they engage in relationships with other medical professionals. I have found that students (and myself when I was starting out) can experience this intersection of two cultures as a crisis of sorts in terms of personal and professional identity development. We can be thrown into a tailspin wondering if we are the right "fit" for collaboration if it doesn't go as we had hoped. I propose that looking at collaboration with physicians through the lens of

ORCA can facilitate our personal and professional growth and help us to establish and maintain high-quality relationships with medical professionals.

Openness

Openness is the interpersonal capacity to respond to and receive what others give. However, just as our openness as therapists can be threatened when we are interacting with challenging clients, so too can our commitment to openness be compromised when working with challenging physicians. I find it is quite common for burgeoning therapists in integrated care to have a strong sense of their skills and level of openness within their personal and professional relationships. However, it is very common that working with medical professionals can challenge that sense of identity and skill level. For instance, it is not uncommon to hear about students feeling out of sorts when they enter an integrated care site and realize that their typical interpersonal skills, which have gotten them a long way in other collegial relationships, do not seem to have the same effect in the medical setting. For example, therapists are sometimes met with cool indifference in response to their exuberant introduction of themselves and expression of their passion for helping patients. When these attempts are not reciprocated in the expected way, it tends to challenge their sense of "who am I" and their preconceived notions of how easy or difficult it is for them to forge relationships. They can quickly begin to doubt themselves and their worth in the medical setting – which subsequently leads to them modifying their own levels of openness to those around them.

During this early stage of therapists' careers an important aspect to consider is that physicians are often trained to leave their personal lives out of their professional relationships. Due to the busy nature of being a medical professional and the emphasis on clinical performance, often there is not enough time to build personal relationships with everyone while on the job, especially during clinic time when one is running from one examination room to the next. In addition, personal self-disclosure is not typically as common or given as early in professional relationships with physicians often due to a difference in training and cultural norms in regards to openness. However, if we perceive these first interactions as simply cold and indifferent, reflective of an overall lack of openness rather than an overall cultural norm for their profession, and representing their focused and diligent priorities towards excellent patient care, we may close off future opportunities to connect with them.

It can be helpful to further define openness in terms of two types: personal and professional. For instance, professionally a physician needs to be able to exhibit openness through taking in the pertinent clinical information a therapist is giving to them. However, in terms of personal openness, physicians are not required to engage in interpersonal openness – nor are you. We may desire some physicians to behave in a more personally open way, but we need to view this as a personal desire rather than a professional need. Thinking of openness in this way can help us to not take their responses personally, but rather to look at their professional behavior in order to determine if their openness is appropriate.

Respect

Similarly to the mindset of openness, a way to think through respect with physicians can be to differentiate the personal from the professional. While many physicians build respectful, collaborative relationships, there are times when we will run across challenging physicians – similar to the times when we have challenging clients and we have to be able to navigate these relationships in terms of respect. In general, the majority of physicians want to give and receive respect as much as we do. However, at times, we may expect respect to look and feel a certain way and we don't feel we are getting that from a physician. What is important is to step back and consider if the physician is treating your professional role with respect. If the physician is not considering your input, ignoring your requests and suggestions, or not providing appropriate referrals or time to spend with patients, then that is a professional issue that needs to be addressed with the physician directly or an administrator. However, if the physician is doing these things, but you are still feeling disrespected, you may need to reflect on what you are expecting from the physician personally and if it is an appropriate expectation.

At times, we conflate respect with warmth or fondness and we need to be careful to separate the professional from the personal in order to help us to see the situation more clearly. Doing this internal self-reflective work is inherent in our professional and personal growth and can result in big payoffs: our own sense of self can be strengthened as we work on our own reactivity and learn to build strong professional relationships with physicians. Contrary to their initial expectations I have seen many interns surprised but highly appreciative of the respect they receive from their physician colleagues. Sometimes it takes a few months for respect to be earned, and focusing on fostering professional respect can lay the groundwork for further development of deeper personal respect from both sides.

Curiosity

I think the crux of being able to be open and respectful with physicians can be accomplished primarily through the cultivation of our curiosity. When it comes to physicians, it can be difficult to find one who has the time to talk with you about all of the pressures and internal thoughts that they experience in their day-to-day work life; this is one of the most difficult aspects of understanding where they are coming from. To feed our curiosity, there are a few resources that can be helpful. An excellent read is *What Doctors Feel* by Danielle Ofri. As an MD, she presents the myriad emotions and vulnerabilities that physicians face on a daily basis and helps us to understand how they cope through some of the behaviors and ways of thinking that can be difficult to reconcile. Jerome Groopman wrote *How Doctors Think* which outlines the thought processes behind a physician's decision-making and communication choices, and helps to illuminate the challenges in physician-patient relationships from the physicians' perspective. Atul Gawande (the author whose quotation is referenced at the beginning of this chapter) has written extensively on physician experiences and presents a call for change in terms of some long-held beliefs and values held by medical professionals in general. In addition, many relevant articles can be found by Googling "professional socialization and physicians," including a recent special issue from the *AMA Journal of Ethics* devoted to "The Culture of Medicine." In addition to books, there are several video resources that can be especially helpful in understanding physicians. *Hopkins* is a documentary that follows residents from Johns Hopkins University as they face the daily tasks and challenges of learning to be a physician. Available on the PBS website, "Doctors' Lives" is a compilation of interviews with physicians regarding their training, current clinical placements, and perspectives on what it takes to be a doctor in general. Beyond books and films, there are experiential activities you can engage in, including interviewing or shadowing a physician in order to get a first-hand personal account of the daunting duties and expectations physicians cope with on a day-to-day basis. The above activities (referenced at the end of this chapter) can help us to cultivate curiosity for physicians that can ultimately help us to understand and build productive relationships.

Accountability

Traditionally, the accountability principle in ORCA is based on the idea that we are the ones who hold the power over our clients and need to be accountable in our actions. While this aspect holds true as we work with patients in the medical setting, we also experience the significant power dynamics and hierarchies inherent in professional medical culture. So how do we apply this principle of accountability to power when collaborating with physicians who often hold a lot of power in the medical setting? The most salient lesson I have learned is that, when we are interacting with someone who holds power, we are prone to misinterpret their behavior as negative and against us personally. In my own professional life, I have seen this dynamic play out as I have recently made the transition from graduate student to professor. When I entered my position, I could tell almost immediately that my actions, gestures, and facial expressions were being scrutinized to a level I had not experienced before – and often were interpreted as being negative or overly critical. This shocked me and didn't resonate with my own sense of how I felt about students. Through discussions with mentors, I came to understand that my newfound power was having unintended effects on my students. While this has been unsettling and challenging to address, it has also given me great insight into some of my own reactions to others who I regard as having power and the reactions of my students to those in power – such as physicians.

An example of how power can beget negative attributions occurred recently for a student at my institution. She was getting to know the health care team members during her first few weeks at her clinical site and told me a story of walking by a physician and saying hello; this physician made very brief eye contact and didn't say hello back. This interaction really bothered the student and it represented for her the larger issue of not feeling valued and respected at this site. She would share subsequent interactions with this physician that continued to build the story of how this physician was dismissive and did not value the student's contribution. However, recently the physician and student have been more closely collaborating about a patient's care. As they were talking in the hallway regarding their coordination, the physician said, "Sometimes when I am coming out of surgery, I can be really focused and not really aware of who's around me. Please know I am not trying to be rude, I am just thinking about the details of the surgery." This proclamation immediately melted away the student's concerns about the physician's dismissive demeanor and her own feelings of worthlessness. They have continued to have a very collaborative relationship, and now when the physician passes by in the hallway without eye contact or saying hello, the student attributes a very different meaning to that interaction and does not let it affect her self-worth or the way she views the physician. While we may not all get the opportunity to hear a physician self-disclose like this, it illustrates how we can incorrectly interpret actions and attribute meaning in relationships that are fraught with power. So, one aspect of being accountable to power in relationships with physicians is for us to be accountable to the *effects* of power in our own lives. We need to be able to recognize and scrutinize our strong reactions to physician behavior, determine if we are taking things too personally, and ultimately challenge ourselves to allow their behavior to be about them and not about us.

Another aspect of accountability to power in the medical setting is to remember that we have the right and the power to be asked to be treated with respect. If a physician is rude, we don't have to put up with that behavior. We can ask to be treated with respect and expect it. In addition, our professional role also includes advocating for patients and family members in the event that they are being negatively affected by power in their clinical care or patient/physician relationship. If we discover that patients are feeling a lack of agency, we can help them to advocate for their own sense of power in their medical care.

Collaborating with physicians can be beneficial to both our clinical work and the lives of our patients. However, it is not without its challenges. Just as a therapist would with a difficult client, it can be helpful to try to see the situation from the physician's perspective. Through using the ORCA principles, we can better attune ourselves to the myriad of influences that are at play as we navigate these sometimes complicated relationships. Committing to openness, respect, curiosity, and accountability to power are crucial aspects of creating meaningful and effective collaborations with medical professionals.

References

Bednar, R., & Wrong, T. (producers) (2008). *Hopkins* [DVD]. United States: American Broadcast Agency Company.

Gawande, A. (2008). *Better: A Surgeon's Notes on Performance*. New York: Picador. Retrieved from https://books.google.com/books?id=hTKrkBmYKDQC&printsec=fro ntcover&dq=Better:+A+Surgeon%E2%80%99s+Notes+on+Performance&hl=en&sa=X &ved=0ahUKEwinkIK10KbhAhUDBnwKHbKdA50Q6AEIKjAA#v=onepage&q=Be tter%3A%20A%20Surgeon%E2%80%99s%20Notes%20on%20Performance&f=false.

Groopman, J. (2008). *How Doctors Think*. New York: Mariner.

Kao, A. (Ed.) (2015). The culture of medicine. Special Issue. *AMA Journal of Ethics* 17(2). Retrieved from https://books.google.com/books?id=RjY2iwqIuIwC&printsec=frontco ver&dq=How+Doctors+Think&hl=en&sa=X&ved=0ahUKEwinkci_0KbhAhWBCXw KHVjhAPkQ6AEIKjAA#v=onepage&q=How%20Doctors%20Think&f=false.

Ofri, D. (2014). *What Doctors Feel: How Emotions Affect the Practice of Medicine*. Boston, MA: Beacon.

NOVA. Doctors' lives. NOVA website. Retrieved from www.pbs.org/wgbh/nova/doc tors/lives.html (accessed November 10, 2015).

30

FINDING MEANING IN OUR WORKPLACES

Steve Maybell

I have learned through 40-plus years in different organizational positions that leaders establish the culture of the work environment, including the values the company lives by and the kind of relationships that are acceptable and unacceptable. Having the relevant technical knowledge about the product or service of the organization is important, but of greater importance is the quality of relationships that leaders facilitate.

There are many factors in the workplace that determine whether a job can be life-enhancing or life-depleting. One of the biggest factors is the quality of leadership. *Forbes* magazine defines leadership as a process of social influence that can enhance the efforts of others toward the achievement of a common goal (Kruse, 2013).

As will be discussed below, research on management emphasizes the important connection between leadership effectiveness and the quality of relationships developed within an organization (Asmus, 2015).

One can argue that the *ORCA-Stance* could inform relationship-focused leadership. As our broader culture evolves, it becomes ever more democratic in nature with people feeling inherently that it is their right to be respected as a person of equal value. No longer do people admire nor are they motivated by leaders who see themselves as superior and treat staff as "less than"; this latter stance breeds resentment and reduces motivation. Egalitarianism is a part of the great social upheaval of the past 100 or so years, which gave us more democracy and many movements toward less hierarchical treatment of people. In particular, some researchers have suggested that a relationship-driven corporate style is needed to keep baby boomer workers in the workforce (Little, 2011). Relationship quality is central for boomers. Using the ORCA-Stance in the workplace can help to provide a relationally oriented dynamic to take place there.

Openness

Collective wisdom holds power for a company. Throughout all my years as a leader in social service and higher education settings, I have, at times, made important decisions solely by myself, relying exclusively on my own knowledge, experience, and judgment. The consequence of this approach, I have learned, is predictable and not always helpful. Staff can become resentful that their voices were excluded, and when other company concerns or resources are not engaged this begets the kind of frustration and anger associated with people who feel devalued. Potential challenges can be addressed before a decision is implemented.

The date June 4, 2014 marked a very sensitive point in my work history as the Director of the Student Counseling Center. The school faced a situation where a mentally ill intruder came to the campus armed with a rifle, shooting and killing one student and wounding two others. Many of our students were emotionally affected by this event and some had significant trauma responses. In my position as Director, I was charged to lead the effort in providing crisis counseling to the students most impacted. At the same time the Counseling Center had many of its own clients who were ending their work with our counselors, and some of them were also affected by this tragic and unexpected event.

Instead of determining things on my own, I was reminded of the ORCA-Stance and its emphasis on openness. I realized that I needed to work out this response with my staff as well as with university personnel from other departments. I invited a group to join me in discussing our options for a response. The ideas generated by many of my colleagues were relevant and creative. I could not have possibly managed this task alone. Inviting the staff's input added value to the decisions being made. This "open" approach takes more time and can be frustrating. The outcomes, however, tend to work better when approached this way.

Respect

The relational stance of respect, when expanded slightly to the phrase "mutual respect," says what is of utmost importance in healthy relationships. Respecting oneself is critical to a healthy life and for being an effective leader. This involves prioritizing our own essential needs, adjusting our lives when we are over-extended, and saying "no" to something we find to be beyond our capacity, that is distasteful, or goes against our values. It also includes standing up for ourselves when faced with demeaning or unjust treatment.

Respecting others is just as important. Staff members are more motivated to fulfill an organization's mission when leaders establish and maintain respect within relationships. A leader who takes time to check in, who demonstrates real interest, who learns about the lives of the staff, who shows appreciation for their contributions, and who asks their opinions about current work projects is weaving together a tapestry of organizational respect. Mutual respect becomes contagious, and staff can often contribute regularly to this culture.

Respect cannot be demanded – it must be won. The only lasting way to win respect is to intentionally show respect to all the people within the organization, no matter their position. The workplace truly relies on everyone for it to run well. Therefore, all staff members have inherent value regardless of their position.

Being raised in a military family with a father who was an officer, I developed the notion that those who are "higher up," who have greater "rank," should be automatically respected. I realized later in life that the civilian world is different. I discovered this in my first job as a counselor following graduate school. The Director of this social service agency frequently treated others in a critical, judgmental, confrontational, and condescending manner. Everyone was treated this way much of the time, including me. His leadership style was one based on holding superior status and seeking control of the staff by generating fear. I am certain that he believed that this stance was the best way to run an organization. The truth was that he could not have been more wrong. Every staff member resented him. The anxiety and apprehension that set in prevented the staff from doing their best work and becoming a team. It was clear to us, through several attempts, that confronting him would only increase the intensity of his behavior. A number of us met together to discuss how his disrespectful leadership was affecting us and damaging the agency. We considered what we might be able to do about it. So, we organized ourselves, decided to take a stand, documented what we had experienced and requested a meeting with the Board of Directors. While it took some time – and there were uncomfortable moments along the way – the meeting with the Board occurred, and they asked for the Director's resignation in exchange for a six-month severance package (and threw a large farewell and appreciation event for him).

Any leader who demands respect without working to earn it is usually disrespected, or even despised. A leader who attempts to impose this much power may eventually lose their power. Cultivating a respectful tone in an organization optimizes its function and stabilizes its workforce. It is beneficial to all.

Curiosity

Taking a curious stance can be difficult for some leaders who believe that it is their job to come up with solutions. Some think that others ask the questions and the leader is supposed to have the answers. I am reminded of the definition of leadership quoted earlier: leadership as a process of social influence that can enhance the efforts of others toward the achievement of a common goal (Kruse, 2013). Arbitrary and unilateral decision-making falls well short of what competent leadership actually does.

I would like to propose a simple but important leadership principle: *a leader's job is not to have the best answers, but to find the best answers*. To do this requires all that the ORCA-Stance has to offer. Openness is critical, because finding the best answers involves tapping into your staff and all the resources and wisdom they hold. Leadership involves developing a culture of respect, whereby staff will feel that they are valued and that they are needed – and so are their ideas. If the ideas are discarded with a dismissive attitude, staff will also withhold their most creative and perhaps transformative ideas.

In order for curiosity to become integrated into a leader's stance and into the organization's way of life, leadership must be humble and grounded. When a leader is curious about the ways in which a problem can be solved, others within the organization might bring the best ideas; the leader must stay humble when this is the case. Curiosity involves patience, as it will take time to hold and facilitate these kinds of conversations. Leaders who want the best ideas from the staff need to maintain the attitude that all their ideas, no matter how irrelevant or outrageous, deserve to be heard and understood.

For a leader to fully employ curiosity as a stance, the concept of *third choices* can be considered a benchmark in the decision-making process. Most of the time possible solutions to work-related challenges can be reduced to two choices, either A or B. For example: decision A: to pay for a piece of new expensive equipment that makes work tasks more efficient; or decision B: to keep the part-time employee. I challenge staff and myself to get curious and not to settle for just two possibilities when coming to a decision about anything. Generating at least three or even four choices often promotes new perspectives and even produces cost-saving solutions. Additionally, taking the time for decision-making processes to include the staff will often save time in the long run. Better decisions are made when collective wisdom is applied. Productivity is strengthened due to the increased ownership and motivation that comes from staff involvement in the process. Most importantly, better outcomes are generated for the organization.

Accountability

Relationship-focused leadership must be aware of accountability to power dynamics. Openly raising the issue of the social power within an organization, as well as to the accountability to the power held by those with more, provides a lens that the entire staff can use to better understand each other and navigate relationships. It is a fact that certain positions within the organization carry more or less power. This is an important reality that allows organizations to function or malfunction. It is also true that there has never been a time in our history when there has been this much skepticism about and sensitivity to power in organizations. To complicate things further, people tend to project upon their leaders problems and feelings from past hierarchical relationships that continue to affect how they see the present. Earlier relationships with parents, older siblings, teachers, coaches, and other leaders in their past, shape their attitude toward how they view their leaders now.

Normalizing how natural reactions are related to power in relationships – involving not only hierarchy between staff and the positions they hold but also gender, race, ethnicity, and age – is an effective way to reduce power's alienating effects. It is especially important for leaders to be accountable to their power, to handle their power with integrity, to not abuse their power, to share power where indicated, and empower others within the organization to bring out their best and have their contributions recognized.

People today are far more likely to admire, trust, and be fully motivated when leaders allow themselves to be real, genuine, open, and even vulnerable. Leaders do better when they are willing to admit when they are wrong, and to apologize when there has been disrespect displayed. When leaders are open about their own imperfections, they become more relatable, and staff can become more open and honest about their own performance. It may seem counterintuitive, but I've seen this repeatedly: leaders are more admired when they are more open and genuine about their humanness.

The ORCA-inspired leader holds the stance that people are the most important asset in the organization. Consequently, developing and maintaining solid relationships with employees and modeling this within the organization as a whole is a leader's most important task.

References

Amanchukwu, R.N., Stanley, G.J., & Ololube, N.P. (2015). A review of leadership theories, principles and styles and their relevance to educational management. *Management*, 5(1), 6–14. Retrieved from www.researchgate.net/profile/Nwachukwu_Prince_Ololube/publication/283081945_A_Review_of_Leadership_Theories_Principles_and_Styles_and_Their_Relevance_to_Educational_Management/links/56292c3408ae04c2aeaee901/A-Review-of-Leadership-Theories-Principles-and-Styles-and-Their-Relevance-to-Educational-Management.pdf.

Asmus, M.J. (2015). The leader you will be. *Aspire-CS* (March). Retrieved from www.aspire-cs.com/the-leader-you-will-be/.

Kruse, K. (2013). What is leadership? *Forbes* (April), 1–4. Retrieved from www.forbes.com/sites/kevinkruse/2013/04/09/what-is-leadership/.

Little, B. (2011). Relationship-driven leaders focus on people, not power. *Training Industry* (May). Retrieved from https://trainingindustry.com/articles/leadership/relationshipdriven-leaders-focus-on-people-not-power/.

31

WORKING WITH INTERNATIONAL RELIGIOUS ORGANIZATIONS[1]

An Explorer's Perspective

Scott Green

My wife Lynne and I have worked as Christian missionaries and pastors for nearly 40 years, and have been blessed to work and serve in some fascinating places: Boston, Hong Kong, China, Seattle, and now Berlin, Germany. Though we have loved this work, traditional retirement years draw nigh apace, and we have recently begun exploring starting our own consulting company – one dedicated to cross-cultural preparation and maintenance for expatriate business families, foreign service families, and even the next generation of young missionaries.

"Exploring" the idea seems apt. We have, in a sense, always been explorers, since our missionary assignments have pushed us, each time, to confront and cross, to the best of our abilities, the boundaries of our own culture and adapt to faraway cities, lands, customs, languages, and peoples. A few months ago, during a visit to Beijing, as we were debating the semiotics of our future company logo, we found our coffee being served in ceramic mugs that featured the image of Marco Polo – the thirteenth-century Venetian explorer who lived in China for 24 years before bringing various kinds of treasure back to Turkey and Italy. Now, in our Berlin apartment, Lynne and I drink coffee – and sometimes tea – from those mugs each morning.

The people who work in international organizations often drink from this cup – the cross-cultural explorer's cup, and the taste can be bitter and confusing at times. When I was first learning Cantonese at the Chinese University of Hong Kong, I frequently experienced our instructors as rigid, authoritarian, and condescending. I resented being treated and scolded like a child, and sometimes addressed this after class, to virtually no effect, not yet comprehending that in China, this was how adult teachers *always* treated students, regardless of age, in accordance with Confucian traditions handed down for over 2,500 years. To the

Chinese, such order fundamentally secured reliable civilization and the preservation of precious knowledge; to student Green, a flag-waving Libertarian American, such order threatened self-esteem, made learning often miserable, encouraged a feeling of disconnection, and inspired exasperation. Something would have to give, and it wasn't likely to be Confucius.

Most of my Hong Kong expatriate acquaintances faced this clash of cultures by hiding from it – in expatriate athletic clubs, in multinational English-speaking business environments free from the mystery of Cantonese, in luxury apartments including English-speaking Filipino maids and drivers, and in hotel lobbies and restaurants catering to expatriate tastes. At that time, in 1987 Hong Kong still had a British Governor, and its citizens were not allowed to directly vote for Legco delegates. The legacy of colonialism kept the local Chinese more interested in business than politics, but also offered institutional safe oases for European, Australian, and American residents. Most of these, and many times myself included, were too grateful for the drink to question whether or not the sand they regarded as a desert might actually be a beach.

It was perhaps easy to anticipate the most obvious cultural friction points: the difference in language and the difference in food, for these were daily things that came up again and again in highly visible ways. We had, in fact, braced ourselves for these. Less obvious, however, and therefore more disorienting, were cultural differences in relationship building, communication, and decision-making. As these differences emerged, and as we navigated some of them successfully, we became more and more aware of the difference between what was happening to us and what was happening to other expats we knew. We posed a series of ineluctable questions about our China "adventure". Were we here to "import" American culture into Hong Kong (surely not)? Were we here to live in an American bubble amid the Chinese cultural typhoon? Or were we here to learn, to understand, to be affected, and to be changed? What would an explorer do?

In those ten years our answers were mixed. Too often I found myself judging aspects of Chinese culture; too often I experienced difference as a threat rather than as an opportunity; too often I felt called to teach rather than observe and learn; and too often I found myself still feeling like an outsider, a lingering deficit that had a strong role in our returning to the United States in 1997. Coming to Seattle, we found ourselves crossing culture again – for America seemed now to be a very different country from the one we left. This felt disorienting, and full of unexpected losses and discoveries, but these experiences again coaxed us into really *paying attention* to what was happening to us. The language for how we navigated these experiences came to me, finally, through the ORCA values we learned because of marriage and family therapy (MFT) training from 2008–2010.

Two years ago, we began our present work with a Berlin Christian church, taking on another challenging language half a life later than when we learned Cantonese. The Berlin congregation has pushed us to reflect differently yet again, because the church has seen itself as having been built poorly at times. The leaders there are experienced and have good questions about how such an organization ought to be built or rebuilt. As we address these questions, it seems that ORCA values provide a clear and cross-cultural framework, informing not only *what* answers we share, but *how* we discuss them, reshape them, and implement them into the German organizational culture.

Good Leadership

What, for example, is "good leadership?" It doesn't take much knowledge of history to guess that the German people, especially the people of Berlin, have a complicated relationship with this question. After the end of World War II, literally in the rubble of Hitler's disastrous Third Reich, Berliners learned to recoil at the dangers and excesses of authoritarian leadership – in the military, in business, in schools, and in their family systems. The traditional words for leadership/leader – Führung/Führer – fell understandably into general disrepute, and were supplanted by synonyms without emotional baggage. Seventy years later, that aversion generally remains, and citizens are quick to criticize political leaders who openly advocate a stronger, more assertive Germany – a road that must not be traveled (Duffield, 1998). At the same time, German education, innovation, and dedication often lead the country to economic excellence and scientific breakthroughs. How do the German people embrace a new story about leadership – one that honors the hard lessons of the twentieth century while allowing the nation to have its day influencing the world for good?

By contrast, America – at least in the dominant culture – has had a relatively untroubled relationship with authoritarian leadership. In theory, in our cultural story, we simply don't allow it. Three branches of government are supposed to "check" such power and keep it at bay. I don't mean to judge here how well or poorly we have lived up to this idea, but rather to show how different the idea itself – embedded in our national *leadership story* – already is. Even our cynicism about Vietnam and the Johnson/Nixon era illustrates a national determination to avoid putting our trust in people and instead put it in principles and due processes. Sometimes this faith is vindicated and sometimes not, yet even our tragedies and injustices are open for debate and revision, something Germany did not begin to experience until 1945. East Germans had to wait until 1989.

In the Berlin congregation we now serve, this began to really matter a few years ago when national leaders questioned the leadership style of founding American missionaries – those who preceded my wife and me. In German eyes, the Americans were "too forceful," "arrogant," "over-confident," "unable to listen," or "convinced they know best." To many of these American leaders, the Germans were being "uncooperative," "obtuse," "paranoid about leadership process," and "inflexible." With this conflict in mind, we have been using ORCA values to address the cultural and historical differences, hoping to build a *both/and* understanding of leadership differences, strengths, and weaknesses. This might not have been possible for me previously; I would have been more committed to comparing leadership styles in a competitive way – which way is "better" for the problem we are addressing? By contrast, we now emphasize the value of openness to help us to find a "third way," our own way, in developing our "story" about what good leadership is. Openness says to us and our German friends that leadership can be interpreted in many different historical and cultural ways, does not depend on finding "the best way," and is free to be judged by and tailored to the community it serves. This gives us the freedom to see leadership as a moving target, never made perfect, never finished in development and therefore something always worth reevaluating. Being afraid of Hitlerism no longer means having to be afraid of leadership itself.

More concretely, we are becoming ORCA-open to many different personal *styles* of leadership. German leaders in today's world tend, for example, to be less dependent on charisma and inspiration than American leaders (Kuchinke, 1999). Without over-generalizing, we might say that American leadership culture often selects for extroversion (Cain, 2012), valuing "speaking up," "being bold," "making decisions," and "taking action." By contrast, German leadership culture today often selects introversion, valuing "listening and understanding," "collaboration," "staying patient," and "avoiding hasty unprocessed decisions." I find it important, and timely as an American myself, to avoid pathologizing either path; rather, we look for "usefulness" in both ways of being. Recently, each member of our leadership team took a Keirsey Myers-Briggs test to see how similar or different we were. We were using openness to embrace the differences rather than lament them or fight them. In another group meeting, we asked each leader to select a historical or fictitious leader with whom they personally identified, then shared these with the group to increase our awareness of each other's different leadership *values*. One person shared "Green Lantern," another "Karl der Grosse" (Charlemagne); unsurprisingly, none of us chose the same character, and we realized from this exercise just how broad the styles of leadership could truly be.

Decision-Making

Second, how do organizations make decisions? With few exceptions, the length and breadth of history has been paved, often tragically, with stones of authority and hierarchy: men dominated women; kings commanded serfs; bishops dictated to priests. War, whether tribal or national, was a way of life for each generation, and military command-and-control paradigms infiltrated the larger social culture (Manchester, 1993). The worst excesses of human history, from the Crusades to the twentieth century's world wars and cruel communist dictatorships, seem to have been enabled by our attachment to authority and command-and-control thinking.

It is not hard to see this influence in schools and in business, including non-profit business. When I was in my twenties, and forging my own ideas about leadership, I devoured as many "business/leadership" books as I could find, and nearly all of them used military combat paradigms in their organizational descriptions. Perhaps the most amusing examples were a series of business books using Sun Tzu's *Art of War* as a blueprint for effective economic "combat." Westerners seemed to love that book in particular because of the "legitimacy" afforded by a non-Western author.

If such authoritarianism has fallen out of Western favor, it is also true the West has had a challenging time articulating a satisfying alternative. The Reformation granted an unprecedented level of freedom – from Catholic authority – but the children of Luther, Calvin, Zwingli, and Knox today still wrestle with organizational credibility: can the church really impress the world with its ability to "make things happen" or "get important things done?" I remember vividly the disillusionment of my father when he, an army colonel, tried to join our local congregation's leadership team only to find that "we have no way to make any substantive decisions." He quit trying after a while.

Similarly, I find today's Americans largely dissatisfied with our political institutions – co-equal branches of government created to keep us away from authoritarianism by the framers of our Constitution. Presidential "approval ratings" are rarely high, and congressional ratings are notoriously low (Riffkin, 2014). From a structural perspective, we really seem stuck: if we cannot hold a public referendum on every issue (Athenian-style "democracy") while rejecting authoritarian dictatorship, how do we get those who represent us to engage processes of decision-making we can live with? Add a layer of international culture and the question gets more dramatic: what about a country like Germany, terrified of Hitlerism and dictatorship, but insecure about how to lead and govern a people who want to "be heard," *right now*, on every issue?

In our Berlin experience, we are using ORCA – especially the value of respect – to shift the focus from structure to culture, namely to flexible structures well informed by a more respectful culture. By keeping our eye on culture, on values, we have been able to navigate the shifting tides of power in our organization – from times when the pastor, by virtue of competence and tenure, has much intrinsic authority, to times when everything seems done more by committee. How has respect created security and liberty here? Respect has shifted us away from the question, "Who has power here?" and towards the question, "Who are the stakeholders?" The former question invites caution, envy, and an intrinsic *demand to be respected*; the latter invites consideration, inclusiveness, security, and is the *gift of respect*. We are paying attention – first and finally, no matter how complex or drawn out our decisions are – to identifying the stakeholders and including them in the decision-making process.

After moving to Seattle in 1997, I remained in a supervisory role with our Hong Kong congregation's leadership team for several years. During that tenure I was invited to help to resolve an internal conflict within the team based on one member being perceived as a "poisonous personality." For several months, I sided with the ostracized member, a good friend of mine. Unsurprisingly, I began to lose credibility with the local team and this was a threat to the entire leadership's unity. At a pivotal juncture, after a personal appeal by another team member ("I don't know if I can really trust Scott anymore"), I had an epiphany that seems obvious now: the many know better than the one, and the people on site know better than a supervisor in Seattle. Without knowing really what to call this sudden value, I deferred to the local team, trusting their combined experiences of the "poisonous" person, and, more importantly, trusting the process they decided to employ in order to remove this person. ORCA respect changed the context of the controversy from danger to safety. Fifteen years later, I can say my mistake was taking my eye off that question, "Who are the stakeholders in this decision about the team?" The stakeholders deserved the loudest voice. Ultimately, this was heard and respected, inspiring, in turn, more trust and respect from the congregation to the team.

Collaboration

A third foundational question emerges from the second: in getting to stake-holder-friendly decisions, what does collaboration look like? When I was a young pastor, my assistant minister would often joke, "If I want so-and-so's opinion, I'll give it to him." As young leaders interested in discovering and developing our own opinions and passions, and in moving from feeling powerless in college to power-endowed as "missionaries", we often overestimated the importance of "strong, executive leadership" while failing to see the need for genuine colla-boration. Perhaps most of this was egotistical, but I suspect some of it was about the bias youth seems to have towards "taking swift action" as a way of defining estimable leadership. The early Steve Jobs was mercurial, ingenious, decisive, abrasive, even abusive, and eventually fired by his board and peers (Isaacson, 2011). It's not clear to me whether or not Jobs became more collaborative when he was rehired years later. Perhaps Apple was just more desperate.

The relative collectivism of both Hong Kong and Germany made the issue of *collaborative process* ineluctable for me. Neither culture admired the exaggerated American "cowboy" prototype, other than in the cinema. While at first the young Chinese leaders we worked with and trained were highly deferential, in time they began to know and articulate their own ideas about how to build the organization. Collaboration had become important to them. Moreover, when we moved to Germany two years ago, we found a seasoned, more mature Berlin leadership team embroiled in the question congregationally. Members wanted excellent communication to and from the leadership team; they wanted genuine feedback mechanisms and dialogue; they wanted clarity around decision-making guidelines and timelines; and they expected the team to expect the same from us as *die Gemeindeleiter* (church leaders). And no *Führer* wanted, thank you.

We needed ORCA's accountability for power, or, as I sometimes call it, awareness of power, to fit into this system. We came with awareness that Europeans often see Americans as being overly powerful, overly assertive, and loathe to listen well. We "feel our power" too easily and too comfortably. In the church missionary community, especially when financial support is coming from the United States, it's easy for American leaders to be paternalistic, taking the one-up position, and treating the Europeans as junior partners. With this kind of power imbalance, true collaboration is not really possible, because *responsibility for the decision is not equally shared.*

We also needed the curiosity piece of ORCA to ignite genuine collaboration, and this is probably self-evident: how can you have collaboration without actually being interested in what the other thinks? This can't be faked, at least not for long. I personally find curiosity to be the most important value I can bring to personal and professional relationships, to conflict resolution endeavors, to team-building and repairing, and to marriage counseling in my role as a licensed marriage and family therapist.

I was asked not long ago to help to mediate a conflict between European missionaries and American financial donors/supporters. The Europeans came into the room with "stories" about the Americans being paternalistic know-it-alls. The Americans arrived with "stories" about the Europeans being inexperienced ingrates for American help. I came into the room armed with my understanding of ORCA and family systems (and the limits of mediation weekends). At first, both sides were unable to entertain alternative stories about each other, and each side felt invisible to the other side.

As one of three mediators, I could play the therapist's role in breaking the deadlock of mutual suspicion with curiosity. I genuinely wanted to understand at a different level the story each side brought – not the story about the other, but their own story: what did they truly want? What did they care most about? What crucial things did they hope the other might know or learn about them? Curiosity re-invited a previously exiled authenticity and sincerity into the room. This catalyzed a tremendous shift of how the leaders experienced each other, and a great deal of healing began to take place. Curiosity was salve for the conflict and savior of the collaborative process so desperately wanted and needed by both sides.

The Final Frontier

Nearly 100 years ago, explorer George Mallory, who ultimately perished on Mount Everest, explained with poetic economy why he wanted to climb the world's highest mountain: "Because it is there." The unknown frontier need say no more to the true explorer, who then finds or makes the tools needed for the journey. For me, mutual understanding, team-building, and true dialogical communication are the mountain, the frontiers worth exploring in this twenty-first century, promising incalculable windfalls for community-building, for the business world and developing world, and for our scarred and scared political leadership landscape. Tools like ORCA can make such a difference in these endeavors, and I am more glad, hopeful, and (I hope) adept, than I have ever been at using them.

Note

1 This chapter was developed several years before final publication. In some sense, it is unfinished due to Scott's untimely death. We kept it, as written and with his wife's permission (Lynne Green), in order to honor our amazing colleague and friend.

References

Cain, S. (2012). *Quiet*. New York: Random House. Retrieved from https://books.google.com/books?id=Dc3T6Y7g7LQC&printsec=frontcover&dq=Quiet&hl=en&sa=X&ved=0ahUKEwij6rH20KbhAhXSv54KHdrXCK8Q6AEIKjAA#v=onepage&q=Quiet&f=false.

Duffield, J. (1998). *World Power Forsaken*. Stanford, CA: Stanford University Press. Retrieved from https://books.google.com/books?id=-vxH-VcQekMC&printsec=frontcover&dq=World+Power+Forsaken&hl=en&sa=X&ved=0ahUKEwixx9u20bLiAhVDgp4KHSO1D5IQ6AEIKjAA#v=onepage&q=World%20Power%20Forsaken&f=false.

Isaacson, W. (2011). *Steve Jobs*. New York: Simon & Schuster. Retrieved from https://books.google.com/books?id=-vxH-VcQekMC&printsec=frontcover&dq=World+Power+Forsaken&hl=en&sa=X&ved=0ahUKEwj50ZGJ0abhAhUN854KHXMpCLgQ6AEIKjAA#v=onepage&q=World%20Power%20Forsaken&f=false.

Kohut, T. (2012). *A German Generation*. New Haven, CT: Yale University Press. Retrieved from https://books.google.com/books?id=9MZGNokj2owC&printsec=frontcover&dq=A+German+Generation&hl=en&sa=X&ved=0ahUKEwj55YCR0abhAhWGv54KHZrWAFEQ6AEIKjAA#v=onepage&q=A%20German%20Generation&f=false.

Kuchinke, K. (1999). Leadership and culture: Work-related values and leadership styles among one company's US and German telecommunication employees. *Human Resource Development Quarterly*, 10(2), 135–154. Retrieved from https://pdfs.semanticscholar.org/3405/21e308199cd973678b6236b27182124e33a7.pdf.

Manchester, W. (1993). *A World Lit Only by Fire: The Medieval Mind and the Renaissance*. Boston: Little, Brown & Company. Retrieved from https://books.google.com/books?id=Ku2PNGO5Y6sC&printsec=frontcover&dq=A+World+Lit+Only+by+Fire:+The+Medieval+Mind+and+the+Renaissance&hl=en&sa=X&ved=0ahUKEwjs4MWn0abhAhWClp4KHfn2Bf4Q6AEIKjAA#v=onepage&q=A%20World%20Lit%20Only%20by%20Fire%3A%20The%20Medieval%20Mind%20and%20the%20Renaissance&f=false.

Riffkin, R. (2014). *2014 US Approval of Congress Remains Near All-time Low*. Gallup, December 15. Retrieved from www.gallup.com.

Trapp, J. (2012). *Sun Tzu's The Art of War*. New York: Chartwell Books. Retrieved from https://books.google.com/books?id=4fZBBAAAQBAJ&printsec=frontcover&dq=Sun+Tzu%E2%80%99s+The+Art+of+War&hl=en&sa=X&ved=0ahUKEwjBy4q00abhAhXE3J4KHcZcAV8Q6AEIKjAA#v=onepage&q=Sun%20Tzu%E2%80%99s%20The%20Art%20of%20War&f=false.

32

CULTURAL HUMILITY AND BEYOND WITHIN YOUR OWN CONTEXT

Scott Edwards and Rachel Baska

> Do nothing out of selfish ambition or vain conceit. Rather, in humility value others above yourselves, not looking to your own interests but each of you to the interests of the others.
>
> *(Philippians 2: 3–4; The Message)*

Humility requires that our heartfelt values, physical posture, social position and actions be congruent. It is a practice which takes energy, intentionality, and at times, correction. Cultural humility, specifically, holds both intrapersonal and interpersonal components, and includes an authentic view of self with an awareness of and ability to acknowledge personal limitations to others. Furthermore, the practice of a culturally humble stance is more than an active quality of an individual; it is a process experienced in relationship with others when there are differences over time – past, present, and future.

Within our cultural context of Seattle Pacific University, the *ORCA-Stance* (openness, respect, curiosity, and accountability) supports humility within relationships, especially when there are differences between us. We emphasize relational qualities throughout our program and foster regular meetings within our community to help with the practices of the ORCA-Stance. Congruent with our Christian worldview and the calling of being Christ-like, we look to a continuous process of attending to and developing cultural humility.

How might humility be developed and practiced on a personal level within your own relationships? What values might you punctuate in the practice of humility? How might humility be defined and developed in your particular context? What community aspects of structure, rituals, and events might punctuate and foster practices of cultural humility?

In considering these thought-provoking and reflective inquires, you may begin to gain a better understanding of the place and culture in which you work, practice, or teach. Imagine you are asked, called, and/or inspired to begin to explore and develop intentional practices of humility and specifically, cultural humility within your own clinical context. Where might you begin? Who would you invite to the conversation? What cultural values might you identify?

We suggest that you first select those persons whom you would need to invite into these conversations. Second, it will be important to review the particular historical, contextual, and cultural processes impacting your relationships and to examine the organizational structure of your setting. The next step will be to identify the specific commitments you wish to make within your context. Finally, you must begin to operationalize those commitments into particular behaviors, interactional styles, and potential rituals. In these ways you will begin to support the development of cultural humility within your context.

Invitations to the Table

In developing practices of cultural humility within your setting, it will be imperative to identify and engage a broad, diverse group of individuals who represent the breadth of the stakeholders within your setting. For example, within our marriage and family therapy program, the key communities of interests for developing competent therapists are students/graduates, faculty, the department, university context, clients and agency supervisors. Below are some guiding questions in considering which stakeholder voices you may invite to the table for conversation:

- Who already has voice within your community?
- Which groups are presently represented and already have a seat at the table?
- Are there past leaders or key members to include?
- Who does not have voice and needs an invitation to the table?
- Are there under-represented groups with a stake in your community?
- Does each constituency group within your setting have voice? Are some louder voices than others? How might this impact the conversation on humility?
- Who participates in your system? Who is present yet does not participate?

The richer the perspectives, roles, and qualities of those at the table, the more valuable this endeavor may be for you. The types and frequency of conversations will vary based on your context, as the development of practices from a culturally humble stance will take time. You may find it necessary to invite additional groups and individuals to the conversation as you begin to develop clarity around humility within your context and whether or not structures exist to support its practice. To ensure that all relevant voices are able to participate, it will be important to have those at the table reflect and discuss who has voice.

History, Purpose, and Structure of Your Context

Once you identify voices and communities of interest within your own cultural context, it will be important for your constituents to explore the historical foundation and purpose of your setting. Below are some guiding questions to identify, examine, and more fully understand your contexts where differences exist:

- How did your context come to be and what was/is its mission?
- Who/what influenced or shaped its formation: funding, school, religious organization, particular group, an individual?
- How long have these settings existed? Have any changed significantly?
- Are there several layers of organization that influence your setting? Define them.
- What is the history of any mission and/or vision statements?
- Whose voices were around the table when these statements were developed? What voices were under-represented? What might they have contributed then and/or now to the conversation?
- What are your current mission and/or vision statements? If none, what creates barriers to developing them?
- Do your mission, vision, and/or purpose statements need to be revisited?
- What is the current size/scope of your setting?

The more complex your organizational structure, the more beneficial intentionally exploring your purpose, history, and values with various constellations of voices and processes may be as you develop richer understandings of your cultural context over time. Beginning with both a historical frame and current mission clarification, you will begin the task with a sense of "appreciative inquiry" (Coopperider & Whitney, 2005). You may become more appreciative of where your context began as well as moving in some direction toward where you might need to go in order to expand so as to develop practices of cultural humility.

Finally, after revisiting, affirming, and/or developing core purposes within your setting, it will be important to examine the organization and hierarchical power structures. Are there structural diagrams or flow charts of roles? If not, what would your organizational structures look like if you developed a diagram of the relationships? Do some people hold a position "above" or "below" or "next to" each other in the decision-making processes of your organization? Identifying differences of power within your organizational structure will later assist in identifying spaces in which to invite cultural humility.

Identify Commitments to *YOUR Stance* of Humility

Begin first with personal conversations together, identifying the words, values, and activities that would indicate your commitment to the practice of humility within your own cultural context. It is often helpful to begin this activity at an individual level and then share your ideas using a corporate and visual display (e.g., a large sheet of paper posted on a wall or a shared computer display). Whether you are in a small private practice, church, academic, or mental health agency setting, the following questions may be useful:

- What are some core and essential values for you to work well together?
- When do you currently experience humility in your relationships where differences exist?
- How is conflict managed? How are differences managed?
- What personal qualities support your expression of humility?
- What do you notice in your relationships when humility is amplified?
- How might humility be developed and practiced in your particular context?
- What values might you punctuate in the practice of a culturally humble stance?

Once you have identified a list both personally and through collective dialogue, you might highlight the concepts which are most prominent or consistently recognized. Sometimes a few key words become evident and an acronym may surface. In our departmental exercise the words respect, openness, accountability, and curiosity became central, and then the acronym ORCA was proposed (Grauf-Grounds, Edwards, MacDonald, Quek, & Schermer Sellers, 2009) because orca whales are part of our Pacific Northwest culture. As another example, the former elementary school of one of our faculty members recently revisited its core values. The school identified welcoming, value of learning, encouragement, and responsibility. Since their school mascot is a dolphin, they developed the acronym WAVE: welcome everyone, act responsibly, value learning, and encourage each other. As we will emphasize in the following section, the next step will be to determine behaviors that embody these values. At the elementary school, waving to one another began to be associated with their listed values and is congruent with the values identified within their stance.

Embodying YOUR Stance of Cultural Humility

The development of practices in cultural humility will be more than just identifying a list of values followed by decisions to practice them. For example, you may identify respect as a foundational quality, but it is not enough to choose to be respectful at a given time for a specific purpose. Embodying YOUR Stance of cultural humility will be a continuous and intentional process, not an end goal or state of being. The exploration, identification, and purposeful attending to values that promote humility are an important and synergistic process.

How might YOUR Stance of cultural humility be practiced and embodied within your relationships? What behaviors would you do? What interactions would you observe? What activities at meetings or organizational structures and processes support these interactions? As you entertain the purpose, mission, and vision of your setting, the following questions may be useful as you identify structures and processes which will impact the practice of YOUR Stance of cultural humility:

- How is YOUR Stance already showing up? Being experienced? Specify how you know and what you observe.
- Discuss what contextual aspects (history, purpose, mission, and vision) are congruent with the practice of humility. What may constrain the practice of YOUR Stance?
- Identify events, activities or community practices that might highlight your humility commitments.
- What organizational structures, power differences, or leadership styles are congruent or amplify the practice of YOUR Stance? What may constrain the practice of cultural humility?

After exploring these questions, you will have identified structures, leaders, processes, and community practices that may constrain, align with, and/or support the embodiment of YOUR Stance within your cultural context. For example, you may determine that certain voices in your community are not heard from regularly in a significant decision-making process. Maybe they do not attend regular staff meetings. Say, for example, your organization needed to hire someone new. In order to practice cultural humility, you might structure a time and invite those with less "regular" voices to provide input for this important decision.

To enhance the capacity for your system to support the practice of a culturally humble stance, it is important to evaluate how you may modify any of the organizational, structural, or cultural processes that constrain or limit the practice of YOUR Stance. You may even begin to develop new structures, processes, and rituals which more fully and intentionally embody YOUR Stance of cultural humility. For example, our program added a ritual towards the end of student training that allowed students, faculty, and supervisors to experience together the burden that hearing trauma stories had on them. Rather than a hierarchical training, the trauma ritual allowed people to hear, feel, and recall their own experiences and to hold them together (Grauf-Grounds & Edwards, 2007).

The Challenge of Isomorphic Accountability

The development of practices of cultural humility within your own setting will occur and be informed by multiple layers – both within personal relationship interchanges, groups, and your broader context. When processes and/or structures of an organization are the same between its various layers, these parallel processes and/or structures are isomorphic. By intentionally attending to the congruency between relational processes and program structures, we practice what we call "isomorphic accountability" (Edwards, Grauf-Grounds, & Cheon, 2011). By keeping isomorphic accountability in mind, you may develop practices that embody YOUR Stance of cultural humility within the relationships that you encounter.

As noted earlier in this chapter, we believe that by defining our core values within our context, we will function better within our relationships, both professionally and personally. The ORCA-Stance is a powerful foundation for opening and maintaining the therapeutic relationship, while also keeping therapists both humble and teachable by allowing for continual learning from others, especially when there are differences. Practicing through the lens of the ORCA-Stance not only empowers clients, but therapists as well. This stance allows therapists to disregard our "expert" role in clients' lives and our authority in the therapeutic relationship.

We encourage you to identify and develop intentional practices of humility within your own context. Cultural humility is essential for challenging therapists when they become both comfortable in their profession and when working to master therapeutic expertise. It requires a willingness to sit with new learning and contradicting perspectives, as well as with clients' inability to change. For those within a faith perspective, cultural humility broadens our ability to walk alongside those who suffer (Romans 12:15). We hope to encourage you to think about how you want to show up in the world, both personally and professionally, empowering you to live purposefully.

References

Cooperrider, D.L., & Whitney, D. (2005). *Appreciative Inquiry: A Positive Revolution in Change.* San Francisco, CA: Berrett-Kohler. Retrieved from https://books.google.com/books?id=sTl9HgheQBgC&printsec=frontcover&dq=Appreciative+Inquiry:+A+Positive+Revolution+in+Change.&hl=en&sa=X&ved=0ahUKEwiP2M7W0abhAhWosFQKHb89AAEQ6AEIKjAA#v=onepage&q=Appreciative%20Inquiry%3A%20A%20Positive%20Revolution%20in%20Change.&f=false.

Edwards, S., Grauf-Grounds, C., & Cheon, H. (2011). Competencies with an ORCA-Stance: Developing the self of the therapist. *Family Therapy Magazine, 10*(5), 45–47.

Grauf-Grounds, C., & Edwards, S. (2007). A ritual to honor trauma: A training community's witness. *Journal of Systemic Therapies, 26,* 38–50. Retrieved from https://guilfordjournals.com/doi/pdf/10.1521/jsyt.2007.26.1.38?casa_token=Aa0ghlgbvvIAAAAA%3AgNCUNNVUyyggm61Thzge7UgT0qcXEfvTRiBHX4vn1wL_8gnwEkGoTZvVwJf4aMAIAykR2mg&.

Grauf-Grounds, C., Edwards, S., MacDonald, D., Quek, K., & Schermer Sellers, T. (2009). Developing graduate curriculum faithful to professional training and a Christian worldview. *Christian Higher Education, 8,* 1–17. Retrieved from www.tandfonline.com/doi/pdf/10.1080/15363750802134931?casa_token=PJMjVAcDUv4AAAAA:Cv6mCsfZDx76ZdAMHETPwKN7yPCGUY4H0dl49STrWHiVeYdfL8–XywB-yd9jxuDYHu-ZMloaw.

INDEX